Pragmatism and the American Mind

Other Books By Morton White

THE ORIGIN OF DEWEY'S INSTRUMENTALISM
SOCIAL THOUGHT IN AMERICA:
The Revolt Against Formalism
THE AGE OF ANALYSIS (ed.)
TOWARD REUNION IN PHILOSOPHY
RELIGION, POLITICS AND THE HIGHER LEARNING
THE INTELLECTUAL VERSUS THE CITY (with Lucia White)
PATHS OF AMERICAN THOUGHT
(ed., with Arthur Schlesinger, Jr.)
FOUNDATIONS OF HISTORICAL KNOWLEDGE
SCIENCE AND SENTIMENT IN AMERICA
DOCUMENTS IN THE HISTORY OF AMERICAN
PHILOSOPHY (ed.)

To
My Students at Harvard University
in the Years 1948–1970
In Grateful Recognition
of How Much They Taught Me

Preface

In this volume I have gathered together a number of pieces previously available only in widely scattered places, hoping that when gathered together they will show how philosophical analysis may illuminate the history of ideas and contribute to the resolution, or at least the clarification, of some important problems concerning the central institutions and disciplines of civilization—for example, science, history, religion, and education. The volume as a whole reflects a combination of interests that I have maintained for more than thirty years. The unusualness of this combination of interests among contemporary American philosophers and, as I think, its intellectual and social value, encourage me to collect these essays in one place.

My notion that a philosopher may fruitfully unite an interest in logical analysis with one in the history of ideas and another in what is sometimes called cultural criticism, has not been accepted—to put it mildly—by many thinkers who have been influenced, as I have been, by analytic philosophy. Those who subscribed, for example, to logical positivism in the nineteen-twenties and -thirties rarely went beyond studying the logic of science because positivists declared that philosophy was nothing but the logic of science; that moral judgments could not express knowledge; that the so-called analytic truths of philosophy were radically different from all other kinds of truths; and that since philosophy, properly conceived, began somewhere in the nineteen-twenties, there was no point studying the pseudo-philosophy of earlier times. Such constrictive views of the philosopher's province were very different from those held in the so-called Golden Age of American philosophy by James, Royce, and Santayana. That generation's more generous views of philosophy's task were scorned by those who preferred quantification to pontification, and therefore the new men held that philosophers should not be concerned with many of the questions discussed in the present volume.

Although the deflationary views of the positivists had a beguiling plausibility, I have never subscribed to them even though I have learned much from studying them. In spite of having begun my philosophical education after the gold standard, as it were, had been abandoned by the ablest American philosophers, I have long felt a kinship with James, Dewey, and Santayana that most of my contemporaries did not feel. Like James and Dewey I am generally suspicious of dualistic epistemology and metaphysics; like Santayana and Royce I am sympathetic to the historical spirit of the nineteenth century; and like all of them I think that the light of philosophy should be spread as far as possible—into all minds and all fields that are able to receive it. Having said this, however, I must ask that I not be taken for a philosophical reactionary or a sentimental victim of nostalgia. I know as well as anyone the limitations of the golden philosophers and I also know that logicians who came upon the scene after them have raised standards of rigor to the point where it is impossible for philosophers to carry on as, say, Royce did in some of his more pontifical efforts to survey all existence and knowledge. On the other hand I do not think that philosophers should be persuaded to avoid the search for a coherent view of such matters as history, law, politics, religion, or education by monitory analysts who cry: "Remember Royce!". And to philosophers who are led by similar warnings to avoid the history of their subject I say, as Santayana did: "Those who cannot remember the past are condemned to repeat it".

By giving up the greater intellectual ambitions of earlier thinkers, some of our narrower philosophical minds have abdicated momentous questions to obscurantists; and many distinguished philosophers of our time have not deigned to criticize pundits and publicists who have debased the coin of philosophy. Yet it is well to remember that Locke did not think it unimportant to criticize the errors of so minor a figure as Filmer, that Kant did not think it beneath him to attack the anti-intellectualism of Jacobi, and that for almost a century Bertrand Russell and John Dewey led the fight against all forms of irrationalism. Philosophers who take seriously their commitments to truth and clarity must often expose idols and the philosophasters who worship them, and with this in mind I have here reprinted a number of pieces that are less than kind to writers who rest their politics on Natural Law, their religion on Original Sin, their educational theories on an indefensible variety of anti-intellectualism, and their view of history on an attachment to the big battalions.

My main aim, however, is not to pummel pundits; and to make this quite clear I have gathered together at the end of this volume a group of pieces in which I express my admiration for Dewey, Moore, and other twentieth-century heroes of the intellect. I hope in this volume to illustrate how ideas and their history may be illuminated by an analytically inclined philosopher; and also how he can contribute to the resolution or clarification of fundamental problems of civilized life. To this end I have divided this book into three parts. The first, which I entitle "The Mind of America", consists of a number of pieces on more general aspects of American intellectual history. Some of those historico-philosophical essays deal with topics that I have written about at greater length elsewhere: the revolt against formalism in American social thought at the turn of the century, the long-standing antipathy of American writers toward the American city, and the deep strain of anti-intellectualism in American philosophy. No one of these tendencies in the history of ideas can be neglected by the historian who wishes to explain the current demand for relevance in the universities, the fear of the American city, and the widespread distrust of the intellect.

In the second part of this book I turn from such general tendencies in American thought to pragmatism, which is linked in many ways to the revolt against formalism and the currents of anti-intellectualism described earlier. Although in this part, which I entitle "Pragmatism and Analytic Philosophy", I deal with certain technical philosophical questions, most of the essays in it were originally written for a general audience. They deal with concepts like truth, necessity, value, and moral obligation, but they bear directly on a question of great practical moment: the nature and scope of science. One of the main theses of these essays is that a distinction between analytic truth and scientific truth is very hard to defend, and that the methods of philosophy and science are not as different from one another as some philosophers have made them out to be.

My desire to link philosophy with other disciplines is also manifested in the third part of the volume, where I try to show how philosophy can play a part in our cultural life by addressing itself to such matters as the nature of history, the aims of education, the foundations of law, and the problems of religion. In general, my philosophical credo commits me to building bridges; and I hope, therefore, that this collection will make some contribution toward showing that analytic philosophy is not a tiny intellectual island and that it has many important connections with the mainland of thought and culture. I also hope that these essays will strike a blow for rationality at a time when rationality is once again under severe attack. That is the least a philosopher can do for the world if he wishes to live up to the ideals of his greatest predecessors.

I am happy to see, moreover, that more and more analytically minded philosophers are taking a generous view of the scope of their subject. One of the more encouraging features of recent American philosophy is its renewed interest in the history of philosophy and in the application of philosophy to public affairs.

I wish to thank all those who hold copyright on my pieces for having given me permission to reprint them. Most of them appear here in their original form except for minor stylistic or typographical changes. In some I have made substantive changes which show, I hope, that I have learned something since they were originally published. Several of them appeared originally as book reviews but I have included only those reviews in which I have said something that I think worth rescuing from the oblivion into which even the best samples of that genre quickly fall. Throughout the years in which these essays were written and during the period in which I was revising them and preparing them for republication, my wife has read them and criticized them with unflagging patience and devotion. For the tenth time, therefore, I thank her in a book that she has virtually written with me. I also wish to thank James Anderson of the Oxford University Press for his wise counsel and encouragement; and I am indebted to Vivian Marsalisi of the same press for her expert editorial advice. I am grateful to Barbara M. Sullivan, who typed the final version of the manuscript.

Princeton, N.J.   M. W.
November 1971

Contents

III PHILOSOPHY AND CIVILIZATION

I. THE MIND OF AMERICA

1. Coherence and Correspondence in American Thought[1]

Parallel to the division of American history into a colonial, a federal, a national, and an international period, there is a division to be made among the ideas that dominated these periods. This intellectual pattern comes into view when we ask about the degree of internal coherence among leading ideas in each of the periods, and also about the extent to which these ideas correspond with the facts of social life. Just as a dream may be logically consistent and yet not be a record of reality or a guide to social action, so it is logically possible for a whole era of literature and philosophy to be internally integrated and yet out of touch with the major social problems of its age. And conversely, the thinkers and writers of an era may be engaged, as the existentialists say, but fail to produce a uniform climate of opinion.

If we approach the history of American thought with these possibilities in mind, we can see an interesting evolution. In

1. This essay was first printed as my prologue to a collection of essays by many hands, *Paths of American Thought*, edited by Arthur M. Schlesinger, Jr., and Morton White (Boston, Houghton Mifflin Company, 1963). It is reprinted by permission. Some changes have been made, mainly in the last few pages.

the colonial age the dominant ideas formed a unity and were in relatively close touch with the social and political life of the colonists. In the federal era that ideological unity declined, as did the ambition of intellectuals to be in touch with the major social and political issues of their day. In the national phase after the Civil War the American mind was once again dominated by a comparatively coherent set of ideas closely linked to the world and capable of guiding action. But in the present age that begins with the First World War we find something unique in our history: intellectuals close to a complex reality, yet unable to find intellectual coherence among themselves.

I

From today's perspective the thought of Revolutionary times seems eminently coherent and exceedingly realistic. While Americans fled from Europe, conquered a wilderness, and freed themselves from foreign domination, they forged a set of beliefs that helped them guide their revolutionary energies and form their new political structure. Colonial America was dedicated to a set of propositions, conceived in flight from political tyranny and religious persecution, and these propositions dominated and unified the age before Independence. There was not only a considerable degree of intellectual concord among thinking men, but what they thought was created and used in the crucible of action. Fear of nature and of threatening foreign powers brought the colonists together in spite of geographical and ethnic differences. They became a consciously united group whose internal disagreements, great as they were, seemed minor by comparison to their disagreements with the rest of the world. They had decided to live together under one government, and their collective decision was the result of long and serious reflection. They had fought hard for their precious liberties and were deeply suspicious of those—inside or outside of America—who might wish to take their liberties away.

Colonial consciousness of man's failings was a tough thread that bound together the sermons of Calvinist divines and the pamphlets of Revolutionary leaders. The divines had feared the depravity of individuals, whereas their politically minded successors of the time of the Revolution were more exercised by the depravity of peoples and governments. And out of this second preoccupation there grew fundamental principles designed to guard against the effects of depravity in politics: that people of one region ought not to exercise dominion over those of another; that a people is distinct from its government and should protect itself from the dangers of tyranny inherent in all governments; and that even majorities could be tyrannical and hence should be checked.

II

Once Independence had been achieved, the colonial intellectual unities began to dissolve. The dissolution of Calvinism and the controversy over slavery threatened the nation with serious division. The closest approximation to "the" Church in America was fragmented into churches, which were in turn separated from a State that promised to split up into states. Henceforth there was nothing like an Establishment in religion, and no agreement on slavery. The age of provincial community—or, as the German sociologists called it, *Gemeinschaft*—was over in America. If there was to be new spiritual unity, it would have to be on altogether different terms.

With the decline of religious agreement and with the growing conflict between Northern and Southern ways of life, the America of 1840 was understandably seen as Henry James saw it forty years later in his book on Hawthorne. Not only could New England writers find no sovereign, no court,

no aristocracy, no church, no clergy, no army, no diplomatic
service, no country gentlemen, no manors, and no ivied ruins,
but as James also remarked, they found "no State, in the European sense of the word, and indeed barely a specific national name". The absence of all these things helps explain
the American writer's failure to produce novels about those
"items of high civilization" that James missed. American literature of the time was more interested in reflecting the emotions of a thwarted Calvinism and an ambiguous frontier. It
expressed itself in the romance rather than the novel; it
lacked a sense of history and culture, and was preoccupied
with the Self. It found no high civilization to describe, and
what it saw in the American city it feared or despised.

If one turns to the socio-political scene at the time—to that
"simple, democratic, thinly-composed society" as James
called it—one finds a poverty of abstract social thought. Understandably, Tocqueville said in 1835: "I think that in no
country in the civilized world is less attention paid to philosophy than in the United States". The forces that united
against Whiggery were not guided by any profoundly articulated political philosophy. Their movement was the result of
a shrewdly managed, large combination of democrats operating without benefit of a unifying metaphysics or theology.
The absent State, in that European sense of which Henry
James spoke, could not have its theorists, just as the nonexis-
tent Church and Society could not have their novelists. The
life of the mind went its own transcendental way, more concerned with Nature and the Over-Soul than with the underbrush of Washington or the underworld of New York.

III

The Civil War officially ended a struggle between the Northern and Southern systems of value, but the old forces tending
toward diversity continued to act and were augmented by
others. The war that preserved the Union prepared the way

for new forms of diversity and conflict in America by encouraging industrialization, urbanization, and immigration. After the Civil War, new social types entered American society and soon their ideals were described and espoused by intellectuals. A character of William Dean Howells succinctly portrayed the change in American society and values between Independence and the end of the nineteenth century. In reply to a Utopian traveler's question, "Who is your ideal great man?", Howells' character of 1894 said: "Before the [Civil] War, and during all the time from the revolution onward, it was undoubtedly the great politician, the publicist, the statesman. As we grew older and began to have an intellectual life of our own, I think the literary fellows had a pretty good share of the honors that were going. . . . When the war came, it brought the soldier to the front, and there was a period of ten or fifteen years when he dominated the national imagination. That period passed, and the great era of national prosperity set in. The big fortunes began to tower up, and heroes of another sort began to appeal to our imagination. I don't think there is any doubt but the millionaire is now the American ideal".[2]

The millionaire was not the only new social type on the American scene. He was accompanied by his opposite number, the industrial worker, and by the new European immigrant. Socially and economically the time seemed ripe for political and ideological conflict. Still, the seventy-five years following the Civil War witnessed an accommodation. Those seventy-five years were therefore very different from the seventy-five that had separated the Civil War from the Revolution. The national phase of America's history recorded dramatic progress toward a liberal, pluralistic society, and in this progress intellectuals played a prominent part. The period between Reconstruction and the First World War was, like

2. William Dean Howells, *A Traveler from Altruria* (New York, 1894), pp. 208–9.

the colonial era and unlike the federal era, doubly integrated from the point of view of the historian of ideas. Its liberal intellectuals formulated a coherent philosophy that was self-consciously and deliberately in correspondence with social reality and social action.

However, the emergence of that philosophy as the dominant philosophy of the age was not immediate. Although the millionaire—unlike the Revolutionary statesman and the literary transcendentalist—was (except for Andrew Carnegie) too busy to give literary expression to his convictions and his aspirations, he did not lack for sociological and legal spokesmen. Social Darwinism (better called Social Spencerism) and the doctrine of laissez-faire provided the rationale and the apology for the accumulation of great fortunes, and for a period these two doctrines dominated the intellectual scene.

But soon the liberal and radical reply was presented, and the evils of unchecked capitalism were fully catalogued. The acrimonious contest between the Spencerians and those who rejected their social philosophy of fatalism was striking evidence of the intellectual's active interest in the world around him. Novelists might still contend with the traditional notion that literature required a moral purpose, and to some extent with the continuing paucity of Jamesian items of high civilization, but they found new excitement in the immense energy of the industrial society and their imaginations were set fire by it. Unlike the partisans of laissez-faire, the novelists did not defend the predatory aspect of the new society, but they were nonetheless fascinated by it. It stimulated them as it did the pragmatic philosophers, the institutional economists, the realistic lawyers, the new historians, and the sociologists and social workers who turned their sympathetic attention to the problems of a new urban world. It was the era of the revolt against formalism—of realism and naturalism in the novel, of pragmatism in philosophy, of practicality in science, of opposition to scholasticism in jurisprudence and the social sciences. The age's preoccupation with practical achievement afforded a climate more hospitable to the scientific technologist than to the scientific theorist; in philosophy it encouraged the pragmatists to reflect more seriously than Western philosophers ever had before on the relations between scientific theory and experimental practice. Universities and colleges were brought into closer contact with a society that was becoming more and more secularized. John Dewey urged that the education of the young be transformed as radically as social life itself had been transformed at the end of the nineteenth century. By the end of the First World War the liberal philosophy of society and social science had emerged as the typical expression of the American intellect at its best, unified within itself and in touch with reality.

IV

As we come to the present era, the lack of perspective makes it of course more difficult to fix the outlines. But having made this disclaimer we may say that whereas American intellectuals of the middle period of the twentieth century remained in touch with the realities of contemporary life, it is not easy to discover a unifying doctrinal theme in their responses to it. A depression and two world wars diminished their confidence in the more optimistic messages of the earlier liberalism, and many became hostile to totalitarian pretensions after their encounter with Marxism. The result was a greater degree of toughness and heightened respect for technical expertise, but a failure to converge on a set of substantive principles comparable to those that guided the Founding Fathers, or to those that united Progressive politics and Progressive scholarship in the first half of the century.

Quite apart from whether or not one approves of it, one must acknowledge the development of a principled aversion —outrunning even that of the philosophical pragmatists—to the formulation of general principles, an incapacity to put down in simple formulae the aspirations and philosophy of

the age, and a cautious skepticism that kept certain intellectuals from being lured into facile generalizations or towering
systems. The three most admired literary figures between the
two wars—Faulkner, Fitzgerald, and Hemingway—were, we
are told, more in search of a moral style than of a moral system to replace what they saw pulled down in the First World
War. From the thirties onward, the metaphysical urge was in
great measure suppressed by philosophers as the method of
logical positivism and linguistic analysis superseded the more
relaxed, more embracing reflections of the early pragmatists.
In sociology, statisticians of market research and voting behavior gradually replaced the older, more philosophical sociologists. In foreign policy, theory lagged cautiously behind
the event. The result was not only a worship of technique
and toughness but also a lack of any world-view, moral philosophy, or political theory which embraced and articulated
America's convictions on basic questions. Whether this is
good or bad is a question that transcends history; it is a question on which serious and honest thinkers may differ. For
some it is a sign of moral weakness, of a lack of intellectual
originality, or of enervating agnosticism. For others the shun-
ning of metaphysics and ideology represents the height of
mature wisdom, a refusal to be trapped by a rigid system in
an age that is more complicated, more dynamic, and more in
need of intellectual resilience than any of its predecessors. In
any case, since the death of Dewey, America has not produced a philosophy that compares with his in scope, intellectual power, and public influence; and the years since his
death have witnessed a resurgence of anti-intellectualism, especially since the beginning of the Vietnam War. I am encouraged, however, by the fact that earlier waves of American irrationalism have come and gone; and I hope that an
end to our maddest war will lead to an increase of sanity in
our intellectual life. Once that nightmare is over it will be
easier for intellectuals to deal with the problems of American
life in a more rational and more coherent way.

2. The Philosopher and the Metropolis in America[1]

In *The Intellectual Versus The City*, Lucia White and I advanced and documented the view that dismay and distrust have been the predominant attitudes of the American intellectual toward the American city.[2] This is true not only of famous American novelists, sociologists, social workers, and architects, but also of influential philosophers and philosophically minded writers from the eighteenth century to the twentieth. In our study, we tried for the most part to examine the views of philosophers side-by-side with those of social workers, sociologists, literary men, and other intellectuals who speak during the same periods, and to similar concerns about the American city. Therefore, we devoted no sys-

1. This essay originated as a paper presented to the Faculty Seminar on Foundations of Urban Life and Form at Washington University in St. Louis during the academic year 1961–62. It was printed in *Urban Life and Form,* edited by Werner Z. Hirsch (New York, Holt, Rinehart and Winston, Inc., 1963). The essay, copyright © 1963 by Morton White, is reprinted without change.

2. Morton and Lucia White, *The Intellectual Versus The City: From Thomas Jefferson to Frank Lloyd Wright* (Cambridge, Mass., 1962); see also their "The American Intellectual Versus The American City", *Daedalus,* Volume 90 (1961), pp. 166–79, reprinted in *The Future Metropolis,* edited by Lloyd Rodwin (New York, 1961), pp. 214–32.

tematic attention to the history of the philosophers' reactions
to the city; we presented no continous examination of what
our major philosophical thinkers have said or felt about
urban life in America. But, as a philosopher, I may be for-
given my special interest in what the American heroes of my
discipline have said about the American city, and I am
moved primarily by that interest to limit myself here to examining their words, thoughts, and feelings on urban affairs.

There are important reasons for lifting Jefferson, Emerson,
William James, Josiah Royce, John Dewey, and George Santayana from the stream of American intellectual history, and
focusing on them as a philosophical group. For one thing,
they were all distinguished and influential minds, whose writings on urban problems often have intrinsic interest or value.
But more important is the fact that they represent an extraor-
dinary variety of philosophical doctrine and point of view,
and therefore demonstrate that distrust and fear of the American city is not the exclusive possession of one system of
thought or one *Weltanschauung*. Also, the fact that Jefferson,
Emerson, Thoreau, Dewey, Royce, and Santayana reacted
critically to the American city shows how deep and pervasive
antiurban feeling has been in America, and that it cannot be
identified simply with roughneck prejudice, ignorance, or
philistinism. To see this critical reaction in the writings of our
most sagacious and civilized Americans may help explain
why the efforts of the contemporary city planner and friend
of the city meet with opposition on so many levels of our national life. Not only farmers and their political spokesmen
have criticized the American city, but also philosophers
whom one might have associated with a very different set of
attitudes on this question. On this issue, poet, peasant, and all
sorts of philosophers have united.

Major Phases in American Philosophy

Before trying to show this, I must say a word about the different sorts of philosophies that Americans have produced or

espoused since colonial times. The history of American philosophy has gone through four major phases: the age of Enlightenment in the eighteenth century, the age of Transcendentalism in the early nineteenth century, the so-called golden age from the 1890's almost to World War I, and the present age of analysis. I do not mean to say that these are the only phases or movements, for I have not mentioned the impact of Scottish philosophy in the nineteenth century, nor Hegelianism and the various species of realism that were advocated and criticized by American philosophers between the turn of the twentieth century and the nineteen-thirties.

In the age of Enlightenment, the empiricism of the eighteenth century predominated and expressed itself with vigorous practical intent in the writing and thinking of Jefferson. But his empiricism and, as it was called by its enemies, his materialism and agnosticism, were repudiated and scorned by Emerson, Thoreau, and their Transcendentalist friends. They turned their backs on the empiricist philosophy that had nourished Jefferson and Franklin, and they built upon Coleridge's interpretation of Kantian idealism a romantic world-view which was fundamentally antithetic to the empiricism of the Enlightenment. After the Civil War, the philosophical influence of these Concord pundits began to be undermined by intellectual forces that corresponded to more pervasive ones radically transforming American society. In New England, after the death of Emerson in 1882, the transcendental era gave way to the golden age of American philosophy. It began with William James, who was later joined by Royce and Santayana to form at Harvard one of the most powerful academic triumvirates ever to dominate a single philosophical department. James spoke for pragmatism, Royce for idealism fortified by mathematical logic, and Santayana for materialism tempered by classical wisdom and good taste. James and Royce of the golden trio had been influenced by the erratic genius Charles Pierce, and all three had great impact on the dogged, monumental, scientifically oriented John Dewey. Partly under the influence of all five of these figures, the most recent age of American philosophy emerged, the age of the pragmatic, analytical, logical, linguistic tendencies which dominate America today.

In this essay I wish to confine myself to the views of certain major figures in the first three of these periods, and to ask the question: What views of urban life have been advocated, sponsored, or encouraged during these three phases of American philosophy? Let me begin by saying that the answer is "none" if we are thinking of the systematic analysis or description of urban life. That was left for sociologists. But, even though American philosophers, unlike Aristotle, did not think of the city as the fundamental political or social unit and hence did not concentrate their attention on it systematically, they certainly expressed deep feelings and thoughts about it, from 1784 when Jefferson's *Notes on Virginia* appeared, to John Dewey's *The Public and Its Problems*, published in 1927.

Jefferson's Empirical Antiurbanism

What were those feelings and thoughts? Let us begin with Jefferson. In the eighteenth century, the American city was too small and inconspicuous to cause any great concern to Jefferson. But when he looked across the Atlantic at the European cities he knew, he expressed his anxiety about having such things in America. In spite of his attachment to the values of civilization as conceived by the enlightened philosophers of the eighteenth century, Jefferson despised the manners and morals of the urban crowd and prayed that they would not be imported to America, the home of the brave and innocent farmer. Even when his concern for national interests led him to revise his views after the War of 1812, Jefferson plainly showed that he was persuaded, not because of any change of heart about the ways of the urban crowd, but rather by a rational respect for the value of urban industry to a new country faced by threatening powers across the sea.

Jefferson's final acceptance of the American city was grudging and military rather than fulsome and loving. Moreover, Benjamin Franklin, of whom one thinks automatically when one thinks of the colonial American city, was not an ideological partisan of urban life, but rather a city-builder. Indeed, Franklin was an agrarian pamphleteer who was certainly not prepared to conduct an intellectual crusade in behalf of the city and against the country.

For those who think of the Enlightenment as a period of calm intellectual activity in which the values of reason and the graces of urban civilization were greatly admired, the reaction of Jefferson to the city may cause some surprise. But no matter how much a stereotyped view of the Enlightenment philosopher might lead one to think that the urbane Jefferson would have welcomed the urbanization of America, the fact is that he did not. It is true that he had to fight hard at times in order to convince himself that the nation should stay down on the farm. Especially after he had seen Paris and had been overwhelmed by its charm and its concert halls. But not even Parisian chamber music, which he dearly loved, could move Jefferson to change his mind about the defects of urbanization. While he admitted that the great cities of Europe encouraged the fine arts, he thought that the cities' elegance and elevating qualities could not outweigh the danger of their sapping or damming America's moral and spiritual strength. Even after he had demonstrated his practical wisdom by conceding that we needed cities for our national defense, he continued to express deeply felt horror at their spirit and style. In short, the philosophical representative of the Enlightenment in American thought was an antiurbanist in feeling who conquered that feeling only because his first concern was to keep the nation free from foreign domination.

Because Jefferson was an empiricist and an active political man, he could not assess the city in purely emotional terms. But the Transcendentalists who came after him in the history of American thought were literary men rather than states-

men, and their metaphysical aspirations were more abstract
than Jefferson's. They could not control their antiurban ani-
mus as effectively as Jefferson controlled his. The War of
1812, which had stimulated Jefferson to adopt a more concili-
atory tone about the American city, had increased the similarity between the American city and the European city that
had occasioned Jefferson's earliest fears about urbanization.
The age of Jefferson had ended on an irenical note so far as
the American city was concerned, but soon the trumpets of a
more militant antiurbanism filled the intellectual air, played
by romantic metaphysicians with little sympathy for colonial
epistemology and with no inclination to serenade the American city.

Emerson's Metaphysical Antiurbanism

While Jefferson was an empiricist, Emerson was in sharp reaction against the traditions of British empiricism and French
materialism. With the details of Emerson's metaphysics and
theory of knowledge we need not be concerned, nor need we
trace his views back beyond Coleridge to Kant. But it is important for our purposes to note that Emerson explicitly
linked his own epistemology to his distaste for the city.
Emerson distinguished sharply between the Understanding
and the Reason. The Understanding, according to Emerson,
"toils all the time, compares, contrives, adds, argues; near-
sighted but strong-sighted, dwelling in the present, the expe-
dient, the customary", while the Reason, which was for him
the highest faculty of the soul, "never reasons, never proves;
it simply perceives; it is vision".[3] Reason was for Emerson the
soaring faculty of the forest-philosopher and the peasant-
poet, while the Understanding was that of the city-bound,
lumbering scientist. Reason, Emerson asserted, is characteris-

---

3. *The Letters of Ralph Waldo Emerson*, edited by R. L. Rusk (New
York, 1939), Volume I, pp. 412–13.

tically exercised in the country, while the Understanding is an urban faculty. The city, he declared, "delights the Understanding. It is made up of finites: short, sharp, mathematical lines, all calculable. It is full of varieties, of successions, of contrivances. The country, on the contrary, offers an unbroken horizon, the monotony of endless road, of vast uniform plains, of distant mountains, the melancholy of uniform and infinite vegetation; the objects on the road are few and worthless, the eye is invited ever to the horizon and the clouds. It is the school of Reason".[4]

Faith was another faculty that Emerson preferred to the empirical Understanding, and faith too was absent from the city. In 1840 he wrote to Carlyle: "I always seem to suffer some loss of faith on entering cities. They are great conspiracies; the parties are all maskers, who have taken mutual oaths of silence not to betray each other's secret and each to keep the other's madness in countenance. You can scarce drive any craft here that does not seem a subornation of the treason".[5] In 1854 he developed the same theme of urban deception in his *Journal:* "Rest on your humanity, and it will supply you with strength and hope and vision for the day. Solitude and the country, books and openness, will feed you; but go into the city—I am afraid there is no morning in Chestnut Street, it is full of rememberers, they shun each other's eyes, they are all wrinkled with memory of the tricks they have played, or mean to play, each other, of petty arts and aims all contracting and lowering their aspect and character".[6]

However much Emerson distrusted the city, Emerson was

4. *Journals of Ralph Waldo Emerson,* edited by E. W. Emerson and W. E. Forbes (Boston, 1909–14), Volume V, pp. 310–11; see Sherman Paul, *Emerson's Angle of Vision: Man and Nature in American Experience* (Cambridge, Mass., 1952), pp. 79–82.

5. *The Correspondence of Thomas Carlyle and Ralph Waldo Emerson* (Boston, 1883), Volume I, pp. 269–70.

6. *The Heart of Emerson's Journals,* edited by Bliss Perry (Boston, 1937), p. 264.

too sociable and too instinctively democratic to shun cities altogether. He was a great conversationalist and was always prepared to give up a night in the country for elevating talk at the Saturday Club. For Emerson, the urban clubs encouraged good words in a naughty urban world. Like so many Americans after them, Jefferson and Emerson thought of cities as great places to work in or to visit, but not to live in. Jefferson saw them somewhat as arsenals for the young Republic, Emerson admired them mainly for providing hotel rooms in which the Saturday Club might meet. But their dominant reaction to the city was that of distrust.

The distrust that they felt, however, was differently related to their respective philosophies. Emerson's view of the American city was intimately linked with his world-view and epistemology, but Jefferson's antiurbanism was more peripheral to his philosophical thinking as well as to the spirit of the Enlightenment of which he was such a distinguished American representative. Although in his *Notes on Virginia* Jefferson expressed great distaste for the ways of the citified artisan, Jefferson did not try to justify this distaste by referring to an elaborate metaphysics or system of values in which art was held to be inferior to untouched nature. As a child of the eighteenth century and as a Deist in theology, Jefferson did not disparage artifice as such, nor did he share Emerson's degree of concern about transcending the findings of empirical science. For a Deist like Jefferson, God Himself is the Great Artificer whose existence one can establish only by scientific induction from signs of design in the world. Therefore the sheer artificiality of the city, the fact that it was an artifact, could not have supplied Jefferson with the metaphysical objections to city life that it supplied to the romantic Emerson in his essay, *Nature*.

Emerson wove his anticity feelings more tightly into his metaphysics than Jefferson did, but more basic for our purposes is the fact that they both disapproved of the idea of an urban America. The empiricist Jefferson and the Transcendentalist Emerson could easily forget their philosophical differences as they made common cause against urbanism. If Jefferson was, in later life, prepared to encourage the growth of the American city, that was partly because he had not lived long enough to see it come to resemble the European cities he distrusted in 1784. But Emerson faced a more highly developed and more menacing American city, and his militant reaction to it set the tone of a great deal of American literature in the middle of the nineteenth century. Above all, it is certain that three famous American philosophers, or if one prefers, three famous philosophically oriented American thinkers—Jefferson, Emerson, and Emerson's comrade, Thoreau—did nothing to encourage the American to love the American city. They preferred life in Monticello, Concord, or Walden. From those retreats they looked with suspicious eyes at Philadelphia, Boston, and New York.

James' Critique of Bigness

We have now traversed two stages in our story of the American philosophers' reaction to the American city. Both stages precede the Civil War, that great divide in our national history, and so, when we come to the period after it, we are minded to ask whether our philosophy, like so many other elements in our culture, was drastically altered. The answer is, of course, "yes", but it applies more to matters of high philosophical doctrine and style than to attitudes toward the American city. A generation after the Civil War, William James, Josiah Royce, and George Santayana possessed a technical expertness, originality, and power in philosophy that had been absent in the period of the preprofessional sages, Jefferson and Emerson. The philosophers of the golden age were professors who lectured to future professors, and their standards of rigor were raised far above those of their predecessors. While the love of wisdom continued, it was accompanied by a kind of analytic acumen that was missing from the writings of Jefferson and Emerson. Pragmatism came upon the scene in the wake of Darwinism; idealism was armed by Royce with logical weapons that Emerson was incapable of supplying; Santayana courageously called himself a materialist. Science, technology, and logic were no longer scorned, as they had been by the transcendentalists. After the Civil War, philosophers lived in an age that was becoming more and more urbanized, and they focused their attention on its characteristic intellectual products.

Yet once again we may observe the old refrain of fear, dismay, and distrust so far as the concrete American city is concerned. Of the three, William James was by philosophical and personal impulse the most sympathetic to what he called the new New York at the turn of the century; and, more than any other single American of his generation, he won the love of all kinds of urban personalities, from immigrants to their patrons in the settlement houses. Unlike his brother Henry, he was not offended by what Henry called the primary stage of alienism, nor did he want to escape from New York into a cozier past. But, in 1899, William James penned a credo that served as a text for a whole generation of progressive reformers of the city. He wrote to a friend: "I am against bigness and greatness in all their forms, and with the invisible molecular moral forces that work from individual to individual, stealing in through the crannies of the world like so many soft rootlets, or like the capillary oozing of water, and yet rending the hardest monuments of man's pride, if you give them time. The bigger the unit you deal with, the hollower, the more brutal, the more mendacious is the life displayed. So I am against all big organizations as such, national ones first and foremost; against all big successes and big results".[7]

James' notion that the big unit was hollow and brutal inspired reformers like Jane Addams to try to fill the urban void, but that is a path that I will not here describe in detail

7. *The Letters of William James*, edited by Henry James (Boston, 1920), Volume II, p. 90.

because of my resolution to confine myself to philosophers. Later I shall describe part of it when I come to the views of James' disciple, John Dewey. But here I want to emphasize the fact that James' distaste for bigness was part of a more general set of attitudes that he shared with Royce, his idealist opponent, and with Santayana, his materialist critic. Once again we find the American philosophical mind united on the subject of the city no matter how it might have been divided on the questions of God, freedom, and immortality.

Royce's Provincial Community

While the reforming disciples of William James worked hard in the cities, doing their pragmatic best to restore in them feelings of local neighborliness and in this way to combat the bigness and hollowness of the post-Civil War cities, Royce proposed a different solution. Royce was an admirer of life in the provincial community, which, he thought, would help eradicate the three main evils he saw in America at the turn of the century. One evil was the presence, as he put it, "of a considerable number of not yet assimilated newcomers" who were often a boon and welcome but who constituted, he thought, a "source of social danger".[8] Another was the leveling tendency produced by centralization and consolidation in an urban society, the same leveling tendency of which Kierkegaard and John Stuart Mill had complained a half-century earlier in the name of the individual. The third evil was the spirit of "the mob" as it had been described in Gustave Le Bon's popular work of the times, *The Crowd*.

Royce, in his *Philosophy of Loyalty*, which appeared in 1908, described the malaise of the times in more general terms with the help of Hegel's concept of alienation or estrangement, much as Karl Marx had earlier with a very different political goal in mind. Hegel, Royce recalled sympa-

8. Josiah Royce, *Race Questions, Provincialism, and Other American Problems* (New York, 1908), p. 73.

thetically, had pointed out that in certain periods of European history the social mind of the Spirit had become "estranged from itself", notably during the decline of the Roman Empire and during the period of political absolutism in Europe in the seventeenth and in the early eighteenth century. On the other hand, the social spirit had not been self-estranged, Royce said, in the period of our thirteen colonies, which were small provinces. "In the province," he said, "the social mind is naturally aware of itself as at home with its own." [9] By the twentieth century, however, America had become the scene of urban alienation, in which the individual saw himself confronted by powers that he could not understand and to which he submitted without love or loyalty.

This spirit of alienation might be overcome, Royce thought, if the American spirit were to come to know itself better, if Americans were to combat the forces leading to detachment and loneliness by repairing to the provinces. In the romantic era, the poet Schiller could hope to escape from a self-estranged world to a world of dreams, but Royce was not drawn in that direction. Instead he found hope in the province. "There must we flee from the stress of the now too vast and problematic life of the nation as a whole. There we must flee . . . , not in the sense of a cowardly and permanent retirement, but in the sense of a search for renewed strength, for a social inspiration, for the salvation of the individual from the overwhelming forces of consolidation. Freedom, I should say, dwells now in the small social group, and has its securest home in the provincial life." [10]

Santayana's Aristocratic Antiurbanism

Royce's pupil, Santayana, could not have been more different from him in philosophy. Royce was an idealist, Santayana a

9. Josiah Royce, *The Philosophy of Loyalty* (New York, 1908), p. 239.
10. Royce, *Race Questions,* pp. 97–98.

materialist. One was a dialectician, the other a poet. One received his nourishment from Kant and the post-Kantian idealists, the other went back to ancient Greece for philosophical insight and practical wisdom. And while Royce was above all a learned professor who was admired by the young philosophical "pros" who looked forward to their own chairs in philosophy, Santayana was a cosmopolitan esthete, a fastidious man of culture, and a devotee of the arts who despised most of the eager professional aspirants who sat in his graduate classes. In spite of these differences, however, Royce and Santayana were both uneasy about urbanization.

Santayana resembled those mobile, unassimilated strangers whom Royce had in mind when he spoke with anxiety of the newcomers who were filling the American cities. Born a Spaniard and a Catholic, Santayana was hardly at home in the Protestantism of New England in his day. He was contemptuous of the commercial path to success that was characteristic of Boston in his youth; by temperament he was cool and detached. Throughout his writings, especially his autobiographical writings, he expressed his antipathy to the ideals of what he calls Judaism, Liberalism, and Positivism, all of which were heavily represented in the New York he knew. And therefore New York, in spite of the great admiration that its philosophers felt for Santayana's work, was always a source of disturbance to him. There, he said, everything was "miscellaneous, urgent, and on an overwhelming scale". There, he complained, "nothing counts but realization".[11]

The tendency to think of Santayana as urbane and anti-romantic in his philosophy has perhaps obscured his hostile attitude toward metropolitan life in America. But the fact is that he thought of commercial towns as feeding on, and levying a toll on, everything transportable. "However much they may collect and exhibit the riches of the world they will not

11. *The Philosophy of George Santayana,* edited by P. A. Schilpp (La Salle, Ill., 1940), pp. 560–61.

breed anything original." [12] Even London of the 1880's,
which Henry James admired so much, was for Santayana a
"Babel of false principles and blind cravings", and Paris to
him was "false, cynical and covetous".[13] He said he loved the
earth while he hated the world, and he thought that ideal
communities, like moral ideals, should be rooted in the earth.

In the end, therefore, Santayana did not differ very much
in his opinion of urbanization from Royce, his philosophical
antithesis at Harvard. Santayana believed that the modern
world had become monstrous in certain of its aspects, that a
leveling tendency was abroad in the world, and even perhaps
that the world was suffering from an excess of strangers and
Hegelian alienation. Being so estranged himself from the
modern world, and lacking Royce's reforming zeal, Santayana
did not officially advocate a return to the provinces, but his
views on the city were not far from Royce's. Just as Santayana's moral philosophy required that ideals be anchored in
natural impulses, and that, as he says somewhere, one must
be a beast in order to be a spirit, so his ideal city had to be
rooted in the land. Once again we find a meeting of philosophical extremes against the city, an occasion for Royce the
idealistic provincialist and Santayana the naturalistic alien to
compose their differences, far from the madding urban
crowd.

John Dewey and the Concept of Community

Up to this point I have considered every one of the major
philosophers on whose views of the city I wish to concentrate, with the great exception of John Dewey. Dewey's
views on the city, as one might have expected, resemble
those of William James, his great predecessor in the history
of pragmatism, more than they resemble those of any other

12. George Santayana, *The Middle Span* (New York, 1945), pp. 25–26.
13. *Ibid.*, p. 22.

philosopher I have been discussing. As a pragmatist, Dewey admired most of the forces that were urbanizing America at the end of the nineteenth century: technology, science, industrialization, and the matter-of-fact outlook which they encouraged. And, as one who lived most of his adult life in Chicago and New York, he, more than any other major American philosopher, knew at first-hand the spirit of the metropolis. It was unlike anything that Jefferson could have known or dreamed of in Monticello, immensely far from Concord and Walden, and a world away from the Cambridge of James, Royce, and Santayana. To the practical problems of the metropolis, political and educational, Dewey addressed himself with more vigor and courage than any other major philosopher in our history. Like William James, he was free of all prejudice against its immigrant residents; like James, he opposed urban corruption and national departures from high ideals; and, like James, he loved the active quality, the hurry, the eagerness, and even the miscellaneousness of urban experience. He was no agrarian, no Transcendentalist, no absolute idealist, no snob, no antisemite, no esthete. And yet he was terribly worried by the forces that we associate with urbanization. This, of course, does not make him, or anyone, for that matter, an antiurbanist in the sense of a city hater. But when one examines some of Dewey's ideas about altering, improving, or eradicating the external causes of his worries about the city, one becomes aware of his link with the tradition of antiurbanism that lies behind him in American thought.

Here Dewey converges with Jane Addams and Robert Park, those other disciples and admirers of William James. The essential point of agreement is their localism, their respect for the values of what the sociologists call the primary group, their notion that only by somehow regenerating these groups could one combat the hollowness of which James spoke when he attacked blind, brutal bigness. In contrast to Royce, who advocated a higher provincialism, the urban

reformers—and here I mean Jane Addams, Robert Park, and
John Dewey—advocated what Park called a new parochialism, a way of life that would re-create some of the values of
an earlier world in the urban context. It is in this spirit that
one may view the emphasis that Jane Addams put on the settlement houses and Dewey's notion that the schoolroom contained within itself the method for improving our way of life.

Perhaps the most articulate expression of this appears in
Dewey's *The Public and Its Problems* (1927). Echoing some
of Royce's fears, Dewey wrote: "The Great Society created
by steam and electricity may be a society but it is no community. The invasion of the community by the new and relatively impersonal and mechanical modes of combined human
behavior is the outstanding fact of modern life".[14] An age
that had expanded the physical means of communication had
failed to use them properly. The revolution that had brought
Bangkok and New York closer together had turned New York
into a vast hotel in which neighbors did not communicate
with one another in spite of having telephones in each room.
And so *the* problem of America in 1927, according to Dewey,
was that of converting the Great Society into a Great Community. How this was to be brought about he did not say in
detail. But he outlined his proposal with sufficient clarity to
make it possible to conclude that he, like Robert Park, was an
advocate of the new parochialism. Dewey emphasized the
need for increased communication, and communication, he
urged, was essentially and necessarily face-to-face in character. *Immediate* community had to be established if the great
society was to be successfully converted into a great community.

It should not surprise us, therefore, to find Dewey return-
ing to two familiar figures in our story. He had always had a
fondness for Emerson, whom he once identified as *the* moral
philosopher of democracy, and he now called upon Emerson

14. John Dewey, *The Public and Its Problems* (New York, 1927), p. 98.

at the end of *The Public and Its Problems:* "We lie, as Emerson said, in the lap of an immense intelligence. But that intelligence is dormant and its communications are broken, inarticulate and faint until it possesses the local community as its medium".[15] The second familiar figure is, of course, Jefferson. At the age of eighty-one, Dewey presented an exposition of Jefferson's political philosophy in which Dewey insisted that Jefferson was not merely a spokesman for states' rights as against the claims of the nation, but that he also attached immense importance to self-governing communities of much smaller size than the state or the county. Impressed as Jefferson was by the virtues of the New England township, he thought that the counties had to be divided into wards if democracy was to work properly, and it was his affection for the wards as immediate communities that captivated the aged Dewey.

Jefferson said that he might have concluded every speech with the words, "Divide the counties into wards". And in a similar spirit, Dewey might have concluded every one of his with the words, "Divide the cities into immediate communities", just as Jane Addams might have declaimed, "Divide the cities into settlement houses", and Park, "Divide the cities into primary groups". The new parochialism was their proposal in the first quarter of the twentieth century for the solution of some of the problems created by urbanization. It was an effort to fill the emptiness of the great city in a nostalgic spirit. This was not a call to revive the unestranged spirit of the colonial provinces, but it shared with Royce's viewpoint the idea that the city was lacking something that older preurban American communities possessed, and which had to be *re*-created. As such, the new parochialism was not an effort to provide *new* forms of association for city dwellers, but rather an effort to revivify old ones and to plant them in a new urban context.

15. *Ibid.*, p. 219.

I have now completed my survey of the three major phases of philosophers' reflections on urban life: the age of Jefferson, the era of Emerson, and the time of James, Royce, Dewey, and Santayana. My purpose has been exclusively historical, and I hope I have established my historical point, which is that in different ways and in varying degrees American philosophers of very different points of view have been distrustful of, or dismayed by, the American city. It would appear that our nation's philosophical history has been characterized by a persistent distaste for urban life, which has at times been more pronounced than at others. This distaste has been associated in different instances with different kinds of feeling—with a preference for the farmer's life, for the hermit's life, for life in the wilderness, for life in a provincial community, for life in a city rooted in the soil. And where the American city was not condemned or escaped by our philosophers, they made an effort to reform it in a nostalgic spirit.

Transcending Antiurbanism

I conclude with some more general remarks. First of all, I want to point out that the history of the philosophers' reactions to the city is paralleled in other fields of intellectual and literary endeavor: the philosophers have not been idiosyncratic. Secondly, the philosophers' reactions reflect the fact that they—even the youngest of them, Santayana, who was born in 1863—lived the formative years of their lives in a preurban phase of American history. They do not transcend the preurban ethos of their times. Thirdly, we cannot explain the phenomenon in purely ideological terms. Too many different kinds of philosophers have shared similar feelings about the city.

In connection with this last point, one special kind of nonsense must be avoided, and that is the idea that the intellectual critique of the American city may be explained by the allegedly inherent romanticism of the American mind. The fact is that of all our major thinkers only Emerson may be seriously interpreted in this way. Among the philosophical thinkers I have discussed, he alone tied his attack on the city to a romantic ideology in which the wilderness was superior to the artificial city. Jefferson's attitude was more a matter of practical political concern about the impact of urbanization on a democratic rural America, and the attitude of the philosophers following Emerson was also unromantic. Even the idealist Royce refused to fly to a dream world, and both Dewey and Santayana made their criticism of the American city as *partisans* of civilization rather than as romanticists drugged by the love of untouched Nature. One of the most striking features of the history of intellectual criticism of the American city is the fact that after the Civil War it comes to be made more and more in the name of the civilized values of order, rationality, and communication, and not in the name of the wilderness. The urbanization of the nation after the Civil War brought about a decline of romantic ideology in the highest reaches of our intellectual life. Hence the city was criticized for reasons that were the very opposite of those advanced by doctrinaire romantics. In the age of Transcendentalism the city was too civilized for the intellectuals; in the golden age of American philosophy it was not civilized enough.

When the American city was found wanting by Royce, Dewey, and others who were not gripped by romantic metaphysics, it was criticized on grounds that cannot be brushed aside as the expression of irrational prejudice or metaphysical doctrine. And it is from the very fact that we cannot subsume all the attacks on the city under one alleged trait of the intellectuals, their romanticism, that we may draw hope. We are not all heirs of Natty Bumppo, not all worshipers of the forest. The forces of American intellectual history do not, of themselves, preclude the possibility that intellectuals will create a set of useful ideas for the improvement of the American city. Some day we may have a coherent philosophy of urban life, a philosophy based not on distrust of the American city but rather on affectionate, sympathetic concern for its well-being. In creating such a philosophy we shall demonstrate that we can overcome the persistent strain of antiurbanism in our philosophical tradition from Thomas Jefferson to George Santayana.

3. Two Studies of William James: Some Problems of Philosophical Biography[1]

The reader of the history of American philosophy who begins at the beginning inevitably sighs with relief when he finally reaches the world of William James, for in James' writing he finds something not only original and exciting, but also philosophically profound. After the reader escapes earlier imitators of British and continental philosophy, he discovers in the case of James a new intellectual globe, a luminary about whom the American philosophical world rotated for a generation beginning with 1890, when James' great *Principles of Psychology* appeared. James may have been anticipated by Charles Peirce and revised by John Dewey, but he was unquestionably the central figure in the pragmatic movement at the turn of the century, the major spokesman for America's distinctive philosophy.

1. This essay is the product of joining together a review of Ralph Barton Perry's *The Thought and Character of William James: Briefer Version* (Cambridge, Mass., 1948) in *The Sunday Bulletin Book Review* (Philadelphia), 28 March 1948, p. 6, copyright 1948 by the Bulletin Company; and a review of Gay Wilson Allen's *William James: A Biography* (New York, 1967), copyright © 1967 by Morton White, in *Perspectives in American History*, Volume III (1969), pp. 491–96. Few substantive changes have been made in the previously published material. The review of Perry is reprinted by permission.

Ralph Barton Perry's *The Thought and Character of William James* makes all of this evident. The longer version of Perry's book is a remarkable monument to James, created by one who studied under him, understood him, and obviously loved him; while the briefer version is a charming, informative, and succinct account for the general reader, a miniature replica of the two-volume work which won Perry a Pulitzer Prize. Perry is primarily interested in James' philosophy, but both versions of his book are crammed with material of interest to students of more general aspects of American life and thought.

One of the more intriguing chapters of the story concerns William's relationship with his great brother, Henry. After reading *The Golden Bowl* William complained of Henry's "interminable elaboration of suggestive reference" and asked: "But why won't you, just to please Brother, sit down and write a book, with no twilight or mustiness in the plot, with great vigor and decisiveness in the action, no fencing in the dialogue, no psychological commentaries, and absolute straightness in the style?". To this Henry replied in exasperation: "I'm always sorry when I hear of your reading anything of mine, and always hope you won't, you seem to me so constitutionally unable to 'enjoy' it. . . ." . Those who view William as the naïve, practical, fresh-air philosopher, and Henry as the sensitive, introverted seer, might regard this exchange between the brothers as indicative of a fundamental conflict in the James family—a conflict between the bully, strenuous life of pragmatism and the delicate feeling of a complicated literary genius. But there is little evidence for such an easy dichotomy. William James, for all his praise of action, was no philosophical Theodore Roosevelt, no pragmatic Rover Boy. "Of all the naked abstractions that were ever applied to human affairs," he began his reply to T. R.'s famous speech on the strenuous life, "the outpourings of Governor Roosevelt's soul in this speech would seem the very nakedest. Although in middle life . . . and in a situation of responsibility concrete enough, he is still mentally in the Sturm and Drang period of early adolescence, treats human affairs, when he makes speeches about them, from the sole point of view of the organic excitement and difficulty they may bring, gushes over war as the ideal condition of human society, for the manly strenuousness which it involves, and treats peace as a condition of blubberlike and swollen ignobility, fit only for huckstering weaklings, dwelling in gray twilight and heedless of the higher life."

The theory that the James brothers were in fundamental conflict is also faced with the difficulty of explaining Henry's reading of William with "rapture". In spite of William's criticism of his novels, Henry thought of himself as a pragmatist, and marveled (in the manner of M. Jourdain) at his having unconsciously "pragmatized" all his life; philosophically, he said, he was "with" his brother completely. Henry's failure to brush pragmatism off as a celebration of the strenuous life, capitalism, imperialism, and acquiescence revealed his own insight and good sense. In spite of his own snobbishness he did not fall in with that long line of literary misinterpreters from Lewis Mumford to Julien Benda who have painted William James as the ideologist of opportunism and private gain, the high priest of American smugness.

In addition to providing us with a great opportunity to achieve greater understanding of James' philosophy and its intellectual background, Perry also provides us with considerable insight into James' personality—though psychology is not Perry's long suit. We learn of James' courageous humanity, his feeling for the underdog, his hatred of sham and the official, and his willingness, even eagerness, to translate his feelings into action. We also learn that "he was a mugwump, an anti-imperialist, a civil-service reformer, a pacifist, a Dreyfusite, an internationalist, and a liberal"; and that he possessed what Perry calls both morbid and benign traits. However, Perry avoids trying to give a "clinical diagnosis" and this is not a book for those who might wish to see James

psychoanalyzed. It is therefore a very different study from
the one to which I now turn.

Upon turning from Perry's book—in either of its two
versions—to Gay Wilson Allen's *William James: A Biography*,
one is inclined to observe that although it is extremely difficult to write a biography of a philosopher when you don't
know much philosophy, Allen's book unfortunately demonstrates that the temptation to do so can be irresistible. Distinguished philosophers like Jonathan Edwards, Emerson, and
James frequently attract biographers who cannot follow a
philosophical argument. Sometimes, of course, this deficiency
in a biographer may not be a defect. In fact, if his subject is
Emerson, it may be a virtue, since it may prevent him from
seeking arguments where there are no arguments to follow.
And if his subject is William James, a biographer may have
enough work cut out for him without digging into what he
may think of as the catacombs of epistemology and metaphysics. I have no doubt that a very interesting book could
be written about James even if the author of that book were
to avoid discussion of his philosophy and his psychology. He
was a hero, as Elizabeth Hardwick has said in her thoughtful
introduction to a volume of his letters, "courteous, reasonable, liberal, witty, expressive, a first-rate writer", and, one
may add, a man with enough sickness in his soul to provide
most biographers with enough of their usual material. For
this reason Miss Hardwick shrewdly observes that James'
pragmatism, his pluralism, and his radical empiricism need
not be her province; and she wisely remarks, as she steers
clear of metaphysics and epistemology: "Reworking the sod
from whence so many crops have come in their season seems
profitless for the enjoyment of James's letters, letters that are
nearly always personal, informal, nontechnical".

Unfortunately, however, Professor Allen has not seen the
possibilities of a philosophy-free biography of James. Al-

though Allen's irrepressibly human subject is vividly presented in this book—no biographer, however ignorant of philosophy, could quote some of his marvelous letters without introducing us to that genial, warmhearted, neurotic "Irishman among the Brahmins", as Santayana called him—wherever Professor Allen tries to connect, as the saying goes, the charmer and his philosophy, the result is really embarrasing.

In his Preface, where Professor Allen states his main concern, he writes:

> James's son Henry was still alive when Ralph Barton Perry wrote his two-volume *Thought and Character of William James* (1935), and he refused to divulge any personal information about his mother, simply because he regarded the publication of such information as an invasion of the family's privacy. Consequently, Perry was not able to write a full account of William James's life, for he was forced to omit almost altogether the important role James's wife played in his biography. Perry's work, though it gives a masterly analysis of James's ideas and of his relationships with other philosophers, was not intended primarily to be a biography. The strictly biographical account is confined to a few chapters in the first volume, preceded and followed by detailed discussions of James's work and his ideas. This plan not only subordinates James's private life to his professional life but obscures the *growth* of his mind and character, depriving the reader of a sense of participation in the experiences being narrated. The present biography is strictly chronological, and attempts to trace the relationship between James's emotional and intellectual life—certainly important for a man who enthroned *feeling* with *thought* in philosophy.

It is the last sentence which is crucial and damaging. For if it states Professor Allen's primary intention, his book must be judged a failure. It is true that because Perry's splendid book concentrates on James' ideas, it cries out for supplementation by a work that would link James the thinker with James the human being. But unfortunately Professor Allen has not forged that link. He has not traced the relationship between James' emotional and intellectual life, because it takes two terms to make such a relationship, and one of them is virtually missing from Allen's account. To be sure, he makes occasional efforts at describing the thought of James, his forerunners, and his contemporaries, but those efforts are so feeble, so skimpy, and so misleading as to be almost worthless.

Let me recite some of the evidence for my conviction that Professor Allen shows little grasp of James' intellectual work or its background:

(1) Every student of James knows that Darwin influenced James enormously, and one might expect his biographer to reveal some understanding of the theory of natural selection. But how does Allen summarize Darwin's great contribution in the *one* sentence he devotes to it? In this misleading way: "Darwin's theory of mutability, whereby variations useful for survival had caused all living creatures to acquire and transmit new characteristics, accounted for the development and separation of species".[2] And after referring to James' Darwinian view that the mind has operated so as to enable the human organism to adapt and survive, Allen writes: "Incidentally, if we extend this concept to all living organisms, then even the most primitive biological creatures have minds similar in kind though not in degree to those of higher organisms, and this raises the possibility that the processes of evolution have not been entirely fortuitous and blind—though this extension goes beyond James's purposes in his book. Yet it seems clearly implied by his words, and he would doubtless have approved of the statement of the twentieth-century biologist, John Langdon-Davies, in *Man and His Universe* that even plants have survived not because they were lucky but because they were clever".[3] If this is what Allen thinks is "clearly implied" by James' words, and what he would

2. Allen, *op. cit.*, p. 95.
3. *Ibid.*, pp. 319–20.

"doubtless have approved of", then it seems to me that Allen fails to understand not only James but also Darwin's influence on him.

(2) A fitting companion of Allen's one-sentence summary of Darwin's views is the following pointless statement about the significance of Ernst Mach: "Mach is best known for his formula giving the ratio of the speed of an object to the speed of sound in the same atmosphere, but he was, as James said, a 'genius of all trades,' and had made important contributions to psychology".[4] So much for Mach.

(3) Finally, consider this incredible remark on "pragmatism": "He [James] had borrowed the term from his old friend Charles Peirce, who, however, had used it in the sense of a rational well-ordered life, whereas James made it a means of judging true from false by looking at results".[5]

We have seen that Professor Allen thinks of his work as different in emphasis from Ralph Perry's, and this is quite true. But whereas Perry was more interested in James' ideas than in psychoanalyzing him, and hence concentrated on presenting a stunning account of James' thought, Allen's book consists of twenty-three superficial chapters on James' personality, sprinkled with misunderstood versions of James' ideas, and a final chapter and Epilogue that hardly compensate for the previous paucity of intelligent philosophical comment. Instead of being connected organically with the tree of James' life, Allen's comments on ideas resemble nothing so much as Christmas decorations that are loosely hooked onto it, feeble little bulbs that flash uncertainly and throw no sustained light on the material or the shape of the tree itself.

As one reflects on the shortcomings of this work, one may ask why there are so many books of this kind. And if anybody doubts that there are such books besides Allen's, let him try to extract from certain studies of Jonathan Edwards a clear

4. *Ibid.*, p. 248.
5. *Ibid.*, p. 392.

statement of what he meant by "necessity", or what he meant
by saying that the will is determined by the strongest motive.
Why do many so-called profound interpreters of early American philosophy lack a philosophy undergraduate's insight
into the meaning of the words they are interpreting?

Here I can only sketch an answer. In part because of the
great historical and literary interest in early American philosophers, books and articles on their thought are often written
by scholars who are inadequately trained in philosophy. And
they are inadequately trained in part because of the vacuum
which sucks them into the task for which they are inadequately trained: philosophers themselves are not interested
enough in the history of American philosophy. While this vicious circle rolls along, those who write on Edwards and
James, for example, without a proper understanding of them
try to transcend their ignorance by offering "deep" interpretations of their hero's thought. Hence they fail to communicate
and analyze what the philosopher in question may have been
most concerned to communicate, because the less one is able
to expound the philosopher's thoughts, the more one is impelled to dilate on his feelings alone. One begins by trying to
connect the ideas and the feelings but soon one loses one's
grip on the ideas, and the whole enterprise collapses into the
kind of thing represented by this book: an entertaining
biography which is adorned with useless snippets about
Peirce, Darwin, Mach, Bain, Stumpf, Renouvier, Bergson, Pil-
lon, *et al.*, about whom the author knows very little and
about whom, I venture to say, he couldn't care less.

The basic failure, therefore, can often be attributed to a
lack of education, but how shall we remedy the situation?
How shall we train aspiring biographers of American philosophers to develop the requisite knowledge of their subject's intellectual accomplishments if they wish to deal with those accomplishments? It may be said that the answer is obvious:
ask them to take courses in the history of American philosophy. But I am convinced that this is not the answer. For even

if professional philosophers could be persuaded to abandon their indifference to the history of American philosophy, it won't do to send students who are trained in history and literature into such courses with the expectation that they will gain the skill that is necessary for writing the kind of book that Professor Allen has tried unsuccessfully to write. For what is wanted, I think, is an understanding of philosophy that can be gained only from the equivalent of at least one year of graduate study in philosophy. The history or literature student who has this kind of training not only does not need courses specifically devoted to the American philosophers, but where he has the opportunity he should almost always be advised first to seek training in philosophy as such and then to study the American philosophers on his own. Naturally, if he can manage both a year of graduate study in philosophy and courses in the history of American philosophy, he will be in an even better position to produce a successful biographical treatment of an American philosopher, but where he must choose, there is no doubt in my mind as to the courses he should take first. Would we be satisfied with anything less than the equivalent of a year of graduate study in physics if a biographer wished to discourse seriously on the connection between Einstein's physical thought and his emotional life? Why, then, do we suppose that a biographer who wished to do a corresponding study of James could do it without analogous training in philosophy?

It is true that in principle a historian is entitled to study the history of any discipline, and if he is a very gifted man and lives a long life, he will undoubtedly be able to master on his own the rudiments of the relevant discipline or disciplines. But I am confident that in this day and age it is unlikely that he will be able to produce a really exciting work in the history of philosophy or a life of a philosopher if he is an autodidact who reads philosophical works as if they were novels. I do not deny that some philosophers about whom one may wish to write historically or biographically may be less technically forbidding than others and hence require less philo-sophical training for understanding their thought. I have al-ready suggested that Emerson is probably a case in point, and it is unfortunate that such an atypical figure as Emerson dominates the minds of Americanists who think that all one needs to know is the language in which a philosopher writes in order to write his biography. But they forget Edwards, James, Peirce, Dewey, Royce, and Santayana; and they may not realize that the study not only of Aristotle and Kant but even of certain philosophers of perhaps greater interest to historical and literary scholars—I have in mind what may be called the Pico-Vico axis—requires philosophical training if it is to be conducted fruitfully.

By this I certainly do not mean to say that the history of philosophy or the biographies of philosophers should be writ-ten only by philosophers. What I mean is that serious train-ing in philosophy is an indispensable condition for writing its history and for writing the kind of biography that Professor Allen has sought to write. And I would emphasize that this is not asking too much of students of American matters. I can well imagine the comment of scholars who exhaust them-selves learning remote languages and establishing texts: "What? Do you expect us to be philosophers, too?". But even scholars of Greek philosophy have come to recognize that they cannot live on philology alone, and that illuminating work on the major Greek philosophers requires a careful study of philosophy itself. Why, then, should we expect less of those who have the language of William James and who have his legible words in books that are indisputably his? Why shouldn't we ask them to take thought and add several cubits to their intellectual stature?

4. The Revolt Against Formalism in American Social Thought of the Twentieth Century [1]

Historians of American thought and critics of American culture are only too aware of the kinship among some of our distinctive intellectual currents—instrumentalism in philosophy, institutionalism in economics, legal realism in the law, economic determinism in politics and literature, the new history. From a methodological as well as a political and ethical point of view they unite to form the distinctive liberal *Weltanschauung* of twentieth-century America. No great research is necessary in order to establish the surface connections of these influential patterns of social thinking in their mature forms; nor, for that matter, does it require much effort to show a striking similarity in the intellectual origins of Beard, Dewey, Holmes, James Harvey Robinson, and Veblen. But these connections and this similarity can hardly be appreciated without a study of the ideas against which they re-

1. This essay first appeared in the *Journal of the History of Ideas,* Volume VIII (April 1947), pp. 131–52. It then appeared, with some minor changes, as Chapter II of my *Social Thought in America* (New York, Viking Press, 1949), which was reprinted as a paperback in 1957 by the Beacon Press of Boston. The essay has also been reprinted in *Historical Vistas,* edited by R. Wiebe and G. McWhiney (Boston, 1964), pp. 417–38. The present version is virtually the same as the original and is reprinted by permission.

volted in the eighties and nineties of the last century. A good deal has been said on this matter,[2] but no one, I think, has put his finger on a fundamental pattern in the early critical work of these figures; namely, their joint participation in a revolt against formalism and a consequent acceptance of the central importance of historical and cultural analysis.

It is very hard to give an exact definition of "formalism" in advance of our discussion, but I think its meaning will become clearer as we consider examples. It may be that the term as applied to movements in different fields—in law, philosophy, and economics—does not retain precisely the same meaning; but there is a strong family resemblance, strong enough to produce a feeling of sympathy in all who opposed what they called formalism in their respective fields. Anti-formalists like Holmes, Dewey, Veblen, and Beard call upon social scientists in all domains, ask them to unite, and urge that they have nothing to lose but their deductive chains.

This attack on formalism or abstractionism leads to two important positive elements in the thought of these men —"historicism", and what I shall call "cultural organicism". These are frequently identified in discussions of nineteenth-century thought, but it seems to me that they can be distinguished in a rather simple way. By "historicism" I shall mean the attempt to explain facts by reference to earlier facts; by "cultural organicism" I mean the attempt to find explanations and relevant material in social sciences other than the one which is primarily under investigation.[3] The histori-

2. See M. Curti, *The Growth of American Thought*, Chapter 22; V. L. Parrington, *Main Currents in American Thought*, Volume III, pp. 401–13; J. Chamberlain, *Farewell to Reform*, Chapter 7; A. Kazin, *On Native Grounds*, Chapter 5.

3. See Morton White, "Historical Explanation", *Mind*, Volume 52, N.S. (1943), pp. 212–29, and "The Attack on the Historical Method", *Journal of Philosophy*, Volume 42 (1945), pp. 314–31. I am aware that these terms have been used differently, and so I must emphasize that I mean only what I say I mean. In the light of the ambiguity of these terms I suppose it would be desirable to find something fresh and neutral. I have searched for these

cist reaches back in time in order to account for certain phenomena; the cultural organicist reaches into the entire social space around him. In many cases these two tendencies exist side by side in the thought of a single man, and in fact this is precisely what happens with most of the figures we shall treat. They are all under the spell of history and culture. Holmes is the learned historian of the law and one of the heroes of sociological jurisprudence; Veblen is the evolutionary and sociological student of economic institutions; Beard urges us to view political instruments as more than documents; Robinson construes history as the ally of all the social disciplines and the study of how things have come to be as they are; Dewey describes his philosophy alternately as "evolutionary" and "cultural" naturalism. All of them insist upon coming to grips with *life, experience, process, growth, context, function.* They are all products of the historical and cultural emphases of the nineteenth century, following, being influenced by, reacting from its great philosophers of change and process—Darwin, Hegel, Maine, Marx, Savigny, Spencer, and the historical school of economics.

The present essay is an attempt to delineate the early roots of this community of outlook. It lays great stress upon the fact that Dewey violently attacked formal logic in his earliest writings, that Veblen devoted great energy to deprecating the abstract-deductive method of classical political economy, that Beard fought against the formal-juridical approach to the Constitution, that Holmes proclaimed in 1881 what later became the slogan of generations of legal realists: "The life of the law has not been logic: it has been experience".[4]

In the case of Dewey the roots are very clear. His early thought begins under the domination of neo-Hegelianism

without success. It should be pointed out, however, that the terms do have this much value: they indicate the strong ties which exist between these American thinkers and those whom we should call historicists and organicists without much hesitation.

4. *The Common Law* (Boston, 1881), p. 1.

with its unqualified condemnation of the formal and the mechanical. It is supported (in his own mind) by the results of
Darwinian biology.[5] Dewey was first a disciple of G. S. Morris, the obscure American idealist. His first philosophical
work was also under the influence of T. H. Green and Edward Caird. Not only did his views of logic and metaphysics
find their roots here, but also the earliest expression of his political philosophy.[6] Veblen, by an interesting coincidence,
was also a graduate student at Johns Hopkins and he too listened to Morris.[7] But there is no clear indication of any influence of Morris' Hegelianism upon Veblen. If there had been,
it would have turned up in Veblen's first publication, "Kant's
Critique of Judgment", in the form of a Hegelian attack on
Kant. Indeed this essay would have been more like Dewey's
first essay on Kant (which appeared in the same volume of
the *Journal of Speculative Philosophy* as Veblen's essay—the
1884 volume) which *is* a Hegelian attack on Kant.

Although Veblen does not go through an early Hegelian
stage with Dewey, he shares with Dewey a tremendous admiration for Darwin. It is interesting to observe that Veblen
constantly compared the Hegelian and Darwinian conceptions of change, always to the detriment of the former,
whereas there was a period in Dewey's development when he
tried to defend his Hegelianism with arguments from Darwinism.[8] Both Dewey and Veblen are part of a reaction
against British empiricism, and their early thought expresses
this quite vividly. One berates the philosophical wing of the
tradition, the other attacks the economists. And sometimes,

5. See Morton White, *The Origin of Dewey's Instrumentalism* (New York,
1943).

6. See Dewey's *The Ethics of Democracy*, University of Michigan Philosophical Papers, Second Series, No. 1 (1888).

7. See J. Dorfman, *Thorstein Veblen and His America* (New York, 1934),
p. 39.

8. See *Library of Living Philosophers*, Volume I, edited by P. Schlipp, p.
18.

of course, they converge on the same figures, e.g., Hume, Adam Smith, Bentham, John Stuart Mill.

It is extremely important to take into account this aversion to British empiricism—a phenomenon which can only surprise those who casually link Dewey and Veblen with all "empiricists". The paradox, if any, was almost solved by Leslie Stephen when he remarked in his study of the Utilitarians that although they were frequently appealing to *experience*, they had a very low opinion of the value of historical study. Now Holmes was certainly less opposed to the British tradition. Nevertheless Holmes selected for his special attack the prime exponent of Utilitarian jurisprudence—John Austin. Holmes was disputing as early as 1874 Austin's view of the law as the command of the sovereign.[9] For if the law is the command of the sovereign, then the judge is to *find* it, rather than make it, and clearly this conflicts with Holmes' main positive view. I emphasize the fact that Austin is a Benthamite in order to indicate the centrality of Bentham in the camp of the enemy. When Dewey first published books on ethics it was hedonism and utilitarianism which he most severely attacked;[10] when Veblen criticized the foundations of classical economics it was Bentham's felicific calculus that he was undermining; when Holmes was advancing his own view of the law it was the tradition of Bentham he was fighting against; when Beard came to treat the Constitution as a social document and not simply as an abstract system to be logically analyzed, he found Bentham's shadow, and that of Austin, covering the subject. That Robinson, the historian, should not have found a comparable sparring partner among the

9. *Holmes-Pollock Letters*, edited by M. De W. Howe (Cambridge, Mass., 1944), Volume I, p. 3; also *Justice Oliver Wendell Holmes: His Book Notices and Uncollected Letters and Papers*, edited by H. C. Shriver (1936), p. 21.

10. *Outlines of a Critical Theory of Ethics* (1891); *The Study of Ethics* (1894).

Utilitarians does not destroy the generality of my thesis; on the contrary, it confirms it, for there were no utilitarian historians of comparable stature. And it was precisely its alleged failure to deal with social phenomena in a historical-cultural manner that led to the attack on the tradition of Bentham and Mill. Dewey attacks its ethics, psychology, and logic for failing to study the actual workings of the human mind; Veblen attacks the felicific calculus as well as the failure to study economic institutions in their wider cultural setting; Beard opposes the analytical school for treating the Constitution as if it were axiomatized geometry rather than a human, social document; and Holmes regards Austin's theory as an inaccurate account of law as it was practiced.

These general reflections give a fair idea of what I mean when I join all of these men as anti-formalist revolutionaries. I want now to turn to some concrete expressions of this attitude in their early writings, and in this way to clarify as well as confirm my contention.

Oliver Wendell Holmes, Jr.

Because Holmes was the oldest of these men, and because he was the first of them to present a mature and clear statement of his position, I want to treat him first. I want particularly to consider some of the more general aspects of his work *The Common Law* (1881) in order to focus upon its important role in the revolt against formalism.

His purpose, Holmes tells us on the first page, is to present "a general view of the subject". And then, as if to dissociate himself from a view which he might have expected his readers to assign to him, he announces that "other tools are needed besides logic" in order to accomplish this task.[11] May we infer that there were some expositors of the Common

---

11. *The Common Law* (Boston, 1881), p. 1.

Law who believed that *only* logic was necessary as a tool? I
doubt it, but certainly there were some who conceived logic
as the fundamental tool.[12] Of what logic is Holmes speaking?
He had in mind traditional Aristotelian logic. It was syllogistic logic that did not suffice for presenting a general view of
the Common Law. Moreover, we can be sure that Holmes
was not rejecting Aristotelian logic because of any failures
which might be remedied by modern, mathematical logic. Of
the latter he knew almost nothing, and in it he had little interest.[13] No enrichment of syllogistic logic in the modern
manner would have changed the situation for Holmes' purposes. It was simply his conviction that deductive logic did
not suffice, no matter how enriched. Holmes was not about to
give a list of legal axioms in the manner of Euclid and
promptly to deduce theorems with the help of logic. If this
were his sole purpose, he would have needed only to apply
logic to the legal principles expressed in his axioms. But on
this he says: "The law embodies the story of a nation's development through many centuries, and it cannot be dealt with

12. John Stuart Mill, in his essay on Austin, says, "The purpose of Bentham was to investigate principles from which to decide what laws ought to
exist—what legal rights, and legal duties or obligations, are fit to be established among mankind. This was also the ultimate end of Mr. Austin's spec-
ulations; but the subject of his special labors was theoretically distinct,
though subsidiary, and practically indispensable, to the former. It was what
may be called the *logic of law*" (my italics). "Austin on Jurisprudence", *Dissertations and Discussions*, Volume IV. "Jurisprudence, thus understood, is
not so much a science of law, as the application of logic to law." *Ibid.*, p.
167.

13. Holmes, like Dewey, never had a very high opinion of formal con-
structions. In a letter to Pollock he has the following to say of Hohfeld's attempt to classify jural relations: "Hohfeld was as you surmise an ingenious
gent, making, as I judge from flying glimpses, pretty good and keen distinctions of the kind that are more needed by a lower grade of lawyer than they
are by you and me. I think all those systematic schematisms rather bores;
and now Kocurek in the *Illinois Law Review* and elsewhere adds epicycles
—and I regard him civilly but as I have written don't care much for the
whole machinery". *Holmes-Pollock Letters*, Volume II, p. 64.

as if it contained only the axioms and corollaries of a book of mathematics".[14]

We see at once the historical emphasis in Holmes. It is because the law embodies the *history* of a nation that it cannot be treated deductively. Although Holmes does not explicitly formulate them, we may indicate at least two questions which are introduced by his statement, in order to be clearer about what he is saying. (1) Can we formulate the law accepted at a given time in a deductive fashion, beginning with legal axioms or fundamental principles? (2) Has the law in its actual historical course developed in a logico-deductive manner? In other words, did the axioms, for example, reveal themselves to man before the theorems? Now we must not forget that in this place Holmes is concerned with the latter question, and his answer is that we cannot explain legal history in terms of logical processes alone. Legal history does not unfold as if it were created by a logician. The life of the law has not been logic in this sense.[15] He follows this statement with a statement of other factors to which we must refer if we are to understand *why* and how certain legal rules were developed: "The felt necessities of the time, the prevalent moral and political theories, intuitions of public policy, avowed or unconscious, even the prejudices which judges share with their fellow-men, have a good deal more to do than the syllogism in determining the rules by which men should be governed". The theory, we see, is predominantly a theory in the philosophy of the history of law, to use Mill's

14. *The Common Law,* p. 1.

15. I am not suggesting that Holmes was not interested in the first question. Indeed he has considered it too. But I wish to suggest that the anti-formalism in *The Common Law* was the product of a negative answer to the second question. On this point it may be instructive to examine Mill's comparison of Maine and Austin. The latter is the logician of the law; the former investigates "not properly the philosophy of law, but the philosophy of the history of law". *Dissertations and Discussions,* Volume IV, pp. 161–64.

phrase in describing Maine's work. And it is anti-formalistic insofar as it rejects a certain theory of the development of the law, the theory that it evolved in accordance with a logical pattern.[16] What Holmes insists is that the law does not develop as formally as some thinkers have maintained.

The positive implications of this attack on formalism are fairly obvious. Holmes is led to an intensive study of the history and theories of legislation in order to explain the meanings of certain legal terms and rules and why they emerged when they did. The first chapter of *The Common Law*, for example, is an exercise in historical explanation: it is a study of early forms of liability in order to show that they are rooted in passion and vengeance. The entire study, the details of which we need not consider, is permeated with a historical outlook, specifically with the spirit of epoch-making work in anthropology. *The Common Law* followed the publication of E. B. Tylor's *Primitive Culture* by ten years, but the impact of Tylor's book was still considerable. Not only is Tylor cited on certain factual questions [17] but some of his

16. It should be pointed out that although Holmes would probably answer the first question in the negative, it is not at all clear that this is entailed by a negative answer to the second. One might formulate the two questions with the word "physics" in place of "law" and conclude that the answer to the second is no, but that the answer to the first is yes. The entire question of Holmes' attitude toward logic in the law is a difficult one. Fearful of the effect that some of his statements may have had in furthering irrationality and illogicality, philosophers like Dewey and Morris R. Cohen have tried to interpret these statements in a manner consistent with their own views. See Dewey's "Justice Holmes and the Liberal Mind", *New Republic*, Volume 53 (1928), pp. 210–12 (reprinted in Dewey's *Characters and Events*), and Cohen's "Justice Holmes", *New Republic*, Volume 82 (1935), pp. 206–9. Other problems are raised concerning his relations with C. C. Langdell, often described as the great exponent of inductive methods in the law and yet someone of whom Holmes says: ". . . to my mind he [Langdell] represents the powers of darkness. He is all for logic and hates any reference to anything outside of it. . . ." *Holmes-Pollock Letters*, Volume I, p. 17 (letter written in 1881).

17. *The Common Law*, p. 11.

general ideas are also absorbed. For example, Holmes remarks on what he calls a very "common phenomenon", and
one which is "very familiar to the student of history":

> The customs, beliefs, or needs of a primitive time establish
> a rule or formula. In the course of centuries the custom, be-
> lief, or necessity disappears, but the rule remains. The reason
> which gave rise to the rule has been forgotten, and ingenious
> minds set themselves to inquire how it is to be accounted for.
> Some ground of policy is thought of, which seems to explain
> it and to reconcile it with the present state of things; and
> then the rule adapts itself to the new reasons which have
> been found for it, and enters on a new career. The old form
> receives a new content, and in time even the form modifies it-
> self to fit the meaning which it has received.[18]

The point of view expressed here is closely related to Tylor's conception of survival, treated at length in Chapters 3
and 4 of *Primitive Culture*. In the case of Tylor, the study of
primitive culture is motivated, in part, by a desire to ferret
out just those elements of his own culture which are mere
survivals of a more backward and less civilized age. The
study of the past is not archaeological or antiquarian for
Tylor. He urges that we try to get rid of those practices
which have nothing to commend them but the fact that they
are survivals of the past. It is for this reason that he concludes his great work with the following statement:

> It is a harsher, and at times even painful office of ethnogra-
> phy to expose the remains of crude old culture which have
> passed into harmful superstition, and to mark these out for
> destruction. Yet this work, if less genial, is not less urgently
> needful for the good of mankind. Thus active at once in aid-
> ing progress and removing hindrance, the science of culture is
> essentially a reformer's science.[19]

Tylor's conception of the science of culture as a reformer's
science must be underscored if we are to appreciate the link

18. *The Common Law*, p. 5.
19. *Primitive Culture*, 1st U.S. edition. (1874), Volume II, p. 453.

between the historicism and the liberalism of our American thinkers. Tylor's view shows conclusively that historicism is not necessarily associated with a veneration of the past. Here the study of the past is construed as instrumental to the solution of present problems—the elimination of contemporary irrationality. The student of the past need not have a stake in the past.[20] If the example of Marx is not sufficient to show this, certainly that of Tylor is worth mentioning. This fact is of great value in helping us to understand the evolutionary and historical orientation of Holmes, Veblen, Dewey, Beard, and Robinson. It helps us distinguish the motivation of their historicism and organicism from that of European reactionaries in the nineteenth century.

John Dewey

In 1882, one year after the publication of *The Common Law*, Dewey's first published contribution to philosophy appeared. With it he began a series of investigations in philosophy and psychology under the influence of British neo-idealism which was to continue until the emergence of his distinctly instrumentalist, pragmatist, or experimentalist outlook.[21] Dewey was even more anti-formalist than Holmes. Under the influence of George S. Morris, his teacher at Johns Hopkins, he came to scorn the epistemology of the British empiricists, and to single out for attack their dualistic separation of mind from the object of knowledge. This separation was construed by Dewey as "formal" and "mechanical" and hence attacked in the manner of Hegel. The "New Psychology" was a movement, according to Dewey, which was to free psychology

20. At a later date Holmes explicitly announced his sympathy with this point of view when he said: "It is revolting to have no better reason for a rule of law than so it was said in the time of Henry IV". "The Path of the Law" (1897), *Collected Legal Papers*, p. 187.

21. I have treated this period in detail in *The Origin of Dewey's Instrumentalism*.

from the analytical dissections of associationism.[22] Hegel provided him with the concept of a universal consciousness which embraced everything and which provided the link between individual consciousness and the objects of knowledge, the link which supposedly showed them to be more than formally related. The *objective mind* of idealism was made central,[23] and as Dewey tells us later, it was the ancestor of his insistence upon the "power exercised by cultural environment in shaping . . . ideas, beliefs, and intellectual attitudes".[24] It was this which united him with the spirit of *The Common Law*—this emphasis on the need for regarding human action (in Holmes the special case of legal action) as part of what Dewey later called a "cultural matrix". Although Holmes was not a Hegelian, I think there is no doubt that he and Dewey were motivated by similar considerations in their attack on formalism. In the light of this great similarity in their early years, their mutual respect in later years and the convergence of pragmatism and legal realism should occasion little surprise.[25] It was in the eighties that Dewey was also at-

22. "The New Psychology", *Andover Review*, Volume II (September 1884), pp. 278–89.

23. John Dewey, *Psychology* (1887).

24. Quoted in the *Library of Living Philosophers*, Volume I, edited by P. Schilpp, p. 18.

25. The connections between the later Holmes and the later Dewey are well known. Indeed something of a literature has already grown up on the intellectual links between pragmatism and legal realism. Dewey has written of Holmes in several places (see M. H. Thomas, *A Bibliography of the Writings of John Dewey*). Holmes' admiration for Dewey is expressed throughout the Holmes-Pollock correspondence and also in H. C. Shriver, ed., *Justice Oliver Wendell Holmes: His Book Notices and Uncollected Letters and Papers*. On some aspects of their intellectual links, see M. H. Fisch, "Mr. Justice Holmes, the Prediction Theory of the Law, and Pragmatism", *Journal of Philosophy* (1942), pp. 85–97. Dewey was familiar with Holmes' *The Common Law* quite early, citing it in his *The Study of Ethics: A Syllabus* (1894) for Holmes' treatment of legal motive and the "external standard". It is also interesting to examine in this connection Dewey's early essay "Austin's Theory of Sovereignty", *Political Science Quarterly*, Volume IX (1894), pp. 31–52. In the latter, Dewey criticizes Austin in a manner quite consistent with what I have called organicism. He objects to his view that "the residence of sovereignty can

tacking formal logic.[26] Now Holmes was no admirer of Hegel's *Logic;* certainly he would not have agreed that it represented "the quintessence of scientific spirit", as Dewey maintained in 1891. But the classic excerpt from *The Common Law* about the life of the law not being logic can be matched with several from Dewey, the most striking being Dewey's claim in 1891 that formal logic was *"fons et origo malorum* in philosophy".[27]

In addition to sharing Holmes' attitudes toward the role of formal logic, and toward what I have called cultural organicism, Dewey shared Holmes' respect for the historical or genetic method.[28] I have already stated briefly how this functioned in Holmes' early work. I want to turn now to its position in the early work of Dewey. In Dewey's thought the use of genetic method is positively motivated, whereas his opposition to formalism is the product of a polemic on Hegelian grounds against British empiricism. I do not mean that the historicism to which I have referred has no connections with his Hegelianism. What I wish to emphasize is the fact that his Hegelianism directed him *against* formalism, but that his Darwinism came later as a support to those tendencies in his thought which had already grown out of contact with idealism. It is not surprising, therefore, to find his use of genetic method taking on an *evolutionary* cast. For this reason we find among his earliest contributions which are historicist in character, attempts to approach morality from an evolution-

be found in a definitely limited portion of political society" (p. 42), and also objects to it for making "a complete gap between the social forces which determine government and that government itself" (p. 43). There is a related attack on Maine in "The Ethics of Democracy" (1888) cited above.

26. Dewey, "The Present Position of Logical Theory", *Monist,* Volume II (1891), pp. 1–17.

27. *Ibid.,* p. 3. The community which is expressed by these outbursts against formal logic does a good deal to explain the ease with which Roscoe Pound has united Dewey, Hegel, and Holmes in his own attacks on *mechanical* jurisprudence.

28. For a discussion of certain other aspects of this tendency in American thought, see Schneider, *op. cit.,* Chapter 33.

ary point of view—e.g., his attempt in the paper "The Evolutionary Method as Applied to Morality".[29] This concern links him not only to Holmes but also to Veblen, as we shall see when we examine the latter's regretful complaint in 1898 that economics was not then an evolutionary science.

Dewey's application of evolutionary method to morality is not only useful for establishing his connection with Holmes and Veblen; it also helps us see some of the ties between his experimentalism and his historicism, between his early Hegelian emphasis on change and history and his later pragmatic emphasis on experiment and control. In expounding the nature of evolutionary method, he tries to formulate the sense in which experimental method is itself genetic. His answer is rather simple. In conducting experiments on the nature of water, to use Dewey's example, we perform certain acts of mixture and we see that water is formed as a consequence. The entire process is one in which water is "brought into being". The experimental process, therefore, is viewed as genetic in character, precisely because it "brings into being" certain phenomena as a result of experimental manipulation. Now there are some domains, Dewey thought at the time, in which experimental control is impossible. We are able to use experiment in chemistry, he argues, but we cannot apply it to "those facts with which ethical science is concerned".[30] "We cannot," he says, "take a present case of parental care, or of a child's untruthfulness, and cut it into sections or tear it into physical pieces, or subject it to chemical analysis." What we can do, however, is study "how it came to be what it is", that is, study it historically. History, therefore, is construed as "the only available substitute for experiment", according to Dewey. "The early periods present us in their relative crudeness and simplicity with a substitute for the artificial operation of an experiment: following the phenomenon into the

29. *Philosophical Review*, Volume XI (1902).
30. *Ibid.*, p. 113.

more complicated and refined form which it assumes later, is a substitute for the synthesis of experiment."

We see then that for Dewey at this time, history was the only available substitute for experiment and, moreover, experiment itself was a kind of historical enterprise. Now the notion of history as a possible substitute for experiment was not original with Dewey; in fact the whole discussion is reminiscent of the kind of discussion one finds in *A System of Logic*, especially where Mill considers the various methods— experimental or chemical, physical or direct deductive, historical or inverse deductive—and their applicability in the social sciences.[31] Mill also concluded that experiment was not possible in at least one of the "moral sciences", namely, economics, but he argued that the best substitute was the abstract-deductive method, not history. That Mill and Dewey should have divided in this way is quite understandable in the light of Dewey's avowed opposition to formalism. It is important to see, moreover, how this permits us to bring Veblen into the picture. For it was precisely this aspect of Mill's methodology which Veblen attacked in his own critique of classical economics. And Veblen, like Dewey, appeals to history, to the need for an "evolutionary science".

Thorstein Veblen

Like Holmes and Dewey, Veblen was strongly influenced by new developments in anthropology. If anything, he was more interested and more learned in that field than they were. So strong was this influence that he began his famous attack [32] on all previous schools of economics by approving the following statement:"Anthropology is destined to revolutionize the political and social sciences as radically as bacteriology has

31. See Book VI of the *Logic*, entitled "On the Logic of the Moral Sciences", in which these various methods are compared.

32. "Why is economics not an evolutionary science?" (1898), reprinted in *The Place of Science in Modern Civilization*.

revolutionized the science of medicine". But economics, he complained, was not then in tune with this new note. In short, it was not an evolutionary science.

Now what, according to Veblen, is an evolutionary science? What was he opposing? To understand this we might best turn to John Stuart Mill for the light he sheds on Veblen's lament, and in this way observe concretely how he represents, with Bentham and Austin, the ideology against which so many of the pioneers of American social science revolted. The doctrine of economic method associated with Mill is well expressed in the *System of Logic,* but it is even more sharply defined in a brilliant essay which he wrote in 1829 when he was twenty-three years old, "On the Definition of Political Economy; and the Method of Investigation Proper to It".[33] For Mill, political economy is to be distinguished from what he calls social economy or speculative politics—the latter treating "the whole of man's nature as modified by the social state". Political economy is rather a branch of social economy because it does not deal with the *whole* of man's nature. It is concerned with man "solely as a being who desires to possess wealth, and who is capable of judging of the comparative efficacy of means for attaining that end".[34] "It predicts only such of the phenomena of the social state as take place in consequence of the pursuit of wealth. It makes entire abstraction of every other human passion or motive; except those which may be regarded as perpetually antagonizing principles to the desire of wealth, namely, aversion to labor, and the desire of the present enjoyment of costly indulgences." [35] The important point in Mill's statement of the nature of political economy is his use of the subjunctive conditional mode of assertion in the following passage: "Political economy considers mankind as oc-

33. This appears in Mill's *Essays on Some Unsettled Questions of Political Economy.*
34. *Ibid.,* p. 137.
35. *Ibid.,* pp. 137–38.

cupied solely in acquiring and consuming wealth; and aims at showing what is the course of action into which mankind, living in a state of society, *would* be impelled, *if* that motive, except in the degree in which it is checked by the two perpetual counter-motives above, *were* absolute ruler of all their actions".[36] I emphasize the subjunctive mood of the statement, for it is clear that Mill is not saying that in fact the pursuit of wealth *is* the sole motive of man. Indeed he goes on to say that the economist does *not* put this forth as a description of man's actual behavior. He denies that any "political economist was ever so absurd as to suppose that mankind are really thus constituted".[37] But future critics of Mill, preeminently Veblen and his followers, have treated this view of the economic man as though it were an unconditional assertion in the indicative mood about man's actual psychology. We can see, therefore, why Veblen rejects the view and why he should find himself in agreement with Dewey on this point. For Veblen, this is the acme of "faulty psychology", and what is worse than a faulty psychology for an institutionalist? It is simply not true that man is governed by this single motive (even if the qualifications about counter-motives are made). And since this is an "assumption" of classical economics which is false, everything which is "deduced" from it is suspect in the eyes of Veblenians.

There are other aspects of Mill's methodology of economics which contribute to an understanding of what was troubling Veblen. Mill suggests that the economist ought to treat man much as the astronomer treats planets. The astronomer frequently talks about what *would* happen to a planet if it were not subject to the sun's attraction. (This, of course, occurs when he considers it as a particle subject only to Newton's first law of motion.) In this sense, Mill says, he *abstracts* and considers the planet *as if* it were a body outside the sun's

36. *Idem*. The italics are mine.
37. *Ibid.*, p. 139.

gravitational field (although he *knows* it is not). Just as astronomers pursue this method successfully, so, it is urged, may economists. Mill believes that economists, by asking how men *would* behave if they were simply dominated by a single motive, will come to a good approximation of how men do in fact behave. "This approximation," he points out, "is then to be corrected by making proper allowance for the effects of any impulses of a different description, which can be shown to interfere with the result in any particular case." [38]

There can be no doubt that this was the tradition against which Veblen was rebelling when he rejected the method of classical economics. I don't think he ever clearly formulated for himself the methodological tenets of Mill in a way that left them defensible, but it was a doctrine of this kind that he rejected. I say *of this kind,* not to exclude the possibility that there were classical economists who were less able than Mill in methodology and less cautious about what they asserted about the actual psychology of man. In any case, it should be evident that classical economics was formalistic for Veblen in a sense related to that in which formal logic was formalistic for Dewey, and Austin's jurisprudence was formalistic for Holmes. Dewey in his earliest attacks on it construed formal logic as a description of how we think, and contemptuously dismissed it. Holmes insisted that when we study law "we are not studying a mystery but a well-known profession", and what could be more mysterious than the abstract dicta of Austin, formally conceived and having nothing to do with the "bad man"—the man who pays the lawyer to advise him how to keep out of jail? It is for this reason that Holmes, Dewey, and Veblen found themselves arrayed against three apostles of empiricism—Bentham, Mill, and Austin—and for an ironic reason—they thought they weren't empirical enough!

When Veblen complained that economics was not an evolutionary science, he was voicing precisely this attitude. Now

38. This appears in Mill's *Essays on Some Unsettled Questions of Political Economy*, p. 140.

what was evolutionary science as Veblen understood it? In his essay on it he is not sufficiently concerned with saying what an evolutionary science is. He insists that some things which might be expected to make a science evolutionary really don't. Hence the historical school—Schmoller, Hildebrand, Ashley, Cliffe Leslie—was "realistic" insofar as it dealt with "facts", but this is not enough, according to Veblen. They fail, in his opinion, to formulate a *theory* concerning those facts. For him an evolutionary science must present a "theory of a process, of an unfolding sequence".[39] When he comes to the classical economists, he finds that even where they do refer to empirical data, and even where they try to present a theory of process, they still fall short of the evolutionary ideal.[40] What, then, is the difference? As we press on we find a statement to the effect that the difference is one of "spiritual attitude"—a rather tender expression for one so tough-minded as Veblen. We press further and find that what he is disturbed about in the classical economists is their addiction to the idea of *Natural Law*. He is opposed to their for-

39. Veblen, *op. cit.*, p. 58; see also J. K. Ingram, *A History of Political Economy* (New York, 1888), on the "realism" of the historical school, esp. p. 213. In addition, see H. Grossman, "The Evolutionist Revolt Against Classical Economics", *The Journal of Political Economy*, Volume 51, Nos. 5 and 6 (1943); this treats the revolts in France and England. H. W. Schneider considers Veblen in his discussion of genetic social philosophy in America, *op. cit.*, Chapter 33.

40. Naturally, some members of the classical school were sensitive to the growing historicism of the nineteenth century and made many attempts to connect with this tendency, e.g., Mill's attempt to deal with dynamics in the *Political Economy*. But evolutionists and historicists were not satisfied with these overtures. Veblen's attitude on this point is very similar to Dewey's attitude toward the "inductive logicians" of the nineteenth century—e.g., Jevons and Venn—who tried to go beyond formal logic to formulate a theory of scientific method, ostensibly a goal he shared with them. Thus Dewey says, "whereas we might expect empirical logic to advance beyond formal logic, it virtually continues the conception of thought as itself empty and formal, which characterizes scholastic logic". "The Present Position of Logical Theory", *Monist*, Volume II, p. 5; White, *The Origin of Dewey's Instrumentalism*, p. 91.

mulating an ideal situation and generalizing about that situation without attending to actual economic facts. In some of Veblen's writings this amounts to an objection to the use of a subjunctive conditional like that used by Mill. We cannot, Veblen seems to urge, use hypotheses like "if man were subject to only one motive" and "if perfect competition prevailed" because they are false. At other times Veblen seems to be objecting not so much to the use of such hypotheses in science but rather to the fact that certain classical economists also had a moral attitude toward them. They thought either that they formulated socially and morally desirable states, or that society was tending toward those states. In both cases Veblen held that some kind of belief in Natural Law was present. The first alternative involved a moral judgment on society; the second, a faith in progress.

We may become a little clearer about Veblen's objection if we compare the situation of the student of mechanics with that of the classical political economist. The former tells us how the distance fallen by a freely falling body depends on the time it takes to fall. He points out, of course, that this law holds only in a vacuum. Thus far his procedure is analogous to that of the economist who insists that his laws hold only for economic vacuums, so to speak—cases where only one motive is in operation. But the physicist does not add: "And indeed the vacuum is a highly prized state," or "The atmosphere tends more and more toward a vacuum." But the analogous economist, according to Veblen, not only used ideal concepts like "economic man" and "perfect competition", but also admired these kinds of men and states of society, and looked upon them as ends toward which man and society were moving.

Thus far we have considered Veblen's attack on the use of *abstraction* in classical economics, but we have not considered his attitude toward the use of *a priori* method in economics. To understand this we must return to Mill's view.

Mill distinguished between two types of minds—the *practi-*

cals and the *theorists,* as he called them. The difference
between them may be exhibited by an illustration. Suppose
we were faced with the following question: Are absolute
kings likely to employ the powers of government for the welfare or for the oppression of their subjects? How would the
practicals go about settling it? They would try, Mill says, to
examine the conduct of particular despotic monarchs in history and to find out how they behaved. But the theorists, he
says, "would contend that an observation of the tendencies
which human nature has manifested in the variety of situations in which human beings have been placed, especially observation of what passes in our own minds, warrants us in inferring that a human being in the situation of a despotic king
will make a bad use of power; and that this circumstance
would lose nothing of certainty even if absolute kings never
existed, or if history furnished us with no information of the
manner in which they had conducted themselves".[41] The
practical uses the *a posteriori* method, the theorist the *a
priori* method.[42]

We see how Mill regarded economics as both abstract and
a priori in method. Abstract because it abstracted one aspect
of man's behavior and tried to discover how he would behave
if he had only one motive; *a priori* because it avoided the la-
borious and painstaking methods of statistical research. To
verify hypotheses by reference to history was for Mill "not
the business of science at all, but the application of science".

41. Mill, "On the Definition of Political Economy", *loc. cit.,* pp. 142–43.
42. This distinction, it must be urged in fairness to Mill, is not based
upon the fact that one method "appeals to experience" and that the other
does not. Mill is anxious to disown any mysticism, authoritarianism or dogmatism. With reference to the phrase *"a priori"* he says in this essay: "We
are aware that this expression is sometimes used to characterize a supposed
mode of philosophizing which does not profess to be founded upon experience at all. But we are not acquainted with any mode of philosophizing,
on political subjects at least, to which such a description is fairly applicable". A similar point is made in the *System of Logic,* Book VI, Chapter IX, section 1.

It should be evident why Mill's doctrine was opposed by historicism and institutionalism. It is plain how Dewey's early views also ran counter to Mill's. Dewey's suggestion that we use history as a substitute for experiment where the latter is not available was clearly the method of the "practical" for Mill—an appellation which the later Dewey would have accepted gladly.

It is evident now, I hope, how much the historical, evolutionary, cultural attitude united Dewey and Veblen against the abstract and *a priori* method of Mill. It is also clear why American thinkers rejected so much of the "empiricism" of Bentham and Mill—because they were revolting against the least empirical elements of the tradition—*a priorism, abstractionism,* the felicific culculus, the formal jurisprudence of Austin. The grounds of Veblen's rejection of the method of classical economics are very similar to those which led Dewey to reject what he called scholastic formalism in psychology and logic. They also resemble the considerations which led Holmes to reject the so-called mechanical theory of the law as existing in advance and awaiting the judge's discovery of it. Furthermore, to complete the pattern, Veblen also turns to history and culture, to a cross-sectional study of the institutional context of economic behavior as well as to a study of the temporal development of society.[43] Like Dewey and Holmes he looks to temporal antecedents and cultural concomitants. For this reason we may say that Dewey, Holmes, and Veblen are united in an attempt to destroy what they conceive as three fictions—the logical, the legal, and the

43. In addition to Dorfman's book see the study by John S. Gambs, *Beyond Supply and Demand: A Reappraisal of Institutional Economics.* This last came to my attention after this paper was prepared. For a succinct statement on Veblen's "system", see K. L. Anderson, "The Unity of Veblen's Theoretical System", *Quarterly Journal of Economics,* Volume 48 (1933). Naturally there is an enormous literature on Veblen, but I cite only items of general interest, especially since I am concerned only with a segment of Veblen's career.

economic man. In this way they begin a tradition in recent American thought which Beard and Robinson continued in political science and history.

James Harvey Robinson and Charles A. Beard

The connections among Robinson, Beard, and the revolt against formalism were evident as early as 1908—when the two scholars delivered lectures on politics and history, respectively, at Columbia University, in a series devoted to science, philosophy, and art.[44] Considered in terms of the revolt, Robinson's work is an expression of historicism, the evolutionary movement in social science, and genetic method. Robinson was anxious to establish the scientific character of history, but at the same time to distinguish his own from Ranke's version of scientific method in history.[45] According to Robinson the earliest historians from Thucydides to Macaulay and Ranke examined the past "with a view of amusing, edifying, or comforting the reader". None of these motives, however, can be described as scientific, according to Robinson. He says:

> To scan the past with the hope of discovering recipes for the making of statesmen and warriors, of discrediting the pagan gods, of showing that Catholic or Protestant is right, of exhibiting the stages of self-realization of the *Weltgeist*, of demonstrating that Liberty emerged from the forests of Germany, never to return thither,—none of these motives are scientific although they may go hand in hand with much sound scholarship. But by the middle of the nineteenth century the muse of history, *semper mutabile*, began to fall under the po-

44. Dewey delivered a lecture entitled "Ethics" in the series.
45. For a discussion of the attitudes of American historians on this question and others, see *Theory and Practice in Historical Study: A Report of the Committee on Historiography*, published by the Social Science Research Council, especially Chapter II by J. H. Randall, Jr., and Geo. Haines IV, "Controlling Assumptions in the Practice of American Historians" (1946).

tent spell of natural science. She was no longer satisfied to celebrate the deeds of heroes and nations with the lyre and shrill flute on the breeze-swept slopes of Helicon; she no longer durst attempt to vindicate the ways of God to man. She had already come to recognize that she was ill-prepared for her undertakings and had begun to spend her mornings in the library, collating manuscripts and making lists of variant readings. She aspired to do even more and began to talk of raising her chaotic mass of information to the rank of a science.[46]

It is evident from this passage that Robinson was anxious to free historical research from moralism and estheticism, and this concern links him with Holmes and Veblen in their attempt to distinguish their disciplines from morals; it is also connected with the early (though not the later) views of Beard, who held in 1908 that "it is not the function of the student of politics to praise or condemn institutions or theories, but to expound them; and thus for scientific purposes it is separated from theology, ethics, and patriotism".[47]

We must remember that this a-moralism occurs at a time when the confusion of factual and ethical questions was usually viewed as an instrument of conservatism and reaction. Objectivity was eagerly sought. Social theorists wanted to *expose*, to rake the facts, and so they were moved by a desire to achieve scientific status. Indeed, on this point they were not so violently opposed to the tradition of Bentham, Mill, and Austin. Like the Utilitarians, they were part of a reforming movement, and they too sought to distinguish between what was and what ought to have been. Nevertheless it should be remembered that the desire to make this distinction was not regarded as incompatible with the view that

46. *History* (New York, 1908); also see J. H. Robinson, *The New History*, pp. 43–44, where this essay is reprinted, with alterations.

47. *Politics* (New York, 1908), pp. 14–15. We must note here the difference between this and Beard's later view concerning the relation between ethics and social science as expressed in *The Nature of the Social Sciences*.

moral judgments are theoretically capable of empirical verification. Certainly this was Dewey's view at the time.[48]

Although Robinson was anxious to exclude moral considerations from the writing of history, he was also anxious to go beyond a mere report of what actually happened. Past historians, he says, "did take some pains to find out how things really were—*wie es eigentlich gewesen,* to use Ranke's famous dictum".[49] Moreover, he says, "to this extent they were scientific, although their motives were mainly literary, moral, or religious". What they failed to do, however, was to "try to determine how things had come about—*wie es eigentlich geworden*". And so Robinson concludes that history has remained for two or three thousand years a record of past events—a definition, he says, which still satisfies "the thoughtless". "It is one thing to describe what once was; it is quite another to attempt to determine how it came about."

Robinson's view of history as itself a genetic account of *how things come to be* emphasized the concept of development, and was therefore part of the movement I have called historicism. It was quite like Holmes' conception of history as something which furnished explanations of the emergence and meaning of legal rules; it resembled Veblen's critique of the historical school; it was like Dewey's view of history as a statement of "how the thing came to be as it is". How did it compare with Beard's view? Let us turn to the latter's lecture on *Politics,* delivered in the same year, in the same place, and before much the same audience.

Beard's major complaint about his predecessors revolved about their error in studying juridical-formal relations in the abstract without attention to their roots in the social process. He warns his audience that "official acts are not really sepa-

48. See, for example, his "Logical Conditions of a Scientific Treatment of Morality", *Decennial Publications of the University of Chicago,* first series, Volume III (Chicago, 1903), pp. 113–39. This was reprinted in Dewey's *Problems of Men* (New York, 1945).

49. *History,* p. 15.

rable from other actions of the governmental agents themselves or from many of the actions of the citizens at large".[50]
Political facts are organically related to the social process as a
whole. "The test of what constitutes a political action draws a
dividing line where none exists in fact, and consequently any
study of government that neglects the disciplines of history,
economics, and sociology will lack in reality what it gains in
precision. Man as a political animal acting upon political, as
distinguished from more vital and powerful motives, is the
most unsubstantial of all abstractions. The recognition of this
truth has induced students of politics to search in many fields
for a surer foothold than law alone can afford".[51] And now
just one more quotation to give the flavor of Beard's early
conception of political science: "We are coming to realize
that a science dealing with man has no special field of data
all to itself, but is rather merely a way of looking at the same
thing—a view of a certain aspect of human action. The
human being is not essentially different when he is deposit-
ing his ballot from what he is in the counting house or at the
work bench. In the place of a 'natural' man, an 'economic'
man, a 'religious' man, or a 'political' man, we now observe
the whole man participating in the work of government".[52]

Robinson and Beard together present us with a historicist
view of history and an organic view of political science. The
connection with the others is only too obvious. In the case of
Beard, moreover, even the influence of some of the others is
evident. He was younger than they and his work appeared
later. I need only point to the fact that he cites Holmes,
Pound, Goodnow, and Bentley in the *Economic Interpretation of the Constitution* (1913) in order to show the intimate
ties between his own cultural organicism and that of the key
figures in some of the most important intellectual trends of

50. *Politics*, p. 5.
51. *Ibid.*, p. 6.
52. *Ibid.*, p. 6.

the century—legal realism, sociological jurisprudence, pragmatism. Many of them, of course, did not accept the main
thesis of his book on the Constitution; Holmes, for example,
did not.[53] But this must not obscure for us the broad grounds
on which Beard was united with the rest in a struggle against
what I have called formalism and in an attempt to break
down artificial barriers between the social disciplines. Like
them he embarked on a historical and cultural study of man.

In the present essay I have tried to describe in some detail
a particular affinity in the early work of some of our outstanding American social thinkers. I have insisted that they
were united in a common revolt against formalism which cul-
minated in an emphasis on historical and cultural factors.
This not only helps us understand some of their early doctrines, but also accounts for a good deal of their mutual attachment in later years. I have not been concerned here with
the value of their work or the work of their disciples. Their
predilection in favor of history and culture as central concepts explains a good deal of their breadth. They necessarily
spread themselves as a consequence of their methodological
credos, and so we find Holmes the most erudite and philosophical lawyer of his day; Veblen a sociologist, anthropolo-
gist, and economist; Dewey a psychologist and educator as
well as a philosopher; Beard a historian and political scientist. For this reason (and others) they tower over their contemporaries in American social thought of the twentieth century. Their example has had many effects, some of which
have been salutary, others questionable. This essay has indicated only some of the historical origins of their reaction
from the formal, the deductive, the mathematical, the mechanical, in favor of the historical, cultural aspects of human
social behavior.

53. *Holmes-Pollock Letters*, Volume I, p. 237; Volume II, pp. 222–23.

5. *A Note in Defense of Historicism* [1]

Although in the previous essay I have avoided any detailed evaluation of the doctrines defended by those I have called anti-formalists, in the present note I want to add a word in defense of what I have called their historicism—their idea that later social events may be explained by reference to earlier ones. On the face of it this idea would seem like a truism but it did have its critics, many of whom were reacting—and, as I think, over-reacting—to what they regarded as the excessively historical orientation of nineteenth-century and early twentieth-century thinkers. Some of these critics, I shall try to show in section I below, attributed to historicists a very narrow conception of history that historicists could not, and usually did not, hold. In section II I shall show that other critics rested their case on a distinction between philosophy and history which is a special case of an indefensible distinction between philosophy and all empirical inquiry. Furthermore, although I grant that some misguided historicists may

1. In this note I have presented in condensed form one of the main theses of an article entitled "The Attack on the Historical Method", *The Journal of Philosophy*, Volume XLII (1945), pp. 314–31. Because my revision has been quite extensive I have used a new title.

have left themselves open to other objections by overstating
the case for historicism, I shall show how a historicist, by
making some simple disclaimers, can parry these objections.
Thus, in section III I shall argue that a historicist need not
maintain the easily refuted view that *all* explanation is historical. Finally, in section IV I shall point out a certain ambiguity in the term "historicist" which should not be allowed to
confuse the issue under consideration.

I

One of the most common criticisms of the historical method
is that history by definition cannot present explanations because explanations must contain general laws. The definition
used by those who level this criticism does not allow the historian to go beyond the utterance or writing of singular statements. In this spirit the learned Sir William Hamilton says:
"The information which we . . . receive,—that certain phaenomena are, or have been, is called Historical, or Empirical
knowledge. It is called historical, because, in this knowledge,
we know only the fact, only that the phaenomenon is; for history is properly only the narration of a consecutive series of
phaenomena in time, or the description of a coexistent series
of phaenomena in space".[2] And if, furthermore, one holds
that a scientific explanation must appeal to generalizations or
laws—that an event or state is explained if and only if the singular statement that records it can be deduced from other
singular statements and generalizations—it is evident that
one must conclude that history cannot explain. If explanation
requires laws, and if history is by definition stripped of laws,
then history yields no explanations. Much of the attack on
historicism rests on just such an argument. Thus Morris R.

2. Sir William Hamilton, *Lectures on Metaphysics and Logic* (New York,
1858), Volume I, p. 38. I cite Hamilton not because he is original in this regard, but because he usually represents a large group of philosophers in his
terminology.

Cohen says: "History deals with particular events, with what has happened at a particular time and place. The consideration of general laws apart from temporal embodiment is not the concern of history".[3] In the same vein, Sidney Hook says that the genetic method can give us no more than a chronicle.[4]

The fact is, however, that this conception of history is not adopted by those thinkers usually associated with the tradition of historicism. Condorcet, for example, in speaking of the progress of the intellect, says: "This progress is subject to the same general laws, observable in the individual development of our faculties; being the result of that very development considered at once in a great number of individuals united in society. But the result which every instant presents, depends upon that of the preceding instants, and has an influence on the instants which follow. This picture, therefore, is historical; since, subjected as it will be to perpetual variations, it is formed by the successive observation of human societies at the different eras through which they have passed. *It will accordingly exhibit the order in which the changes have taken place, explain the influence of every past period upon that which follows it,* and thus show, by the modifications which the human species has experienced, in its incessant renovation through the immensity of ages, the course which it has pursued, and the steps which it has advanced towards knowledge and happiness".[5] According to Condorcet, it should be noted, a "historical picture" involves exhibiting the order in which changes take place and explaining the influence of one

3. *Eleven Twenty-Six: A Decade of Social Science Research*, edited by Louis Wirth (Chicago, 1940), p. 241; also see Morris R. Cohen, *A Preface to Logic* (New York, 1944), pp. 128–29.

4. Sidney Hook, "A Pragmatic Critique of the Historico-Genetic Method", *Essays in Honor of John Dewey* (New York, 1929), p. 161.

5. Antoine-Nicolas de Condorcet, *Sketch for a Historical Picture of the Progress of the Human Mind*, anonymous translation of 1795, pp. 3–4; the italics are mine. In 1955 another translation was made by June Barraclough (New York, 1955).

period on periods which follow it. He also says that the progress of the intellect is subject to general laws. Therefore to construe the historical method as though it involved only the first task—the presenting of a chronicle—is to make it an easy prey to the kind of objection we are here considering; and that is why the objection is not very impressive.

I should add, however, that even if critics of historicism should say that, by definition, history cannot discover laws, so long as these critics do not deny that *there are* dynamic laws or laws of succession, the historicist need not worry. He need not be *too* upset to hear that a historian is not the official custodian of dynamic laws, and that laws are discovered by practitioners of what are sometimes called the generalizing sciences. If this be true, the historian who offers explanations may find the laws he needs in these generalizing sciences, or if he does not find them there, he himself may formulate them and confirm them. The fact that physics is different from pure mathematics did not prevent Newton from creating some of the pure mathematics he needed for his physics. The only serious threat to the student who claims to explain later events by citing earlier ones is made by those who claim to know that there are no—or that there cannot be any—laws of succession. But has anyone ever conclusively established this?

So much then for a very weak argument against the view that history can explain. I want now to say a word in passing about critics of the historical method who, after denying that a historical study of the past can explain the present, go on to assert instead that knowledge of the present explains the past.[6] If they mean by this—as they seem to—that all of the *evidence* that a historian has is in the present insofar as he can look at and read only documents and remains that are contemporaneous with him, they will say nothing that need

6. Among those who make much of the fact that we infer our knowledge of the past from evidence in the present are F. H. Bradley in his *Presuppositions of a Critical History* (1874) and Henry Sidgwick in his *Philosophy, Its Scope and Relations* (1902).

bother the historicist. It is obvious that even though a historian's evidence is contemporaneous with him, he may nevertheless maintain that past states have brought about or caused present states of the universe or of society. The evidence we gather for the premises of an explanation should not be confused with the explanation itself.

II

Some critics of the historical method grant that it can find past causes of events, but they follow this with a warning. "To explain," they say, "is not to understand." Thus it is said of historical systems like monogamy: "Knowing what causes their development I no more know what they are, than knowing the bodily changes which condition the development of affection in a human being, I know what that affection is".[7] However, according to such critics, "knowing what an affection is" seems to refer to the kind of knowledge that is sometimes thought to come upon the performance of a *philosophical* analysis. Such knowledge is thought to be the result of analyzing a concept or an abstract entity rather than the result of causally explaining a concrete event in time. According to this view, only concrete entities have histories and only abstract entities may be logically analyzed. It follows from this same view, however, that *all* empirical disciplines—not only historical disciplines—fail to tell us what an abstract entity is. But if, by contrast to the philosophical analysis of concepts, *all* empirical knowledge is defective, it is misleading to give the impression that where history fails to give *knowledge what,* some other empirical science will succeed. Moreover, if one rejects the dualism that underlies the distinction between analytical knowledge and empirical knowledge, this attack on historical method collapses.

7. Hook, *op. cit.*, p. 171. I should add in fairness to Professor Hook that I am here commenting on something he published over forty years ago.

III

I turn now to two objections to historicism which are easily met by making certain disclaimers.

A. One objection presupposes that the historicist holds that *everything* can be explained historically, so the objector simply points out that it is not obvious that there is always an event or state which is earlier than the event or state for which we seek an explanation. In this spirit it has been said that "the notion that the present characters of the system of matrimony, or any other 'social constellation of forces,' can be explained by reducing it to a previous system, overlooks the fact that no matter how far back we go, we must somewhere begin with characters which are not so derivable".[8] Now, so far as I can see, the "logical difficulty" presented here rests on the assumption that there are first states, and that we are unable to explain a later state by reference to an earlier one because at some point in time there are states having no predecessors. But this argument is not very effective. If there is a first state, then naturally *it* can't be explained by reference to a state earlier than it. But does it follow from this that later social systems can't be explained by reference to earlier ones where they exist? Not at all. To show that history can explain some things, we need not argue that history can explain everything; and the so-called historicist as I view him need maintain only that history can explain *some* things. He can disclaim holding that *all* events and states may be explained historically without abandoning anything that he should miss.

Incidentally, the argument against historicism that I just considered is very much like one offered by Henry Sidgwick, except that he applied it to physical phenomena. In speaking of the nebular hypothesis and what he called speculative ge-

8. Hook, *ibid.*, p. 158.

ology and astronomy, he said: "If we take as given—as our point of departure—the positions and velocities of all parts of the physical world at any point of time, present or past, we may reasonably regard all subsequent changes as ultimately explicable by the known laws of physical motion, and partially known laws of chemical combination. . . . But however far back we go, the state of matter at the point of time that we began with is exactly as inexplicable as the state of matter now; it presents the same unsolved problem to Philosophy, which aims at an explanation of the world as a whole".[9] But if one is not interested in "explaining the world as a whole", one need not fear the impact of Sidgwick's argument. The fact that we cannot explain the first state and that we do not try to explain the world as a whole in no way prevents us from sometimes using an earlier state to explain later ones.

B. Although I have argued that history may present explanations if there are dynamic generalizations which connect later events with earlier events, I have not argued that all generalizations are of this kind. Some are static rather than dynamic, as Comte and Mill correctly maintained. If we ask, for example, why a particular volume of dry air is heavier than an equal volume of moist air, and someone answers: "because the density of dry air is greater than that of moist air", he need not appeal to any dynamic generalizations. And this shows that some historicists have overstated their position: for example, John Dewey in an article published at the turn of the century. At that time Dewey seems to have held that every scientific generalization is dynamic and therefore that every scientific explanation is historical. He seems to have held that all scientific generalizations are equivalent to statements having the following form: If an experimenter institutes certain conditions at time t_1, then he will experience certain phenomena at a later time t_2.[10] I think, however, that

9. Sidgwick, *op. cit.*, pp. 132–33.

10. See John Dewey, "The Evolutionary Method as Applied to Morality", *Philosophical Review*, Volume XI (1902), pp. 107–9.

Dewey's view is not acceptable if it excludes the possibility of static generalizations. Dewey's extreme historicism seems to rest on a confusion. A psychologist who studies the behavior of physicists as they test a static generalization like "Dry air is denser than moist air" may assert that if a physicist institutes certain conditions at a certain time, he will experience certain phenomena at a later time; but this psychological fact about the behavior of physicists does not turn the *physicists'* static generalization into a dynamic generalization. We cannot conclude from the fact that it takes time to test a static physical generalization that the generalization is itself dynamic. The property of being denser than moist air is a property of a particular volume of dry air which is not a later property of that volume than its property of being dry. Therefore we cannot argue, as Dewey seems to have argued, that all explanation is genetic or historical. This, however, should not faze a reasonable historicist. He may defend the possibility of historical or dynamic explanation without insisting that all explanation is historical or dynamic.

IV

It must be borne in mind that historicism as I have defended it is simply the doctrine that we may, by appealing to dynamic laws and earlier states or events, explain later states or events. Unfortunately, however, the word "historicist" is sometimes applied to those who dispute the contention of certain classical economists, like John Stuart Mill, to the effect that we can derive certain laws about the economic process from so-called principles of human nature. These derived laws, moreover, may be static or dynamic. Now it has been argued by some economists that there are no principles of human nature of the kind that Mill had in mind. They have therefore maintained that the only way in which we can test both dynamic and static economic laws is by directly appealing to history. They have maintained, in other words, that the only method that can be used effectively in social science is

the *a posteriori* method as described in the previous essay;
and for this reason they are sometimes called "historicists".
When they are faced with the question whether absolute
kings are likely to employ the powers of government for the
welfare or for the oppression of their subjects, they answer it
by examining the conduct of particular despotic monarchs in
the past. They do *not,* to quote Mill once again, "contend that
an observation of the tendencies which human nature has
manifested in the variety of situations in which human beings
have been placed, especially observation of what passes in
our own minds, warrants us in inferring that a human being
in the situation of a despotic king will make a bad use of
power". But the fact that a man is an *a priori* thinker who
does appeal to principles of human nature when trying to answer the question referred to by Mill does not force him to
renounce historicism in the sense in which I have been defending it in this paper. The *a priori* social scientist may
grant that there are dynamic laws governing behavior, even
though he uses the *a priori* method in establishing those dynamic laws. He may be a historicist in the sense in which I
have been defending historicism even though he is not a historicist in the sense in which that word is sometimes used. He
may hold that there are dynamic laws and therefore explanations of later events or states in terms of earlier events or
states without committing himself on the question whether
these dynamic laws may be derived from principles of human
nature. That question can be settled only by an investigation
which is independent of the question at issue in this note.

Furthermore, the question whether capitalist society is
transitory, as Marx maintained, is also different from the one
I have treated. So is the question whether Mill was right in
saying that "human beings in society have no properties but
those which are derived from, and may be resolved into, the
laws of the nature of individual man" and that "men, however,
in a state of society, are still men; their actions and passions
are obedient to the laws of individual human nature. Men are

not, when brought together, converted into another kind of substance, with different properties; as hydrogen and oxygen are different from water".[11] True, thinkers have been called historicists because they agreed with Marx on the transitoriness of capitalism and because they disagreed with Mill's views just quoted; but no argument against such historicists undermines my contention here. This does not mean that the issues raised by Marx's and Mill's substantive views are unimportant; it means that they are irrelevant to the issue whether historical explanation as I conceive it here is possible.

Before concluding, I should say that I have not written this note to establish the obvious truth that sometimes we can explain later states or events by citing earlier ones. Rather, my purpose has been to show how certain critics of historical method have obscured this truth. Some of them begin with a deflationary view according to which historians cannot establish the generalizations which are essential to explanations, so we are not surprised when such critics conclude that history cannot explain. Other critics begin by *in*flating the claims of history the better to *de*flate them afterwards. One way of doing this is first to attribute to historicists the view that history explains everything, and then to refute this view. Once we see such criticisms for what they are, we can also see that the effort to explain later states or events by referring to earlier ones has in no way been undermined by them.

11. Mill, *A System of Logic*, Book VI, Chapter VII, Section 1.

6. *Anti-intellectualism in America* [1]

One of the more obvious features of the epithet "anti-intellectualist" is its ambiguity. It may refer either to one who is hostile to intellectuals or to one who is hostile to the philosophical doctrine known as intellectualism. And so it would be just as well to begin with a terminological distinction that reflects these two different uses of the term. I shall call a person who is hostile to intellectuals an "anti-intellectual" and I shall use the term "anti-intellectual*ist*" only when referring to intellectuals who are themselves critical of certain views concerning the intellect.

The anti-intellectual is usually an ordinary man, a *non*-intellectual, to whom an egghead is an egghead, whether scientist, historian, or philosopher; rationalist or empiricist; hard-boiled or scrambled. For the anti-intellectual, the important contrast is that between the pursuits of the professor, artist, scholar, and scientist, on the one hand, and those of the busi-

1. This essay originated in a lecture I delivered in 1960 at Marietta College on the occasion of the one hundredth anniversary of its Phi Beta Kappa chapter. The lecture was printed in considerably revised form as "Reflections on Anti-intellectualism", copyright © 1962 by Morton White, in *Daedalus*, Volume 91 (1962), pp. 457–68. In revising this essay for publication here I have made enough changes to warrant changing its title.

nessman, plumber, barber, and politician, on the other. But the salient contrast for the anti-intellectualist is within that world which the ordinary man treats as the uniformly gray world of gray matter. Unlike the anti-intellectual, the anti-intellectualist may press the claims of the heart and the hand against those of the head, or he may think of intuition as a superior faculty to be distinguished sharply from that employed by the mathematician or the experimental scientist.

A Metaphor

Even though the category of anti-intellectuals may be distinguished from that of anti-intellectualists, the fact that both consist of individuals who are opposed to something makes it possible to distinguish analogous subclasses within each of the categories. This may be done by distinguishing different ways in which one may oppose something, and an easy way to do so is to employ a metaphor in which we think of the anti-intellectuals and the anti-intellectualists as conducting a war, or some kind of game, if that is pleasanter to contemplate. Then, if we imagine the anti-intellectuals arrayed against the intellectuals, and the anti-intellectualists against the intellectualists, we may distinguish three kinds of strategies that may be employed in each case.

Let us begin with the campaign of the anti-intellectuals. One of their strategies calls for the total destruction of the enemy; a second calls for his containment; and a third calls for an invasion of his terrain. The destructive critic of the intellectual cannot understand how anyone could possibly follow such trivial, silly, time-wasting pursuits, and would therefore liberate society from the responsibility of supporting such drones. Containment is the slogan of the peasant who resents the philosopher's telling him how to run his affairs, and it can portend nothing more painful than a request that the philosopher mind his own business. The invaders wish to enter the classroom, the study, the studio, or the laboratory, to dictate what shall be done and how. The policy of destruction, if pushed to its logical conclusion, would eliminate schools, colleges, universities, sciences, and the arts. Containment would permit intellectuals to operate, but only if they were properly fenced in or reined in, limited in their influence and allowed to express nothing more than idle curiosity—and the idler the curiosity, the better. The invaders would move in on the intellectual and force him to improve himself by standards provided by the invader.

The vertices of this triangle of destruction, containment, and invasion are conspicuous points toward which the anti-intellectual can gravitate. Of these three, the point of destruction is the least popular in the world today. Most popular is the wish to contain, which springs from resentment at the sight of the professor moving into politics, the scientist making government policy, the doctor advocating birth control, the Keynesian economist seducing the sons of businessmen. Although the desire to invade the intellectual's sanctuary would seem to occupy an intermediate position in terms of popularity today, it must always be reckoned as the more dangerous of the two more popular threats to the intellectual life; and for this reason I shall be primarily concerned with it in this essay.

If one turns to the anti-intellectualists, one may once again speak profitably of a triangle of destruction, containment, and invasion; and once again it is fair to say that the destructive attitude figures least prominently. Here too the most influential strategies seem to be those of containment and invasion. But here the significance of containment and invasion is different from what it is in the case of the anti-intellectual's war, precisely because the anti-intellectual and the anti-intellectualist aim at different opponents.

Since containment and invasion are the more common strategies among anti-intellectuals and anti-intellectualists, it will be useful to say a few words about them. First, containment. We try to contain, restrict, or limit what is, or what seems to be, pushing too far, pressing us too hard, invading our own territory. And we try to restrict it rather than destroy it, either when we find it too powerful to destroy, or when we think it will do a useful job if it minds its own business, not ours. Hence it is the *aggressive* intellectual whom the anti-intellectual wants to contain and the *aggressive* intellectualist whom the anti-intellectualist hopes to restrict. When a society has respect for its intellectuals, it will not wish to destroy them. But if the intellectuals begin to threaten the ordinary man, the ordinary man will seek to draw a line beyond which he will not let the intellectuals move. If the ordinary man continues to admire intellectuals, he will merely try to restrict their movements, to set up a wall between the intellectuals and the territories really or seemingly threatened by them.

Something similar may be said about the anti-intellectualist's attitude toward reason. So long as the philosophical analyst of reason is willing to accept or encourage a limitation on its sphere of influence, he does not incur the enmity of the philosopher who is willing to see reason operating peacefully in its own sphere. But let the intellectualist move too far into forbidden territory, and he will meet the blocking efforts of the restrictive anti-intellectualist.

A Little History

The history of modern philosophy yields striking confirmation of this thesis. When the intellectualist limits the sphere of the intellect to pure mathematics and logic, when he says that only truths in these domains may be established by the workings of abstract intellect, he threatens relatively few philosophers. Pure reason is surely the custodian of pure questions and pure answers. But let the intellectualist be aggressive, as he was in the seventeenth century, and he will have to answer to the empiricist, who is a comparatively mild sort of anti-intellectualist.

In the eighteenth century the empiricist wished to prevent the extreme intellectualist, the rationalist, from invading a territory which the empiricist thought of as the preserve of sensory observation and experiment. The rationalist had claimed, or seemed to claim, that pure reason could solve problems that properly belonged to the realm of experience; and therefore he was checked by the empirical anti-intellectualist, who insisted that we must look, listen, taste, touch, and smell in order to confirm or test statements about the world. To be an empirical anti-intellectualist is to be nothing more than one who insists that there are truths that cannot be detected without recourse to sensory experience. Such empirical truths the empiricist wished to protect from the arrogant incursions of the rationalist's reason, and the result was a containment of the intellect as conceived by the rationalists.

Indeed, so effective were the empiricists in this effort, that they forced an entry into the land of the intellect. They forced a reconstruction of the idea of reason itself, and this, one might say, represented a turning of the tide. Once the empiricist's point was accepted, reason was conceived more broadly and more liberally; pure mathematics could no longer be regarded as the sole example of rational intellectual activity. This empirical phase of anti-intellectualism, however, was only the beginning. Once the tide was turned, the real onslaught on intellectualism began. Now the empiricist had to face *his* critics; and at this point in the history of Western thought, a much more aggressive variety of anti-intellectualism emerged. Even after the empiricists had insisted on broadening the intellect, more extreme anti-intellectualists appeared, demanding greater concessions.

After observation and experiment had won their way into the house of knowledge, it was the turn of passion and sentiment. They too, it was thought, could enter and take their places as reputable providers of knowledge. And this was the point at which the invasion begun by the empiricists was pushed to its extreme. When it came to be thought in the eighteenth century that sentiment could find and establish truth, anti-intellectual*ism* became very popular with anti-intellectuals. The two classes remained distinct in composition if only because the anti-intellectualists were intellectuals while the anti-intellectuals were not, but the aggressive wing of the latter class was emboldened by the aggressive wing of the former class.

A *Digression*

Let me make clear that the extremely aggressive anti-intellectualist, the partisan of passional truth, argued for more than the *existence* of passion. It is one thing to say that there is such a thing as passion, and another to say that there is passional truth. It is one thing to say that we have hearts as well as heads; it is another to say with Pascal that the heart has reasons that the reason can never know. It is one thing to say that logical calculation and experiment are not the only activities worthy of man; it is another to say that there are truths which can be established by other methods. The difference in each case is the difference between a true announcement and one that represents a false and dangerous variety of anti-intellectualism. There is also a difference between calling attention to the existence of know-how and elevating it into a distinctive source of truth.

When philosophers call attention to the existence of native abilities and innate skills, they say something that should be acknowledged by everyone. There is a difference between knowing how to attract people and knowing that all bodies attract one another. There is a difference between knack and knowledge. To win friends is not to write a treatise on how to win friends. To be a sympathetic, understanding person is one thing; to be a psychologist is another. No intellectual and no intellectualist need fear these true propositions. Therefore, the reminder that there is such a thing as knowing how is really not a variety of *anti*-intellectualism. However, those who go further and insist that passion and know-how are respectable avenues to truth *are* aggressive, invading anti-intellectualists. When Pascal spoke of the heart's reasons, Emerson of the heart's truths, and D. H. Lawrence of blood knowledge, they surely did not wish to insist merely on the fact that men have passions: they went further and urged that the passions themselves yield a peculiar sort of truth and knowledge.

I should add that it is a tribute to the importance of knowledge and truth in the Western tradition that so many have thought that truth is the goal of poetry. The prestige of truth and knowledge has been so great that some poets (or their spokesmen) seem compelled to prove to the world that the poet also discovers theorems. Plato banished the poet from his ideal community, presumably for not being truthful enough; but the reply to Plato should have been that he was unable to see that a civilized man could not live on knowledge alone. Instead, self-appointed counsellors of poetry have felt compelled to get their clients back into the Republic by ill-advised appeals to the doctrine of poetic truth.

Now the poet should be granted liberty, and even license, but I see no need for providing him with a disguise too. The greatest poets have provided us with truths about man and the world that we might never have known before, but when we accept these truths, we do so because we can in some sense confirm them by means that are not peculiar to poetry. Poets may help us see the truth, but they do not have special methods for confirming it. Moreover, it is grotesque to suppose that the worth of poetry is directly proportional to the amount of truth it uncovers, a conclusion to which some partisans of poetic truth seem to be driven in their laudable but badly reasoned efforts to squeeze the poet into college departments of literature. He deserves to be there, but not because he reports on ethereal things. The danger of this kind of doctrine is even greater when passion, poetry, and practice are said to be sources of *higher* truth, of knowledge which is real and great by comparison to the arid pedantic knowledge gained by calculation and experience. This is the most aggressive form of aggressive anti-intellectualism, for it not only tries to get the poet into a club he would be wise to stay out of—it tries to make him president.

To deny that the poet is primarily concerned with establishing truth by a peculiar method of his own is not to denigrate poetry. On the contrary, the effort of the poet's lawyer to demonstrate that poets are primarily searchers after truth is less than a tribute to one of the noblest activities of man, for it is a misleading way of getting the poet his proper due. There is a difference between being a poet and being a nuclear physicist, a difference which is not brought out properly by saying that they seek different kinds of truth, nor by saying that they establish truth by different methods. A similar point may be made about the claim that passion can lead to truth. The passions may form the *subject matter* of a truthful study, they may stimulate such a study, and they must often be consulted when one is making a moral decision; but it is disastrously misleading to postulate a kind of truth which passion itself finds according to its own infrared lights.

A Spectrum of Philosophies

To see how an anti-intellectualistic doctrine like that of passional truth can encourage the anti-intellectual, one must realize that it represents an aggressive variety of anti-intellectualism which is often populistic in character. That is why it is admirably suited to encouraging an aggressive attack on the intellectual.

If we begin with the assumption that there are no more than two ways of arriving at reliable knowledge of truth, namely, logic and empirical observation, we may think of the history of philosophy as a story of misguided efforts to present others. These efforts divide into two categories. Philosophers of an aprioristic turn of mind have often spoken of a metaphysical capacity to intuit truth, one that allegedly surpasses the kind of reflection that yields ordinary logical or mathematical truth. Such philosophers occupy a position which is at the opposite extreme from that held by partisans of passional truth. One may imagine a spectrum of faculties, proceeding from the metaphysical intuition celebrated by the superrationalist, through calculation and empirical observation, which are favored by the chastened intellectualist, and on to the subempirical methods of practical skill and feeling. At one extreme we have the superrational faculties of man and at the other his subempirical gropings and impulses. Intuition as here conceived is the faculty to which the ancients, some of the medievals, some of the classical rationalists appealed. It is a form of superscientific mental activity under which one might include the knowledge of innate principles and self-evident propositions as conceived by some philosophers. Philosophers who have urged the existence of such faculties have sometimes thought of them as supermathematical, while philosophers who have moved away from logic and sensory experience in the other direction have insisted on the subsensory capacity of some men to *feel* the truth with their hearts and their hands. Therefore, a spectrum of philosophies may be defined in terms of this spectrum of capacities. In the ultraviolet region we find the superrationalistic doctrine that metaphysical intuition yields knowledge; in the infrared region we find the subempiricist view that skill and feeling yield knowledge. In the visible region we find a variety of intellectualism, according to which reason and experience are the only ways of establishing knowledge.

A Convergence

I am now in a position to say a little more about the convergence of the anti-intellectual and the anti-intellectualist. Although I am keenly aware of the problems that arise when

one tries to associate philosophical doctrines with sociopoliti-
cal attitudes, I wish to put forth a hypothesis. First of all, I
should like to express agreement with the familiar thesis that
those philosophers who urged the existence of supermathematical insight spoke for, or prepared an ideological weapon
for, the few. To urge that there is a mode of insight into truth
which transcends that of even the mathematician is to call attention to a putative capacity which only the most favored
few possess—the priests, metaphysicians, theologians, and
sages. And therefore, *other things being equal,* this is a conservative or aristocratic form of anti-intellectualism. Locke
correctly viewed it in this way when he criticized the doctrine of innate principles and attacked the men it would set
up as "dictators of principles". John Stuart Mill was properly
suspicious of the intuitionism of Coleridge and the Scottish
school on similar grounds.

By contrast, I should like to emphasize that the romantic
anti-intellectualism which celebrates the powers of the
farmer, the artisan, and the red-blooded man is, other things
being equal, a democratic form of anti-intellectualism. The
point is that, as one moves along our spectrum from metaphysical intuition to pure feeling, one is moving from faculties which (in the Western tradition at least) are thought to
be possessed by very few, to those that everyone has. It is
primarily for this reason that the superrationalistic critics of
calculation and experience, who complain that they are not
the only sources of truth, have been aristocratic in tendency;
whereas those subempiricists who urge the claims of passion
and know-how have been, generally speaking, democratic or
populistic in tendency. Moreover, it would appear that super-
rationalism was more typical of a prescientific age, whereas,
of course, the subempirical variety of anti-intellectualism first
flourished after the eighteenth century and became very popular in the romantic era, when the passions, the emotions,
and the feelings came to be regarded as ways of establishing
truth and knowledge. This variety of anti-intellectualism was

primarily a reaction to the scientifically oriented thought of Locke.

American Anti-intellectualism

Because of my special interest in the history of American ideas, I wish to apply what I have said to three key figures in the history of American philosophy—Jonathan Edwards, Ralph Waldo Emerson, and William James. Edwards was a logically acute Calvinist who followed Locke on a number of matters, but one of Edwards' most influential works, his *Treatise Concerning Religious Affections,* was a non-Lockeian defense of religious evangelicalism in which he argued that the Protestant elect have a special "Sense of the Heart", as he called it. This sense, according to Edwards, provided the Protestant saint with an opportunity to know the deepest religious truths; and the saint, he said, was more likely to be a babe or an ignorant farmer than a philosopher or a historian. It is true that Edwards thought he was steering a middle course between religious formalism and the most lunatic forms of evangelicalism, but it is fair to say that his doctrines gave more comfort to what I have called aggressive anti-intellectuals than they did to rational or empirical theologians.

Furthermore, the religious views of Edwards were much admired by the Transcendentalists, whose movement came to a climax in the work of Emerson. American philosophy, as represented by Emerson in the early nineteenth century, was romantically and democratically anti-intellectualistic. In a new country that lacked a feudal tradition, that was filled with a vast wilderness, that celebrated the yeoman's life, that was suspicious of the dialectical minutiae of technical philosophy, one might expect that romantic and populistic anti-intellectualism would flourish. Emerson's thought was permeated by a conviction that the mind has ways of knowing which go beyond calculation, observation, and experiment. His Coleridgian distinction between Reason and Understanding led him to think that the Understanding was the limited faculty celebrated by the empiricists, a faculty which was unsatisfactory, he thought, because it did not transcend logic and experience. By contrast, Reason, as Emerson conceived it, went deeply into the mystery of things; and its truths, he thought, were more easily perceived by the poet than by anyone else. It should be realized, therefore, that Reason as conceived by Emerson was very different from Reason as conceived by Locke and the classical rationalists. For Emerson it was the way of the heart, since the heart led man into a realm which could not be penetrated by abstract reason.

In Emerson's case the claims of the poet were associated not only with an effort to limit the sway of Lockeian empiricism but also with a romantic love of Nature and a distaste for the American city of Emerson's time. The Understanding, empirical science, the city—all these were artificial and hence to be put lower than Reason, poetry, and the country in his scheme of values. And like so many of the romantics, he thought of the heart as a faculty which was more commonly used by the man of the soil than by the sophisticated urban intellectual. He said that poetry brought us closer to vital truth than history. Moreover, Emerson constantly sang the praise of artisans. Although he found himself drawn to rural life, he did not despise practicality. Like Crèvecoeur, he associated rural life with practice as well as with feeling. Both practice and feeling were contrasted by Emerson with supersophistication and hyperintellectuality, and this was a feature of his philosophy that attracted William James.

William James was a grandchild, if not a child, of the romantic movement. His famous essay, "The Will To Believe", was an effort to justify faith as a policy. It was written in opposition to scientifically oriented agnostics like W. K. Clifford, who held that, whenever we have no evidence in favor of a proposition or its contradictory, we must suspend judgment. Yet James thought that we are sometimes justified in accepting a belief even when, as he said, our "logical intellect is not coerced". He sympathetically quoted Pascal's statement about the heart's reasons, and vigorously contended for the view that metaphysical and religious truth may be established by sentiment rather than by reason or experience. There are signs in his later work, *Pragmatism,* of a somewhat different view of the way in which our beliefs are established, but in his most widely read articles—notably those he collected under the title, *The Will To Believe and Other Essays in Popular Philosophy*—he gave much support to the tradition of Edwards and Emerson by arguing for non-rational, non-empirical access to religious and metaphysical truth.

In summary one may say that three of the greatest American philosophers were, in some degree, advocates of aggressive anti-intellectualism because they all challenged the idea that reason and experience alone can establish truth. Edwards sought to carve out a sphere in which not they, but mystical insight settled the fundamental questions of religion; Emerson held that Coleridgian Reason was supreme in the realm of morals and poetry; and James took the daring step of making metaphysics a creature of sentiment. Most important for my hypothesis is the fact that Edwards' babes, Emerson's farmers, and James' ordinary men were empowered to see truths beyond those established by calculation and experiment, beyond those established by trained intellectuals. I hasten to add that I do not maintain that Edwards, Emerson, and James were anti-intellectuals. Nothing could be further from the truth. But I believe that their view that the passions can establish truth encourages the philistine anti-intellectual to suppose that he possesses capacities for arriving at *knowledge* that are superior to those of the scientist and the scholar. This emboldens the anti-intellectual to think that he can tell the intellectual how to run his business; and this is the link that joins the two classes of individuals distinguished on the first page of this essay: the anti-intellectuals and the anti-intellectualists.

In America, therefore, the aggressive anti-intellectual has not been coached or encouraged primarily by superrationalistic, aristocratic theoreticians, but rather by romantically oriented populists. Edwards' and Emerson's campaign against Locke's Understanding and James' against the Intellect were all conducted in the name of the "whole man", and the whole man has often been identified by the ordinary man with himself. While reading all of these philosophies, the ordinary man may easily conclude that "vital truth" can be arrived at by the use of faculties which he, the ordinary man, has, and has in much greater degree than the pedantic, narrow, pale, anemic, clever scientist or philosopher. All people have hearts and know-how, though not all of them have very powerful intellects. They all have emotions and passions, and it is commonly thought that the farmer and the man in the street have more and deeper passions than the dust-ridden scholar in his library. So, when ordinary men are encouraged by anti-intellectualists to think that passion and know-how are superior roads to *truth*, they may come to believe that they are as good or better than the intellectual himself at what the intellectual may regard as his game.

A Moral

Populistic anti-intellectualists have encouraged anti-intellectuals by sponsoring a misconception of the nature of knowledge which has had serious effects on our educational system and on our intellectual life. It is implicitly shared by those who speak of feeling as not merely the subject matter of knowledge, but also as a way of arriving at knowledge. It is at the root of misguided efforts to fill the college curriculum with vocational courses, and courses in the creative arts. And when it is coupled with a certain view of spiritual truth, it can lead to a statement like the following by the Governor of the State of New York: "Knowledge is of value only insofar as it is in accord with the spiritual truths inherent in our Judaeo-Christian tradition".[2]

2. *The New York Times,* 5 December 1959.

In denying that feeling and skill may by themselves establish knowledge, we need not deny the existence of feeling
and skill. But we must realize that there is a difference between the pursuit of knowledge, on the one hand, and the
cultivation of moral feeling, religious feeling, and artistic
creativity, on the other. If we wish to cultivate feeling or
creativity in the arts, let us not confuse ourselves with double, indeed, *n*-tuple, talk about many kinds of truth and
many meanings of "veritas" in order to provide a reason for
doing so in universities primarily dedicated to the pursuit of
truth and knowledge. We demean the very things we wish to
encourage when we try to justify them by the use of trans-
parent casuistry. So long as the scholar or the scientist does
not deny either the existence of non-cognitive capacities or
the importance of cultivating them, he does not sink into a
philistinism which is the reverse of aggressive anti-intellectualism. He merely insists on a distinction of profound human
importance. In doing so, the intellectual does not set himself
up as a priest or a prophet. But he does remind the anti-intellectual and his philosophical adviser that there are many subjects on which the voice of Everyman is not authoritative.

Those who cannot see this today fail to see it at their own
peril as well as ours. Today, when the territory of the intellectual is invaded either by anti-intellectuals or subverted by
misguided anti-intellectualists, we all run greater risks than
ever before. Today, the recognition that knowledge of the
truth cannot be attained by mere feeling or instinctive skill is
a necessary condition for the survival of those who are capable of that recognition as well as of those who are not.

II. PRAGMATISM AND ANALYTIC PHILOSOPHY

7. *Pragmatism and the Scope of Science* [1]

The problem of defining the scope of science has been more fundamental and more persistent than almost any other problem of philosophy. Is the method of checking statements by observation and experiment the only method of achieving knowledge of the truth, or are there others? Are there disciplines which validly arrive at truth by means fundamentally different from those used in empirical science? Is there such a thing as knowledge of the truth which may be reached without recourse to experience? Like their European predecessors and contemporaries, American philosophers have struggled with these questions, and like European philosophers they have offered no single answer to them. Neither American philosophy as a whole, nor pragmatism, the most distinctive American philosophical movement, has described

1. This essay appeared originally in *American Perspectives: The National Self-Image in the Twentieth Century*, edited by Robert E. Spiller and Eric Larrabee (Cambridge, Mass., Harvard University Press, 1961), copyright 1961 by the President and Fellows of Harvard College. It was reprinted with a number of revisions in *Paths of American Thought*, edited by Arthur M. Schlesinger, Jr., and Morton White (Boston, Houghton Mifflin Company, 1963). The present version contains some additional changes and is reprinted by permission of the publisher.

the scope of science in a uniform manner. America has been the home of Emerson and Thoreau as well as of Franklin and Jefferson; and from the eighteenth century onward, American philosophy has oscillated between deflationary and inflationary conceptions of the scope of science. The path from the Enlightenment to Transcendentalism, and from Transcendentalism to evolutionism in the nineteenth century, may be represented by a cyclical curve depicting the fortunes of science in American thought. And even more striking evidence of the lack of any monolithic attitude toward science is the fact that pragmatism—supposedly *the* scientific American philosophy—has been torn on the issue. Not all pragmatists have been, as it were, scientific imperialists; not all of them have maintained that all knowledge is scientific in the sense in which physics, chemistry, and biology are commonly said to be scientific.

Of course, pragmatism, as much as any philosophy in modern times, has proclaimed its respect for empirical science and its sympathy with the spirit of scientific method. The founder of pragmatism, Charles Peirce, was a logician who sometimes spoke of his doctrine as if it were nothing more than a theory of the meaning of scientific words; the great popularizer of pragmatism, William James, occasionally spoke of his theory of mind as a corollary of Darwinian biology; and John Dewey, the youngest member of the pragmatic trinity, devoted most of his long life to extolling the virtues of scientific intelligence and to urging its application to political, social, and moral problems. Nineteenth-century America, so unsuccessful in producing scientific thinkers of the first rank, did give to the world three of science's loudest cheerleaders. In fact, so loudly did they cheer that they did much to encourage the erroneous view that all pragmatists worship at the altar of something called "scientism" and believe that one scientific method rules as a god over all branches of human thought.

And yet, if one conceives of pragmatism as the doctrine

originated by Peirce, popularized by James, applied by Dewey, and more recently refined by C. I. Lewis and W. V. Quine, one may safely say that whereas some pragmatists may believe that one and the same scientific method is applicable in all spheres of intellectual activity, other self-styled pragmatists do not. Some pragmatists may be called methodological monists; some are pluralists; and some think they are methodological monists when they really are not. Therefore, the historian of pragmatism cannot present a pragmatic catechism which will formulate a unified creed concerning the scope and limits of scientific method. This may best be seen by reflecting on the pragmatists' ambiguities and disagreements about the nature of metaphysics, theology, ethics, and mathematics. When one does reflect, one sees that pragmatism, more than any historical movement in philosophy, has had internal disagreements on one of the fundamental problems of the theory of knowledge. Let us turn first to the ambiguous status of metaphysics in the writings of Charles Peirce.

Science and Metaphysics

The pragmatism of Peirce was basically a theory about the meaning of scientific beliefs. Confronted with assertions containing laboratory words like "hard", "heavy", and "lithium", to mention Peirce's own examples, a pragmatic logician must translate them into statements of practice. Peirce recognized, of course, that a scientific statement about the hardness or weight of an object is logically equivalent to what he described as a myriad of other statements; but he held that one type of equivalent is of special significance to the scientist, that which specifies certain experiences that an experimenter would have if he were to perform certain operations on the experimental object. Peirce held that if a statement could not be translated into such an equivalent, it lacked scientific or pragmatic meaning; and that two statements, no matter how different they might appear, meant the same thing if their pragmatic translations were identical or equivalent. One purpose of establishing such a test of translatability was to eliminate what he jeeringly referred to in some of his writings as "ontological metaphysics", but ironically enough his own pragmatic maxim led him to conclusions which were themselves metaphysical. For if every laboratory statement about a particular object is equivalent to a statement which asserts what would happen if one were to perform certain operations on it, then, Peirce held, every such statement covertly attributes a *disposition* to the experimental object. To say that Shylock would bleed if he were pricked is to attribute a disposition to Shylock; hence, Peirce said, to imply the existence of an entity which is a *universal*, a metaphysical entity. It was precisely this metaphysical implication of his version of pragmatism that led him to claim that medieval realism was the consequence of pragmatism, that pragmatism implied the reality of universals.

In saying this, however, Peirce created a puzzle, for how could a maxim dedicated to the elimination of "ontological metaphysics" lead to such a conclusion without violating itself? [2] On the one hand, Peirce urges us to present the pragmatic meaning of a laboratory statement in order to distinguish laboratory statements from pragmatically meaningless metaphysical statements; on the other hand, our very pragmatic translation supposedly implies the metaphysical conclusion that universals are real. But can we translate the statement that universals are real into pragmatic terms? If not, should we not conclude that this statement is scientifically or pragmatically meaningless? And if it has another kind of meaning, are we not led to think that two standards of meaningfulness and hence two criteria of truth are employed in

2. For an illuminating consideration of this question, see Arthur W. Burks' essay introducing his selections from Peirce's writings in *Classic American Philosophers*, edited by M. W. Fisch (New York, 1951).

Peirce's philosophy? Apparently Peirce is forced into the acceptance of two such criteria of truth, but he leaves the criterion of metaphysical truth very obscure indeed. Peirce's predicament, therefore, is not very different from one in which William James found himself when he came to discuss the method of theology.

Science and Theology

James' sense of style led him to avoid the jargon of the schools, his racing intelligence made him impatient of logical minutiae, and his feelings inevitably brought him to religion. But James, like so many of his generation, was caught in the cross fire of science and theology, his sense of conflict exacerbated by his devotion to Darwin's biology. His *Principles of Psychology* applied scientific Darwinism to the mind, and the mind was a place of refuge for those who sought to save something immaterial after Darwin's bombardment of conventional theology. On the other hand, although James shared the Darwinism of W. K. Clifford and T. H. Huxley, he did not share their agnosticism on theological matters. James was too religious in temperament, too much the son of his Swedenborgian father, too quick to resent a short way with dissenters from agnosticism. In 1877 Clifford had said sternly: "It is wrong in all cases to believe on insufficient evidence; and where it is presumption to doubt and to investigate, there it is worse than presumption to believe"; [3] and in the very same year Peirce had spoken scornfully of the man who might say, "Oh, I could not believe so-and-so, because I should be wretched if I did". [4] Yet James, the Darwinist, spoke up against Clifford in defense of what James called

3. W. K. Clifford, "The Ethics of Belief", *Lectures and Essays*, edited by Leslie Stephen and Frederick Pollock (London, 1901), Volume II, p. 205.

4. *Collected Papers of Charles Sanders Peirce*, edited by Charles Hartshorne, Paul Weiss, and Arthur W. Burks (Cambridge, Mass., 1931–58), Volume V, Paragraph 377.

"the religious hypothesis". His first famous attempt in its behalf was his essay "The Will To Believe", which appeared in
1896; the second was his *Pragmatism* of 1907.

"The Will To Believe", as James pointed out, was essentially an answer to Clifford's agnosticism, an argument in justification of religious faith as a policy. According to James,
we do have a right to believe a religious statement even
though "our merely logical intellect may not have been
coerced",[5] even though neither the statement nor its contradictory has been scientifically verified. But, when one examines James' treatment of religious statements, one is struck by
the fact that he does not bother to see whether they can be
translated in accordance with Peirce's pragmatic maxim. The
statement that God exists, is not—or at any rate James does
not bother to persuade us that it is—a statement that is easily
translated into one of Peirce's pragmatic conditional statements. It does not predict certain experiences after the performance of certain operations on an experimental object.
For this reason, an application of Peirce's severe pragmatic
test of meaningfulness might well yield the conclusion that
such a statement was meaning*less*. And this is why James'
predicament is similar to that in which Peirce found himself
when he defended medieval realism. Just as Peirce consciously or unconsciously exempted the statement that universals are real from the need to satisfy the pragmatic criterion of
meaning, so James seemed to exempt the statement that God
exists. Once again a double standard of meaning and truth
seems to emerge—one for science and another for theology.

Even though James' *Pragmatism* shows some signs of a
shift away from this double standard—as I argue elsewhere in
this volume [6]—James' *Pragmatism* does not apply Peirce's criterion of meaning to *all* statements. Before the Peirceian scientist may say that a statement is true, the statement must be

5. William James, *The Will To Believe and Other Essays in Popular Philosophy* (New York, 1898), pp. 1–2.
6. See the essay, "Logical Positivism and the Pragmatism of James".

meaningful. But in order for it to be meaningful, it must be translatable into something analogous to the statement "If I let this body go, I shall see it fall". If a statement cannot be so translated, then there is, in Peirce's view, no scientific point in saying that the statement is true. One may pronounce with satisfying results the *words* "I believe that God exists" or the *words* "It is true that God exists", but if the statement that God exists is itself not capable of Peirceian translation, then according to a Peirceian one is not really believing anything when one utters the words "God exists"; one is not seriously attributing truth even though one thinks or says one is. Yet James in his *Pragmatism* did not insist that religious statements pass muster before Peirce's pragmatic theory of meaning. In effect, James bypassed the crucial rule of Peirce's pragmatism by not requiring that the statements of theology be pragmatically translatable in the manner of Peirce's laboratory statements. James went on, as it were, to the election of statements as true, without bothering to nominate them as pragmatically meaningful.

The conclusion that must be drawn is that neither Peirce nor James was fully consistent or thoroughgoing in his application of Peirce's pragmatic maxim. Peirce failed to apply it to his own realistic metaphysics, and James failed to follow its full implications in his discussion of theological belief. The result is the confusion in which they left the subjects of metaphysical and theological method. One clung to universals, and the other to God; but neither of them provided a rationale for their ontological or theological beliefs which is clearly consistent with Peirce's pragmatic theory of meaning. Both Peirce and James, by implication at least, failed to adopt the view that all knowledge is scientific and empirical.

Science and Ethics

Whereas the use of a double standard of truth is implicit in Peirce's treatment of metaphysical assertions as well as in James' treatment of theological statements, the ambivalence of the pragmatic movement is much more explicit in the field of ethics. John Dewey was an ethical naturalist, who believed that all ethical statements are translatable into empirical statements; but C. I. Lewis, the most distinguished pragmatist of the generation after Dewey (Dewey was born in 1859, Lewis in 1883), emphatically disagreed. In the ethical writings of Lewis one finds an explicit defense of the view that not all ethical knowledge is based on empirical investigation. In particular, Lewis argued, knowledge of what is right and just can never be determined by empirical facts alone. Lewis therefore explicitly rejected the epistemology of "scientism", whereas Dewey insisted that the method of ethics was thoroughly scientific.

As we shall see in another essay in this volume,[7] Dewey and Lewis were united in regarding statements of *value* as empirical, but they divided on the subject of obligation, of what ought to be done. On the subject of value, Dewey's view was close to that of Lewis, who says: "As a first approximation, we might say that attributing value to an existent, *O*, means that under circumstances *C*, *O* will or would lead to satisfaction in the experience of somebody, *S*; or it intends the joint assertion of many such affirmations".[8] Here both Dewey and Lewis follow Peirce's pragmatic maxim, applying its central idea to statements of value; indeed, Lewis points out explicitly that value is a disposition, and that therefore attributing value to a diamond is like attributing a specific gravity to it. In both cases, we imply that certain experiences would occur under certain circumstances, and in both cases we express scientific knowledge.

However, Lewis' distinction between value and obligation upsets any picture of pragmatic uniformity on the fundamentals of ethics. In his own words, "Valuation is always a matter

7. See "Value and Obligation in Dewey and Lewis".
8. C. I. Lewis, *An Analysis of Knowledge and Valuation* (La Salle, Ill., 1946), p. 512.

of empirical knowledge. But what is right and just, can never be determined by empirical facts alone".[9] By contrast, Dewey was not prepared to grant that there is a class of moral statements or beliefs which are established by means that are fundamentally different from those used in science. For this reason, the historian of twentieth-century pragmatism must record its divided view in ethics. It is true that Lewis acknowledges a double standard, whereas Peirce and James seem to slip unconsciously into holding that metaphysics and theology have methods of their own which are distinct from that of empirical science. But, like Peirce and James in their respective treatments of metaphysics and theology, Lewis—in my opinion—fails to make clear just how we do justify judgments of right and wrong. His difficulty is related to his position on the nature of *a priori* knowledge, which is itself a subject on which pragmatists are in considerable disagreement.

Perhaps one of the most distinctive features of Lewis' work in epistemology is his theory of *a priori* knowledge, knowledge that we allegedly justify without reference to experience. The most distinctive characteristic of such knowledge is its necessity: statements expressing such knowledge must be true. By contrast, *a posteriori* knowledge is said to be contingent: statements expressing it may be false. If *a posteriori* statements are true, that is not because they *must* be true but because the world happens to be as they say it is. The classic examples of *a priori* statements have usually come from pure mathematics; whereas the most highly developed variety of *a posteriori* knowledge is to be found in the empirical sciences.

The problem of *a priori* knowledge has often been conceived as the problem of saying how there could be such a thing, and a number of answers have been offered in the history of philosophy. The answer given by Lewis is one of the most widely accepted in the twentieth century and is in

9. *Ibid.*, p. 554.

broad outline similar to that given by logical positivists. He holds that all and only *a priori* statements are analytic; that is, they may be seen to be true merely by inspecting the meanings of their component terms. Therefore he rejects Kant's doctrine of the synthetic *a priori*. In Lewis' view, the truth of the statement that every horse is an animal is a consequence of the fact that the meaning of the word "horse" contains the meaning of the word "animal", and this is why we can discover its truth without engaging in experiment on or observation of horses. Therefore, analytic statements are sharply distinguished by Lewis from synthetic statements, whose truth we cannot determine merely by studying meanings. Moreover, according to Lewis and the positivists in Hume's tradition, all logical and mathematical truths are fundamentally like the statement that every horse is an animal in being analytic. The upshot of Lewis' theory is an exhaustive and exclusive division of knowledge into two kinds: logico-mathematical knowledge which requires no observation of the world for its justification, and empirical knowledge which does.

One can therefore understand why Lewis is involved in a serious problem over the status of statements about what is right and just. He contrasts them with value statements because he claims that value statements are empirical. Yet I do not think that he can successfully hold that *all* statements about the rightness or wrongness of actions are analytic, seen to be true merely by an inspection of the meanings of their component terms. Moreover, he seems to reject the view that ethical statements express no knowledge at all. As a result, he entered a quandary from which he never successfully emerged. In one respect, therefore, statements about the rightness of action are to Lewis what ontological statements are to Peirce and theological statements to James. On Lewis' view their method of justification is not empirically scientific, but the positive nature of their method of justification is not made sufficiently clear.

Science and
Mathematico-logical Truth

This brief discussion of *a priori* knowledge leads naturally to the question of pragmatism's position on the nature of mathematical and logical truth; and once again, there is no uniformly held position. One of the most discerning expositors of Peirce's philosophy writes:

> Peirce's Pragmatism is, primarily, the logic of hypothesis; its aim is to prescribe and articulate the one essential condition to which every genuine hypothesis must conform; and broadly this condition is that a hypothesis must be verifiable experimentally. This being the case, it would be natural to assume that Pragmatism has a bearing solely on questions of matters of fact, questions about the world which is disclosed to us, ultimately through our sensations. It should therefore have no bearing whatsoever on our purely formal *a priori* knowledge, that is, our knowledge of logical truths and of pure mathematics. But, although Peirce's writings on this issue are distressingly scrappy, there can be no doubt that he did *not* wish the scope of his Pragmatism to be restricted to thoughts, statements, or hypotheses concerning questions of empirical fact. Pragmatism, he maintains, has an important relevance to those parts of our knowledge which are commonly described as purely formal, or apodeictic.[10]

But while Peirce's writing on this subject may be "scrappy" and even "confused", as Gallie says, the fact that Peirce did try to extend his pragmatism to the statements of logic and mathematics itself prefigures later pragmatic efforts to erase the sharp line between the analytic and the synthetic. Moreover, there is evidence that James too had serious doubts about the distinction between analytic and synthetic, especially in the last chapter of his *Psychology*. It is entitled "Necessary Truths and the Effects of Experience", and in one

10. W. B. Gallie, *Peirce and Pragmatism* (Harmondsworth, Middlesex, England, 1952), p. 161.

of its notes James says: "Some readers may expect me to plunge into the old debate as to whether the *a priori* truths are 'analytic' or 'synthetic'. It seems to me that the distinction is one of Kant's most unhappy legacies, for the reason that it is impossible to make it sharp".[11]

Contemporary reflection on the sharpness of the distinction between analytic and synthetic statements has led to a serious difference between pragmatists on the subject of logico-mathematical truth. Lewis espouses just such a sharp distinction as James disowns. On the other hand, W. V. Quine argues that his own refusal to make a sharp distinction between analytic and synthetic statements is more thoroughly pragmatic in spirit than the dualism of Lewis.[12] Quine's attack on the distinction between analytic and synthetic is prompted by a number of considerations. It is mainly inspired by the negative conviction that the "meanings" appealed to by Lewis in his account of analytic statements are shadowy, obscure entities, and furthermore that the word "synonymous" as applied to linguistic expressions lacks the clarity to be expected of philosophical terms. Other considerations lead Quine to the conclusion that we must surrender the notion that for each kind of statement there is a separate and distinct method of validation. He advances this view in opposition not only to a sharp methodological distinction between logico-mathematical truth and truth in the natural sciences, but also to the contrast between ontology and natural science which seems implicit in Peirce's acceptance of scholastic realism. Quine contends that there is a basic similarity in the methods of justifying statements of mathematics, statements of physics, and statements which assert the existence of universals. In short, they are all justified pragmatically.

11. William James, *The Principles of Psychology* (New York, 1890), Volume II, p. 661, second note.

12. W. V. Quine, "Two Dogmas of Empiricism", *The Philosophical Review,* Volume LX (1951); reprinted in Quine's *From A Logical Point of View* (Cambridge, Mass., 1953).

Quine may therefore be called a methodological monist, at least so far as mathematics, the empirical sciences, and ontology are concerned. As he has not written on theology or ethics, one cannot say how far his monism would extend. But it is safe to say that such a methodological monism has not been typical in the history of American pragmatism. Either half-consciously, as in the case of Peirce and James, or explicitly, as in the case of Lewis, pragmatists have tended to shy away from the view that Peirce's theory of meaning—or something like it—applies to *all* statements which express knowledge.

In fact even Dewey, who seems by intent to be the most thoroughgoing of all pragmatists in his methodological monism, has wavered in his treatment of questions surrounding the distinction between *a priori* and *a posteriori* knowledge. More than any thinker in modern times, Dewey viewed the history of Western philosophy as a fruitless quest for certainty, a misguided effort to discover a class of truths that would be stable, certain, and self-evident. And for this reason the notion of *a priori* knowledge was always suspect in Dewey's philosophy. For more than a half-century he campaigned against the view that there are two sorts of knowledge, one rational, necessary, and unchanging, and the other empirical, contingent, and merely probable. In his *Reconstruction in Philosophy* Dewey wrote: "Mathematics is often cited as an example of purely normative thinking dependent on *a priori* canons and supra-empirical material. But it is hard to see how the student who approaches the matter historically can avoid the conclusion that the status of mathematics is as empirical as that of metallurgy".[13] And a little further on in the same book Dewey says: "Logic is a matter of profound human importance precisely because it is empirically founded and experimentally applied".[14]

13. John Dewey, *Reconstruction in Philosophy* (New York, 1920), p. 137.
14. *Ibid.*, p. 138.

In such passages Dewey appears to be a methodological monist who puts logic in the same category as one of the most practical of empirical sciences; he adopts a position that is not unlike the extreme empiricism of John Stuart Mill in its methodological monism. And when we read the earlier pages of Dewey's *Logic*, we continue to think of him as a methodological monist, who does not make a sharp distinction between the methods of logico-mathematical science and natural science. But the *Logic* is a very long book, and by the end of it Dewey's monism seems to flag, and he seems to revert to a view which is strongly dualistic in its implications. Dewey makes a distinction between what he calls "existential" and "ideational" propositions, which is a version of the positivistic distinction between synthetic and analytic propositions. "Propositions", he says, "are . . . of two main categories: (1) Existential, referring directly to actual conditions as determined by experimental observation, and (2) ideational or conceptual, consisting of interrelated meanings, which are nonexistential in content in *direct* reference but which are applicable to existence through the operations they represent as possibilities".[15] And this distinction, it would appear, serves to reinstate the sharp distinction between *a posteriori* and *a priori* knowledge that was apparently repudiated in *Reconstruction in Philosophy* and in the earlier pages of his *Logic*. In any case it is a far cry from the doctrine that mathematics is as empirical in its status as metallurgy, for it does suggest that whereas the "existential" truths of metallurgy are established experimentally, the "ideational" truths of mathematics are established by an examination of the interrelationships between "meanings". And it is hard to see how Dewey can view propositions about the interrelationships between meanings as experimentally verifiable. Once again we find a pragmatist speaking by implication of a kind of knowl-

15. John Dewey, *Logic: The Theory of Inquiry* (New York, 1938), pp. 283–84.

edge which is not experimental, and this time it is one of the most anti-dualistic of all pragmatic theorists of knowledge.[16]

Science and Pragmatism

One may sum up the situation as follows. Peirce seemed to exempt the statements of ontology from the need to follow the pragmatic maxim. James seemed to exempt the statements of theology. Lewis unquestionably exempted those ethical statements in which we assert that actions are right or wrong. And while Dewey professed to apply the canons of experimental science to all claims to knowledge, he seems at places to have fallen unwittingly into a variety of dualism. Quine is monistic in his approach to mathematics, logic, physics, and ontology,[17] but through lack of interest fails to commit himself on ethics and theology. In short, not one of these five distinguished American pragmatists has seriously subscribed to the view that all statements by means of which men take themselves to express knowledge may be justified by the techniques commonly associated with experimental science. Because individual pragmatists have not all been consistent about the scope of science and because the movement as a whole has been divided on this question, pragmatism has never been able to present a single face to the world on one of the central problems of modern philosophy. Whether this has been philosophically or socially fortunate is a matter beyond the concern of this essay. But it is a fact that must be acknowledged by any serious historian of ideas in America. In other essays in this part of the present volume, I shall try to document this contention in greater detail.

16. See "Experiment and Necessity in Dewey's Philosophy" below.
17. See "The Analytic and the Synthetic: An Untenable Dualism" below.

8. *Logical Positivism and the Pragmatism of William James* [1]

Any philosopher of whatever persuasion who tries to write the history of his subject in America from its beginnings to the First World War will sooner or later discover that, of all the thinkers he is obliged to study, the two most brilliant and most original were those lifelong friends and partners in pragmatism, Charles Peirce (1839–1914) and William James (1842–1910). Both were sons of intellectual fathers, both were Harvard men, and both began their careers in natural science but soon after their intellectual launchings they sailed into very different seas.

James became an international success upon the appearance of his *Principles of Psychology* in 1890, made a triumphal entry into philosophy in the next decade, and died with the knowledge that he was one of the most famous philosophers in the world. Peirce's luck was very different. He never succeeded in publishing a book in philosophy, never had a

1. This first appeared as a review of A. J. Ayer, *The Origins of Pragmatism: Studies in the Philosophy of Charles Peirce and William James* (San Francisco, 1968), in *The New York Review of Books*, Volume XII, 30 January 1969, pp. 24–27, and is copyright 1969 by Morton White. The present version is only slightly different from the original.

permanent academic position, often lived in squalor, and was constantly forced to keep body and soul together by lecturing, reviewing, and writing dictionary entries. He was a thorny, unconventional mathematical logician who had a genius for being unpleasant to his benefactors, yet he never seems to have driven away the ever-generous James, who made allowances for Peirce's nuttiness and who praised and supported him in every kind of emergency. James handsomely announced to the world in 1898 that Peirce had been the founder of pragmatism, but Peirce's distinction took an inexcusably long time to sink into the American academic mind. It was not until the 1930's, when his posthumous *Collected Papers* began to appear, that Peirce's greatness was generally acknowledged by philosophers.

America had been much too late in discovering its philosophical Cinderella, but better later than never. After Peirce's works joined James' on library shelves, it became evident what a powerful pair they had been. They compared favorably with any philosopher produced by England or the Continent in their time, and alongside their American predecessors and contemporaries they shone with almost solar brightness. Before Jonathan Edwards (1703–1758) there was virtually nothing of lasting philosophical value in what may be called Perry Miller Land after that dedicated explorer of the Puritan mind. And although Edwards was an acute and even powerful arguer on the subject of free will, he hardly seemed like a heavyweight when compared with Locke, Hume, or Berkeley. Emerson (1803–1882) was a great man and a seer, but what little technical philosophy he espoused was connected with his slavish acceptance of Coleridge's distinction between the Reason and the Understanding. Chauncey Wright (1830–1875), often said to be the ur-pragmatist, turns out on careful reading to be better regarded as a highly intelligent and knowledgeable disciple of Darwin and John Stuart Mill. Josiah Royce (1855–1916), the younger colleague of James and the friend of Peirce, is not to be put in the same class with them, for all of his learning and his logic. And if one is thinking of liveliness and originality, the less said the better about the supernumerary Philadelphia materialists, Princeton realists, and St. Louis Hegelians who lurk in the underbrush of American philosophical history.

It is not at all surprising, therefore, that when Professor A. J. Ayer—who does not appear to have any general interest in America's history or its ideas, but who has a nose for good philosophy—was invited by an English foundation to lecture on "the history, literature, and institutions of the United States", he was inevitably drawn to Peirce and James. Ayer was informed by his broadminded hosts that the terms of the lectureship might be taken to cover a comparison of British with American philosophy, and so in 1957 he delivered at University College in London a series of four lectures under the overall title of "Pragmatism and Analysis", in which he tried to trace the main lines of American philosophy from Peirce and James to the present, alongside the main lines of British philosophy from G. E. Moore and Bertrand Russell to the present. Finding the subject of his lectures too vast for a book, Ayer decided at first to narrow it down to Peirce and James as the originators of American pragmatism, and Moore and Russell as the originators of British analysis; but when he discovered how difficult it would be to deal merely with Peirce and James, he settled for a book on them alone. Such is the origin of Ayer's book, *The Origins of Pragmatism*.

Not only has Ayer focused all of his attention on these figures, but he has limited himself to their pragmatism and allied doctrines. Ayer's apparent indifference to the views of other writers on these doctrines will appall many Peirce and James specialists, but it will evoke the sympathy and knowing smiles of every philosophy professor who has had to lecture on a figure in ignorance of the scholarly literature about him. Ayer views his own failure to cite anything in the vast secondary literature on Peirce and James with what can only be called "chutzpah". "It has not been my aim to produce a work of historical scholarship," he says, and neatly disarms his likely reviewers in scholarly journals. "I have read the works of Peirce and James attentively, but I have not tried to situate them in the history of philosophy." "Nor," he adds, "have I studied the writings of other commentators, to see how far their interpretations agree with mine." The space that Ayer saves by not considering the views of other commentators he uses to develop his own theories on some of the main issues raised by Peirce and James.

I confess that I am of two minds about certain aspects of this undertaking. On the one hand, I can't help feeling that it is odd for an interpreter of a philosopher—especially an interpreter of Ayer's empiricist leanings—to ignore what has been written about his subject in this way. The task of discovering what a philosopher has said and meant is empirical, and so one might expect a commentator to seek all possible evidence about him, including that provided by other commentators. I think therefore that this book would have been a much more useful one if Ayer had spent more time dealing with the opinions of other interpreters of Peirce and James, and less on presenting his own ideas on the issues raised by Peirce and James. On the other hand, we all know how easy it is for the interpreter of a philosophical text to be diverted from his main task by wrangling with other commentators. And to make matters worse, anyone who felt obliged to read everything written on Peirce and James would have to go through a dreary cultist literature that has grown up beside a respectable exegetical literature.

Moreover, I need not stress the amount of rubbish that has been written on the alleged alliance between pragmatism and American capitalism, and on the so-called pragmatism of FDR and JFK. I venture to guess, therefore, that if Ayer had, in the manner of an intellectual historian, waded through all of the literature on Peirce, James, their lives and times, we would never have had any book by him on Peirce and James; and that would have been a pity. As it is, we can be grateful for an illuminating and challenging study, which allows us to witness the impact of two of our most distinguished philosophical minds on one of the most lucid and least insular of present-day English philosophical writers.

In the thirties Ayer brought the positivistic doctrines of the Vienna Circle home to England and wrote his provocative *Language, Truth and Logic.* In this book he is bringing home a report, which may be news to some, that two Americans had begun to create an original and powerful philosophy before Russell, Moore, and Wittgenstein were born. Although Ayer has come a long way from his youthful positivism, one of the most interesting things about his latest book is his application of what he learned in Vienna to the pragmatism of James. Therefore I shall concentrate on this aspect of the book even though much of what he says about Peirce is also of great interest. Ayer is especially concerned to refute the view that according to James a man may believe any proposition that he finds it satisfying to believe, and tries to protect James from this charge by viewing him as something like a logical positivist.

So far as I can see, Ayer has never abandoned the positivistic doctrine that there are three fundamentally different types of statements which are supported in fundamentally different ways: those of empirical science which are factual, those of pure mathematics and logic which concern the relationship between ideas, and those which are moral or esthetic. In spite of James' failure to acknowledge such a trichotomy explicitly, Ayer thinks that he really did accept it. When James said that we should adopt only those beliefs that "work", he meant to add, according to Ayer, that the factual beliefs of empirical science work in one way, mathematical and logical beliefs in a second way, and moral and esthetic beliefs in a third. On this interpretation, a factual belief works if and only if it is corroborated by experience; a mathematical or logical belief works if and only if it expresses a relationship between ideas which is "perceptively obvious at a glance";

and a moral or esthetic belief works if and only if it brings satisfaction to the person who holds it. Therefore, only the moral or esthetic belief behaves in the manner usually described by commentators on James, because it alone is at the mercy of the personal caprice that is usually associated with James' doctrine. By contrast, Ayer holds, the grounds on which we accept the statements of science and mathematics are as objective on James' view as they can be on any positivistic doctrine.

What about metaphysical and religious beliefs? According to Ayer, James put them into the same category as moral and esthetic beliefs, because they too are neither empirical nor mathematico-logical; and therefore they too may be said to work if and only if they satisfy the person who holds them. That is why James could appeal to moral sentiment alone in rejecting the metaphysics of determinism and naturalism. The belief that every choice is determined does not square, he said, with our feelings of moral regret; and therefore belief in determinism must give way. The belief that there is no spiritual order beyond nature does not square with equally respectable feelings, and therefore that belief must also give way for non-intellectual reasons. On Ayer's interpretation of James, science, mathematics, and logic are deaf to the claims of feeling; and mathematics and logic are deaf to the claims of sensory experience; whereas a man's metaphysics and his theology respond to his every heartbeat.

There is a good deal to support this interpretation of James, even though there are many passages that provide obstacles to it. Rather than say that it represents *the* correct interpretation, however, I should say that Ayer has put his finger on one conspicuous strain in James' thought, a strain which brought him very close to his predecessors, Jonathan Edwards and Emerson. In order to provide a rationale for evangelical religion, Edwards added a sixth sense to the ordinary ones of Locke; he insisted that the Protestant elect have a "sense of the heart" which allows them to see the glory of divine things, and roundly attacked as formalists those who were content with a more theoretical or more historical knowledge of divine excellency. Although Emerson departed in many ways from Edwards' philosophy and theology, he notoriously relied on his heart more than on his head in coming to his religious, moral, esthetic, and metaphysical convictions.

That was Emerson's main purpose in urging that Coleridgian Reason could see the glory of God in the face of Jesus, the existence of Platonic ideas, and the truth of moral propositions. And that is why we may sum up about 150 years of American philosophy by pointing out that the Calvinist's Sense of the Heart, the Transcendentalist's Reason, and James' Will To Believe were all irrationalist or anti-intellectualist devices. For Edwards, the Protestant saint could be a simple, ignorant man and yet see truth more effectively than the man of learning or the philosopher; for Emerson, the poet who saw the highest truths could be a farmer or a child; and for James in *The Will To Believe,* anyone with feelings had the right to accept a metaphysics or a religion that satisfied him when his logical intellect, as James put it, had not been coerced on the subject.

It is ironic that James should fit more easily into the older American tradition of anti-intellectualism when one concentrates, as Ayer does, on the positivistic strain in his thought. However, this becomes more understandable when one realizes that there is a strong tendency among twentieth-century positivists to treat so-called ontological questions as radically different from scientific questions. When they don't regard them as nonsensical, positivists hold that philosophical questions like "Are there physical objects?" and "Are there universals?" are not settled as we settle questions like "Are there bacteria?" or "Are there electrons?". The latter they regard as factual questions which should be answered by empirical methods, whereas they think that ontological questions call for decisions about the convenience of certain conceptual frameworks, decisions made by appealing to so-called pragmatic considerations. Once a positivist comes to regard ontological questions in this way, we can easily see why he might be sympathetic to the idea that ontological and other metaphysical beliefs are acceptable only in the degree to which they satisfy us. For, as Quine has pointed out, the positivist subscribes to an untenable contrast between the method of ontology and the method of science, putting his pragmatism to work only after his empirical, scientific inquiries have supposedly ended, whereas in fact pragmatic considerations when properly understood play a part in the justification of both ontological and scientific beliefs. A belief in the existence of universals, like a belief in the existence of electrons, is to be tested by—among other things—its capacity to organize our experience effectively. Therefore we do not appeal only to our hearts in metaphysics, religion, and morals while we use only our heads in science.

I should say therefore that if Ayer is right in claiming that James subscribed to an anti-intellectualistic positivism, so much the worse for James. Such a positivism depends on an indefensible trichotomy of physics, logic, and ethics, which is propped up by an obscure distinction between analytic and synthetic statements, and an unsuccessful analysis of the nature of moral judgments. I hope therefore that if Ayer continues his study of American philosophy he will be persuaded that there is no radical methodological distinction between the way in which our ontological beliefs work and the way in which our scientific beliefs work.

If I were writing a book on James, I should call attention to a strain in his thought which Ayer neglects, but which seems to me to be closer to the philosophical truth. It is well expressed in a passage like the following from James' essay, "The Sentiment of Rationality":

> Pretend what we may, the whole man within us is at work when we form our philosophical opinions. Intellect, will,

taste, and passion co-operate just as they do in practical affairs; and lucky it is if the passion be not something as petty
as a love of personal conquest over the philosopher across the
way. The absurd abstraction of an intellect verbally formulating all its evidence and carefully estimating the probability
thereof by a vulgar fraction by the size of whose denominator
and numerator alone it is swayed, is ideally as inept as it is
actually impossible. It is almost incredible that men who are
themselves working philosophers should pretend that any philosophy can be, or ever has been, constructed without the
help of personal preference, belief, or divination.[2]

I would remark that here intellect, will, taste, and passion
are *all* said to cooperate in the formation of a philosophical
opinion, and that intellect is not denied a part. James was interested in giving personal preference a part in the process
but not the only part. The key phrase in the passage is "the
whole man". When he spoke in this way, James did not wish
to deny that intellectual considerations played some part in
his abandonment of, say, determinism. When this strain
comes to the fore in his thinking, he emphasizes that a decision to accept or reject a metaphysics is dictated by a blend
of considerations that are logical, empirical, and emotional.
When he is thinking along these lines, he is far from accepting the idea that a factual belief is tested by experience
alone, a mathematico-logical belief by examining only the re-
lationships between ideas, and a metaphysical belief by con-
sulting only one's emotions.

By the time his *Pragmatism* appeared, James was moving
away, I suggest, from the notion that we test our beliefs individually in accordance with standards that are peculiar to the
discipline from which they come. He was leaning more and
more toward the view that when we think we are testing an
isolated belief, whether metaphysical, scientific, or logical, we
are really evaluating what he called a "stock of opinions" that

2. William James, *The Will To Believe and Other Essays in Popular Philosophy* (New York, 1898), pp. 92–93.

is variously composed and subject to the demands of consistency, experience, and emotion. This comes out most clearly in the following passage in his *Pragmatism:*

> The individual has a stock of old opinions already, but he meets a new experience that puts them to a strain. Somebody contradicts them; or in a reflective moment he discovers that they contradict each other; or he hears of facts with which they are incompatible; or desires arise in him which they cease to satisfy. The result is an inward trouble to which his mind till then had been a stranger, and from which he seeks to escape by modifying his previous mass of opinions. He saves as much of it as he can, for in this matter of belief we are all extreme conservatives. So he tries to change first this opinion, and then that (for they resist change very variously), until at last some new idea comes up which he can graft upon the ancient stock with a minimum of disturbance of the latter, some idea that mediates between the stock and the new experience and runs them into one another most felicitously and expediently. This new idea is then adopted as the true one. It preserves the older stock of truths with a minimum of modification, stretching them just enough to make them admit the novelty, but conceiving that in ways as familiar as the case leaves possible.[3]

Here, I suggest, there is no tendency to insist that physics works in one way, logic in a second, and metaphysics in a third. The emphasis is rather on the idea that a whole man will subject a heterogeneous stock of opinions to a test in which conformity to both experience *and* desire is to be taken into account, that he will balance many considerations against each other in an effort to deal with the challenge that has put the old system to a strain. And although James recognizes the need to preserve that system with a minimum of modification, he regards even the oldest truths in the old stock—those of logic and mathematics—as modifiable in the face of a challenge from experience or emotion.

"How plastic even the oldest truths . . . really are," he an-

---

3. William James, *Pragmatism* (New York, 1907), pp. 59–60.

nounces, "has been vividly shown in our day by the transfor-
mation of logical and mathematical ideas." [4] This is the James
who encourages us to reject sharp positivistic distinctions between the analytic and the synthetic, between metaphysics
and science, and between science and morals. This is the
James who looks forward in the history of American philosophy and not backward to the anti-intellectualism of Edwards
and Emerson. This is the greater James, but the James I don't
see enough of in Ayer's lucid, stimulating examination of
pragmatism.

4. William James, *Pragmatism* (New York, 1907), p. 65.

9. *The Analytic and the Synthetic: An Untenable Dualism* [1]

John Dewey has spent a good part of his life hunting and shooting at dualisms: body-mind, theory-practice, percept-concept, value-science, learning-doing, sensation-thought, external-internal. They are always fair game and Dewey's prose

1. This paper is a slightly revised version of one read on 14 May 1949 at the annual meeting of the Fullerton Club, a discussion group composed mainly of philosophers residing in the Philadelphia area. The paper owes its existence to the stimulus and help of Professors Nelson Goodman and W. V. Quine, with whom I had been engaging in a three-sided philosophical correspondence in the Spring and Summer of 1947. This was initiated by my circulating the manuscript of my paper, "On the Church-Frege Solution of the Paradox of Analysis", later published in *Philosophy and Phenomenological Research*, Volume IX (December 1948), pp. 305–8. The correspondence soon came to focus on analyticity and related notions.

My general attitude on the analytic and the synthetic has also been influenced by Professor Alfred Tarski though I hesitate to attribute to him the specific beliefs defended in this paper. Since I say in the text that I trace my general attitudes to Dewey, I should add in the same spirit that any effort to trace the history of discontent with the distinction between the analytic and the synthetic must not neglect John Stuart Mill, though, as usual, Mill's views on the issue are somewhat complicated (as are Dewey's).

The paper was first printed in *John Dewey: Philosopher of Science and Freedom*, edited by Sidney Hook (New York, 1950). It was reprinted without change in *Semantics and the Philosophy of Language*, edited by Leonard Linsky (Urbana, Ill., 1952), and in *Analyticity: Selected Readings*, edited by rattles with fire whenever they come into view. At times the philosophical forest seems more like a gallery at a penny arcade, and the dualistic dragons move along obligingly and monotonously while Dewey picks them off with deadly accuracy. At other times we may wonder just who these monsters are. But vague as the language sometimes is, on other occasions it is suggestive, and the writer must confess to a deep sympathy with Dewey on this point. Not that distinctions ought not to be made when they are called for, but we ought to avoid making those that are unnecessary or unfounded. It is in this spirit that I wish to examine one form of a distinction which has come to dominate so much of contemporary philosophy—the distinction between analytic and synthetic statements. It must be emphasized that the views which will be put forth are not strict corollaries of Dewey's views; indeed, he sometimes deals with the question so as to suggest disagreement with what I am about to argue. But I trace the source of my own general attitudes on this point to Dewey, even though my manner and method in this paper are quite foreign to his.

Recent discussion has given evidence of dissatisfaction with the distinction between analytic and synthetic statements. A revolt seems to have developed among some philosophers who accepted this distinction as one of their basic tenets a few short years ago. So far as I know, this attitude has not been given full expression in publications, except for a few footnotes, reviews, and undeveloped asides. In this paper I want to present some of the reasons for this decline of faith in such a pivotal distinction of recent philosophy, or at least some of the reasons which have led to the decline of my own assurance. On such a matter I hesitate to name too many names, but I venture to say that some of my fellow revolu-

James F. Harris, Jr., and Richard H. Severens (Chicago, 1970). Pages 144 through 147 of my *Toward Reunion in Philosophy* (Cambridge, Mass., 1956) contain a revised version of some pages in this paper; Part II of that book represents a fuller development of views expressed in this paper.

tionaries are Professor W. V. Quine and Professor Nelson Goodman. As yet the revolution is in a fluid stage. No dictatorship has been set up, and so there is still a great deal of freedom and healthy dispute possible within the revolutionary ranks. I, for one, am drawn in this direction by a feeling that we are here faced with another one of the dualisms that Dewey has warned against.

There is some irony in the fact that formal logicians have played a role in creating doubt over the adequacy of this great dualism—the sharp distinction between analytic and synthetic. It is ironical because Dewey has never looked in this direction for support; indeed he has shunned it. But such a phenomenon is not rare in the history of philosophy. Dewey has told of his attachment to Hegel's language at a time when he was no longer a Hegelian, and in like manner the contemporary revolt against the distinction between analytic and synthetic may be related to Dewey's anti-dualism. Perhaps this is the pattern of philosophical progress—new wine in old bottles.

There are at least two kinds of statements which have been called analytic in recent philosophy. The first kind is illustrated by true statements of formal logic in which only logical constants and variables appear essentially, *i.e.* logical truths in the narrowest sense. For example:

$$(p \text{ or } q) \text{ if and only if } (q \text{ or } p)$$
$$p \text{ or not-} p$$
$$\text{If } p, \text{ then not-not-} p$$

and similar truths from more advanced chapters of modern logic. With the attempts to define "analytic" as applied to these I shall not be concerned. Nor am I interested here in the ascription of analyticity to those which are derived from them by substitution of constants for variables. This does not mean that I do not have related opinions of certain philosophical characterizations of this type of statement, but rather that my main concern here is with another kind of statement usually classified as analytic.

My main worry is over what is traditionally known as essential predication, best illustrated by "All men are animals", "Every brother is a male", "All men are rational animals", "Every brother is a male sibling", and "Every vixen is a fox". I am concerned to understand those philosophers who call such statements analytic, as opposed to true but merely synthetic statements like "All men are bipeds", "Every brother exhibits sibling rivalry", "Every vixen is cunning". The crucial philosophical assertion is made when a predicate like "man" is said to be analytically linked with "rational animal" but only synthetically linked with "featherless biped", although it is fully admitted that all men are in fact featherless bipeds and that all featherless bipeds are in fact men; when it is said that whereas the statement "All and only men are rational animals" is analytic, the statement, "All and only men are featherless bipeds" is true but synthetic. And what I want to understand more clearly is the ascription of analyticity in such a context. What I will argue is that a number of views which have been adopted as papal on these matters are, like so many papal announcements, obscure. And what I suggest is that the pronouncements of the modern, empiricist popes are unsuccessful attempts to bolster the dualisms of medieval, scholastic popes. From the point of view of an anti-dualist, their distinctions are equally sharp, even though the moderns make the issue more linguistic in character. But the similarities between the medievals and the moderns are great; both want to preserve the distinction between essential and accidental predication, and both have drawn it obscurely.

Quine [2] has formulated the problem in a convenient way. He has pointed out (with a different illustration) that the statement "Every man is a rational animal" is analytic just in

2. "Notes on Existence and Necessity", *The Journal of Philosophy*, Volume XL (1943), pp. 113–27.

case it is the result of putting synonyms for synonyms in a logical truth of the first type mentioned. Thus we have the logical truth:

(1) Every *P* is *P*

From this we may deduce by substitution:

(2) Every man is a man.

Now we put for the second occurrence of the word "man" the expression "rational animal" which is allegedly synonymous with it, and we have as our result:

(3) Every man is a rational animal.

We may now say that (3) is analytic in accordance with the proposed criterion. Quine has queried the phrase "logical truth" as applied to (1) and the phrase "is synonymous with" as applied to "man" and "rational animal", but I am confining myself to the latter.

Quine has said that he does not understand the term "is synonymous with" and has suggested that he won't understand it until a behavioristic criterion is presented for it. I want to begin by saying that I have difficulties with this term too, and that this is the negative plank on which our united front rests. I should say, of course, that the complaint when put this way is deceptively modest. We begin by saying we do not understand, but our opponents may counter with Dr. Johnson that they can give us arguments but not an understanding. And so it ought to be said that the objection is a little less meek; the implication is that many who *think* they understand really don't.

Now that the problem is introduced, a few preliminary observations must be made.

First: I am not asking for a clear synonym of "is synonymous with". I am asking only for a clear extensional equivalent. Therefore, I make rather weak demands on those who hold that the expression "is synonymous with" may be used in clarifying "analytic". I ask them to present a usable criterion, a sufficiently clear expression which is extensionally equivalent to the expression "is synonymous with"—in other words, a term which bears the relation to "is synonymous with" that "featherless biped" bears to "man" according to those who hold that these last two terms are equivalent though not synonymous.

Second: whereas Quine appears to require that the criterion for being synonymous be behavioristic or at least predicts that he won't understand it if it's not, I make less stringent demands. The term formulating the criterion of being synonymous will satisfy me when it attains a degree of clarity it does not now possess. It should be said in passing that Quine's behaviorism would appear quite consonant with Dewey's general views.

Third: it is obvious that if the problem is set in the manner outlined, then the statement " 'All men are rational animals' is analytic" is itself empirical. For to decide that the statement is analytic, we will have to find out whether "man" is in fact synonymous with "rational animal" and this will require the empirical examination of linguistic usage. This raises a very important problem which helps us get to the root of the difficulty and to ward off one very serious misunderstanding.

Showing that "All men are rational animals" is analytic depends on showing that it is the result of putting a synonym for its synonym in a logical truth. In this situation we find ourselves asking whether a statement in a natural language or what Moore calls ordinary language—a language which has not been formalized by a logician—is analytic. We find ourselves asking whether two expressions in a natural language are synonymous. But this must be distinguished from a closely related situation. It must be distinguished from the case where we artificially construct a language and propose so-called definitional rules. In this case we are not faced with the same problem. Obviously, we may *decide* to permit users of our language to put "rational animal" for "man" in a language L_1. (For the moment I will not enter the question of how this decision is to be formulated precisely.) In that same language, L_1, which also contains the phrase "featherless biped" in its vocabulary, there may be no rule permitting us to put "featherless biped" for "man". Thus we may say that in artificial language L_1 "All men are rational animals" is analytic on the basis of a convention, a rule explicitly stated. In L_1, moreover, "All men are featherless bipeds" is not analytic. But it is easy to see that we can construct a language L_2 in which the reverse situation prevails and in which a linguistic expression which was analytic in L_1 becomes synthetic in L_2.

Now no one denies that two such languages can be constructed having the features outlined. But these languages are the creatures of formal fancy; they are dreamed up by a logician. If I ask, "Is 'All men are rational animals' analytic in L_1?", I am rightly told to look up the rule-book of language L_1.[3] But natural languages have no rule-books and the question whether a given statement is analytic in them is much more difficult. What some philosophers do is to pretend that natural languages are really quite like artificial languages; and that even though there is no rule-book for them, people do behave *as if* there were such a book. What some philosophers usually assume is that the artificial rule-book which they construct in making an artificial language is the rule-book which ordinary people or scientists *would* construct if they were asked to construct one, or that it is the rule-book which, in that vague phrase, presents *the* rational reconstruction of the usage in question. But suppose a logician constructs L_1 and L_2 as defined above, and now suppose he approaches L_3, a natural language, with them. Can he say in any clear way that L_1 is *the* rational reconstruction of L_3 and that L_2 is not? My whole point is that no one has been able

3. Even here, Quine asks, how do you know a rule when you see one? Only by the fact that the book has the word "Rule-Book" on it, he answers.

to present the criterion for such claims. And the reason for this is that no one has succeeded in finding a criterion for synonymy.

The moral of this is important for understanding the new revolt against dualism. I hope it makes clear that whereas I understand fairly well the expressions "analytic in L_1" and "analytic in L_2", where L_1 and L_2 are the artificial languages mentioned, I do not understand as well the phrase "analytic in the natural language L_3".[4] More important to realize is that my understanding of the first two expressions in no way solves the serious problem of analyticity as I conceive it, and I want to repeat that my major difficulties will disappear only when a term is presented which is coextensive with "synonymous" and on the basis of which I can distinguish analytic sheep from synthetic goats. I want to repeat that I am not doing anything as quixotic as seeking a synonym for "synonym".

Those who refuse to admit the distinction between "analytic in L_1" and "analytic in natural language L_3" will, of course, disagree completely. But then, it seems to me, they will have to refrain from attributing analyticity to any statement which has not been codified in a formalized language; in which case they will find it hard to do analysis in connection with terms in *ordinary language*. They may say, as I have suggested, that people using natural languages behave *as if* they had made rules for their language just like those of L_1 and L_2, but then how do we show that people behave *as if* they had done something which they hadn't done? As we shall see later, clearing up this problem is just as difficult as clarifying "analytic", for it involves the equally vexatious problem of contrary-to-fact conditional statements. I suppose it would be granted that those who use natural language do not make conventions and rules of definition by making a lin-

---

4. For many years Quine has also pointed to the unclarity of the phrase "analytic in L", where "L" is a variable even over formal languages.

guistic contract at the dawn of history. What defenders of the
view I am criticizing want to hold, however, is that there are
other ways of finding out whether a group of people has a
convention. And what I am saying is that philosophers should
tell us what these ways are before they dub statements in
natural languages "analytic" and "synthetic".

The point at issue is closely related to one discussed at
length by Professor C. I. Lewis in *An Analysis of Knowledge
and Valuation* (1946). We agree in seeing a problem here
which is overlooked by what I shall call crude conventional-
ism, but differ in our conception of where the solution must
be sought. Lewis is led to say that whether "All men are rational animals" is analytic in a natural language depends on
whether all men are necessarily rational animals, and this in
turn depends on whether the *criterion in mind* of *man* in-
cludes the *criterion in mind* of *rational animal*. Lewis has
dealt with this matter more extensively than any recent philosopher who advocates a sharp distinction between analytic
and synthetic, and his arguments are too complex to be
treated here. In any case, his views are quite different from
those upon which I am concentrating in this paper. He holds
that I need only make what he calls an "experiment in imagination" to find out whether all men are necessarily rational
animals. And when I try this experiment I am supposed to
conclude that I *cannot* consistently think of, that I cannot
conceive of, a man who is not a rational animal. But how
shall we interpret this "cannot"? How shall we understand
"thinkable"? I suspect that this view leads us to a private, in-
tuitive insight for determining what each of us individually
can conceive. How, then, can we get to the analyticity of the
commonly understood statement? Lewis' most helpful explanation turns about the word "include" in the following passage: "The [answer to the] question, 'Does your schematism
for determining application of the term "*square*" include your
schematism for applying "*rectangle*"?' is one determined in
the same general fashion as is the answer to the question,

'Does your plan of a trip to Chicago to see the Field Museum include the plan of visiting Niagara to see the Falls?' ". The inclusion of plans, furthermore, is a sense-apprehensible relationship for Lewis. One either sees or doesn't see the relationship and that is the end of the matter. It is very difficult to argue one's difficulties with such a position, and I shall only say that I do not find this early retreat to intuition satisfactory. I will add, however, that in its recognition of the problem Lewis' view is closer to the one advanced in this paper than those which do not see the need for clarification of "analytic in natural language". My difficulties with Professor Lewis' view are associated with the difficulties of intensionalism but that is a large matter.

I want to consider now two views which are avowedly anti-intensional and more commonly held by philosophers against whom my critical comments are primarily directed.

(1) "*Analytic statements are those whose denials are self-contradictory.*" Consider this criterion as applied to the contention that "All men are rational animals" is analytic in a natural language. We are invited to take the denial of this allegedly analytic statement, namely, "It is not the case that all men are rational animals". But is this a self-contradiction? Certainly looking at it syntactically shows nothing like "A and not-A". And even if we transform it into "Some men are not rational animals" we still do not get a self-contradiction which is syntactically evident. It might be said that the last statement is self-contradictory *in the sense* in which "man" is being used. But surely the phrase "in the sense" is a dodge, because if he is asked to specify that sense, what can the philosopher who has referred to it say? Surely not "the sense in which 'man' is synonymous with 'rational animal' " because that would beg the question. The point is that the criterion under consideration is not helpful if construed literally and if not construed literally (as in the attempt to use the phrase "in the sense") turns out to beg the question.

Let us then suppose that the criterion is not used in this

question-begging manner. A self-contradiction need not literally resemble in shape "*A* and not-*A*" or "Something is *P* and not-*P*". All it has to do is to produce a certain feeling of horror or queerness on the part of people who use the language. They behave as if they had seen someone eat peas with a knife. Such an approach is attractive but we need an account of the kind of horror or queer feelings which people are supposed to have in the presence of the denials of analytic statements. About this approach, however, I must ask a few questions and make a few observations.

(a) Who is supposed to feel the horror in the presence of the opposites of analytic statements? Surely not all people in the community that uses the language. There are many who feel no horror at seeing people eat peas with a knife, just as there are many who are not perturbed at statements that philosophers might think self-contradictory. Who, then?

(b) Let us remember that on this view we will have to be careful to distinguish the horror associated with denying firmly believed synthetic statements from that surrounding the denials of analytic statements. The distinction must not only be a distinction that carves out two mutually exclusive classes of sentences but it must carve them out in a certain way. It would be quite disconcerting to the philosophers I am criticizing to have the whole of physics or sociology turn out as analytic on their criterion and only a few parts of mathematics.

(c) If analytic statements are going to be distinguished from synthetic true statements on the basis of the degree of discomfort that is produced by denying them, the distinction will not be a sharp one [5] and the ideas of a rigid separation of analytic and synthetic will have been surren-

5. On this point see Nelson Goodman's "On Likeness of Meaning", in *Analysis* (October 1949), pp. 1–7. Also W. V. Quine's *Methods of Logic* (New York, 1950), section 33. (I should add here that readers of Goodman and Quine will know that since 1950 they have written further on this subject.)

dered. The dualism will have been surrendered and the kind of *gradualism* one finds in some of Dewey's writings will have been vindicated. The most recent justification of the distinction between essential and accidental predication will have been refuted. It may be said that sharp differences are compatible with matters of degree. Differences of temperature are differences of degree and yet we may mark fixed points like 0° Centigrade on our thermometers. But it should be pointed out that a conception according to which "analytic" is simply the higher region of a scale on which "synthetic" is the lower region breaks down the radical separation of the analytic and the synthetic as expressive of different kinds of knowledge. And this is a great concession from the view that K. R. Popper [6] calls "essentialism". It is reminiscent of the kind of concession that Mill wanted to wrest from the nineteenth century in connection with the status of arithmetical statements. Once it is admitted that analytic statements are just like synthetic statements, except that they produce a little more of a certain quality—in this case the quality of discomfort in the presence of their denials—the bars are down, and a radical, gradualistic pragmatism is enthroned.

(2) *"If we were presented with something which wasn't a rational animal, we would not call it a man."* Such language is often used by philosophers who are anxious to clarify the notion of analytic in the natural languages. In order to test its effectiveness in distinguishing analytic statements, let us try it on "All men are featherless bipeds", which by hypothesis is *not* analytic. Those who use this criterion would have to deny that if we were presented with an entity which was not a biped or not featherless we would not call it a man. But we *do* withhold the term "man" from those things which we

6. *The Open Society and Its Enemies* (London, 1945), especially Chapter 11 and its notes.

know to be either non-bipeds or non-featherless. Obviously, everything turns about the phrase "we would not call it a man" or the phrase "we would withhold the term 'man'". Again, who are we? And more important, what is the pattern of term-withholding? Suppose I come to a tribe which has the following words in its vocabulary plus a little logic: "man", "rational", "animal", "featherless", and "biped". I am told in advance by visiting anthropologists that "man" is synonymous with "rational animal" in that tribe's language whereas "featherless biped" is merely coextensive with it. I wish to check the report of the anthropologists. How do I go about it?

In the spirit of the proposed criterion I must show that if anything lacked rationality it would not be reputed a man by the people in question. So I show them coconuts, trees, horses, pigs, and I ask after each "man?" and get "no" for an answer. They will not repute these things to be men. I must now show that there is a difference in their attitudes toward "rational animal" and "featherless biped" *vis-à-vis* "man". I originally produced things which are not rational animals, but these very things also lack feathers and are not bipeds and so the negative responses of the natives might just as well be offered as an argument for the synonymy of "man" and "featherless biped" as for the theory that "man" is synonymous with "rational animal". It seems that such crude behaviorism will not avail. They don't call non-featherless-bipeds men, just as they don't call non-rational-animals men. The criterion, therefore, is one that will not help us make the distinction.

We might pursue the natives in another way. We might ask them: "Would you call something a man if it were not a featherless biped?" To which they answer in the negative. "Would you call something a man if it weren't a rational animal?" To which they answer "no" again. But now we might ask them: "Aren't your reasons different in each of these cases?"—hoping to lead them into saying something that will allow us to differentiate their responses. "Aren't you surer in concluding that something is not a man from the fact that it is not a rational animal, than you are in concluding it from the fact that it is not a featherless biped?" If the savage is obliging and says "yes", we have the making of a criterion. But notice that it is a criterion which makes the distinction one of degree. Not being a rational animal is simply a better sign of the absence of manhood than is the property of not being a featherless biped, just as the latter is a better sign than the property of not wearing a derby hat. It should be noticed in this connection that we are precluded from saying that the inference from "*a* is not a rational animal" to "*a* is not a man" is logical or analytic for them, since we are trying to explain "analytic". To use it in the explanation would hardly be helpful.

Probably the most helpful interpretation of this mode of distinguishing analytic and synthetic is that according to which we observe the following: when the natives have applied the word "man" to certain objects and are then persuaded that these objects are not rational animals, they immediately, without hesitation, withdraw the predicate "man". They contemplate no other means of solving their problem. But when they have applied the word "man" and are then persuaded that the things to which they have applied it are not featherless bipeds, they do not withdraw the predicate "man" immediately but rather contemplate another course, that of surrendering the hypothesis that all men are featherless bipeds. Now I suspect that this criterion will be workable but it will not allow us to distinguish what we think in advance are the analytic equivalences. It will result in our finding that many firmly believed "synthetic" equivalences are analytic on this criterion.

I am sure that there are a number of other ways of constructing the criterion that are similar to the ones I have just considered. No doubt students of language who have thought of this problem can develop them. But I want to call attention to one general problem that criteria of this sort face. They usually depend on the use of a contrary-to-fact conditional: something of the form, "if . . . were . . . then . . . would be. . . ." But in appealing to this (or any variety of causal conditional) we are appealing to a notion which is just as much in need of explanation as the notion of *analytic* itself. To appeal to it, therefore, does not constitute a philosophical advance. Goodman [7] has reported on the lugubrious state of this notion. It is small consolation to reduce "analytic" to the contrary-to-fact conditional, for that is a very sandy foundation right now.

After presenting views like these, I frequently find philosophers agreeing with me. Too often they are the very philosophers whose views I had supposed I was criticizing. Too often, I find, the criticisms I have leveled are treated as arguments *for* what I had supposed I was opposing. For example, there are some philosophers who construe my argument merely as an argument to show that words in natural language and scientific language are ambiguous—that "man" is synonymous with "rational animal" in one context and with "featherless biped" in another—and who immediately embrace the views here set forth. But this is beside the point. Many philosophers who defend the view I have criticized admit that a word may have many meanings, depending on context. For example, John Stuart Mill, who admits that a biologist might regard "mammiferous animal having two hands" as the synonym of "man", and not "rational animal". But Mill also holds that in common usage "rational animal" is *the* synonym. Because of this admission of a varying connotation, Mill regards himself (justifiably) as superior to the benighted philosopher who holds what has been called "the one and only one true meaning"-view of analysis. If the be-

7. "The Problem of Counterfactual Conditionals", *The Journal of Philosophy*, Volume XLIV (1947), pp. 113–28; reprinted as Chapter I of Goodman's *Fact, Fiction, and Forecast*, 2nd ed. (New York, 1965).

nighted philosopher is asked, "What is the synonym of 'man'?", he immediately replies "rational animal". If he is a Millian, he says it depends on the situation in which it is used.

I am not concerned to advocate this Millian view here because it is quite beside the point so far as the thesis of this essay is concerned. The difference between the Millian (if I may call him that without intending thereby to credit Mill with having originated the view) and his opponent (I would call him an Aristotelian if such matters were relevant) is comparatively slight. The Millian takes as his fundamental metalinguistic statement-form, "X is synonymous with Y in situation S", whereas his opponent apparently refuses to relativize synonymy. The opponent merely says: "X is synonymous with Y". What I want to emphasize, however, is that by so relativizing the notion of synonymy he is still far from meeting the difficulty I have raised. For now it may be asked how we establish synonymy *even in a given context*. The problem is analogous to the following one in mechanics. Suppose one holds that the question: "Is x moving?" is unanswerable before a frame of reference is given. Suppose, then, that motion is relativized and we now ask such questions in the form: "Is x moving with respect to y?" But now suppose we are not supplied with a clear statement of how to go about finding out whether x is in motion with respect to y. I venture to say that the latter predicament resembles that of philosophers who are enlightened enough to grant that synonymy is relative to a linguistic context, but who are unable to see that even when relativized it still needs more clarification than anyone has given it.

I think that the problem is clear, and that we may have to drop the idea of a sharp distinction between essential and accidental predication (to use the language of the *older* Aristotelians) as well as its contemporary version—the sharp distinction between analytic and synthetic. I am not arguing that a criterion of analyticity and synonymy can never be given. I argue that none has been given and, more positively, that a suitable criterion is likely to make the distinction between analytic and synthetic a matter of degree. If this is tenable, then a dualism which has been shared by both scholastics and empiricists will have been challenged successfully. Analytic philosophy will no longer be sharply separated from science, and an unbridgeable chasm will no longer divide those who see meanings or essences and those who collect facts. Another revolt against dualism will have succeeded.

10. *Experiment and Necessity in Dewey's Philosophy* [1]

John Dewey, more than any other thinker in modern times, viewed the history of Western philosophy as a fruitless quest for certainty, as a misguided effort to discover a class of truths which would be stable, certain, and self-evident. And for this reason the notion of *a priori* knowledge, or knowledge which is supposed to be independent of experience, was almost always suspect in Dewey's philosophy. For more than a half-century he campaigned against the view that there are two sorts of knowledge, one rational, necessary, unchanging, certain; and the other empirical, contingent, and merely probable. Preoccupation with the status of what other philosophers regard as *a priori* knowledge is therefore almost perpetual in Dewey's thought. It dominates not only his work in logic and epistemology but also his discussion of basic politi-

1. This essay originated in a lecture delivered at Brandeis University on 8 April 1959 as one of a series of lectures given by different philosophers under the general title: "John Dewey in the Light of Recent Philosophy", copyright © 1959 by Morton White. It was first reprinted in *The Antioch Review*, Volume XIX (Fall 1959), pp. 329–44, then reprinted in slightly revised form in *Sidney Hook and the Contemporary World*, edited by Paul Kurtz (New York, John Day, 1968). In the present version I have made a number of changes that clarify the argument.

cal, moral, and educational problems. He criticizes proponents of the doctrine of Natural Law when they speak with confidence about self-evident principles, he opposes transcendental moralists who defend prejudice in the name of intuition, and he insists that the pedagogical separation of learning and doing is partly the result of a failure to see continuity in all kinds of knowledge from mathematics to geography.

Dewey continued an old tradition in philosophy when he coupled belief in transcendent principles with a tendency toward political conservativism. To realize this, one need only recall the similar views of John Locke and John Stuart Mill. Both of these great empiricists felt obliged to undermine certain views on *a priori* knowledge, partly because they felt that these views were politically dangerous. And it was from Locke and Mill that Dewey derived a similar concern. Locke, Mill, and Dewey were all fearful lest an excessively anti-empirical view of knowledge encourage political and social tyranny because they thought that a tendency to think of practical matters in an excessively rationalistic way might give the upper hand to those whom Locke called "the dictators of principles". John Stuart Mill testified eloquently to the liberal motivation of his own work in logic when he said:

> The notion that truths external to the mind may be known by intuition or consciousness, independently of observation and experience, is, I am persuaded, in these times, the great intellectual support of false doctrines and bad institutions. . . . There never was such an instrument devised for consecrating all deep-seated prejudices. And the chief strength of this false philosophy in morals, politics, and religion, lies in the appeal which it is accustomed to make to the evidence of mathematics and the cognate branches of physical science.[2]

Dewey's logical work was motivated, as Mill's was, by a desire to examine the methods of natural science and mathe-

2. John Stuart Mill, *Autobiography*, ed. J. J. Coss (New York, 1924), pp. 158–59.

matics in order to drive the rationalists and intuitionists from their stronghold. But, as I shall try to show, he does not always succeed in this effort. On the contrary, there is a part of Dewey's theory of knowledge in which, without realizing it, he provides wonderfully elaborate quarters for a rationalistic Trojan horse. To see this, we must look into a number of questions concerning the distinction between analytic and synthetic statements, which is so intimately associated with the problem of *a priori* knowledge.

In the previous essay I expressed my dissatisfaction with the distinction between analytic and synthetic as developed in the literature of logical positivism, but prefaced my argument by saying:

> It must be emphasized that the views which will be put forth are not strict corollaries of Dewey's views; indeed, he sometimes deals with the question so as to suggest disagreement with what I am about to argue. But I trace the source of my own general attitudes on this point to Dewey, even though my manner and method in this paper are quite foreign to his.[3]

One of the first comments on the previous essay was from a devoted disciple of Dewey. It read: "Unless I have misread Dewey [your paper] is squarely in the context of his thinking. If I had time I could document this". As my friend did not have time, the point was never documented. I took him to imply that criticisms like mine of the positivistic distinction between analytic and synthetic were *completely* Deweyan, and that my qualification about Dewey's dealing differently with the question—on some occasions at least—was the product of ignorance. Since then I have looked into the relevant texts more closely, and I feel more confidently cautious in claiming Dewey as an ally on this point. An inspiration he undoubtedly was, as I have already indicated. But he says so many things which are either inconsistent, or objectionably

3. See "The Analytic and the Synthetic: An Untenable Dualism" above, p. 122.

dark, or unacceptable for other reasons, that I feel we cannot
look to him for a complete view of the subject. In order to
show what I mean, I must begin with a discussion of some
general issues in the theory of *a priori* knowledge.

I

There are three terms that ought to be distinguished in the
discussion of *a priori* knowledge: one is "*a priori* knowledge"
itself, a second is "necessary truth", and a third is "analytic
statement". Some philosophers have held that *a priori* knowledge is knowledge which is independent of sensory experience, that a necessary truth is one that cannot be false, and
that an analytic statement is one that is true by virtue of the
meanings of its terms. If one begins one's philosophical reflections with these three terms in one's vocabulary, one may advance a number of philosophical theses. For example one
may say that the class of necessary truths is identical with the
class of truths known *a priori*, and then explain the existence
of such truths by pointing out that they are all analytic. The
argument would be that if a statement is true merely by virtue of the meanings of its terms, we do not have to consult
sensory experience to know that it is true: we know *a priori*
that it is true. And if the class of truths known *a priori* and
the class of necessary truths are identical, then we have, in
the course of explaining *a priori*-ness, explained necessity as
well. I need not add that a lot of damaging questions may be
—and have been—asked about such an effort at epistemological explanation, but it represents a kind of thinking that has
been very popular in Western philosophy. One of its elements, of course, is a denial that analytic truths are known by
sensory experience. It begins with the assumption that there
is such a thing as *a priori* knowledge and then appeals to the
notion of analytic truth in order to explain the existence of
such knowledge. However, if a philosopher begins with the
supposition that there is no such thing as *a priori* knowledge,

and hence with the supposition that all knowledge is *a posteriori* or dependent on sensory experience for its establishment, he has no epistemological need for a notion of analyticity of the kind previously mentioned. Obviously, if one thinks that *all* knowledge must be established by recourse to sensory experience, then one cannot hold that *some* knowledge may be gained merely by examining the meanings of one's words, since an examination of meanings is usually thought to be non-sensory because meanings are thought to be non-sensory. Often meanings are thought by such philosophers to be universals, abstract entities which are not the objects of sensation.

I should say in passing that this way of thinking is often illustrated in the literature of logical positivism. And if one puts to the side Kant's doctrine of synthetic *a priori* judgments, one sees that Kant shared this point of view. He too seems to have held that the analyticity of *analytic* judgments is what explains the fact that they are *a priori* and necessarily true even though he explained the necessity and *a priori*-ness of some synthetic judgments in a different way.

I want now to outline my argument for the view that Dewey does not subscribe to one consistent position on these questions. First of all, I shall show that there are many places in which Dewey rejects the kind of thinking I have just described. In those places he seems to deny the existence of *a priori* knowledge and therefore does not *need* to appeal to a notion of analyticity of the kind I have mentioned. I shall show this below in section II by considering what he has to say about the principles of formal logic and pure mathematics—those traditional exemplars of necessity and *a priori*-ness. There I shall show that Dewey sometimes rejects the view that the principles of logic and the principles of physics are established in fundamentally different ways.

I shall argue in section III that elsewhere Dewey defends views that are inconsistent with the point of view described in section II. In certain places, for example, he seems to hold

that there *is* a sharp distinction between what he calls "ideational" and "existential" propositions, a distinction that is
reminiscent of the positivistic distinction between analytic
and synthetic statements. This, I submit, is inconsistent with
his denial that there is such a thing as *a priori* knowledge.
But that is not all. When Dewey comes to apply his distinction between ideational and existential propositions, he
moves in the direction of classical rationalism. In other
words, he holds that laws of *physics* are what a positivist
would call "analytic" and hence to be established by an examination of meanings. I should point out, of course, that it
would be bad enough if he had merely reverted to a position
like that of the positivists and Hume, that is to say, if he had
merely said that the principles of pure mathematics and logic
were established by examining meanings or ideas. But no, he
goes further and says that principles of physics like Newton's
First Law of Motion are established in this way. He does this
because he can find no better way of dealing with the difficult problem of scientific law or causal necessity; and the
irony is that he treats physical necessity in a way that he
once thought inadequate for the treatment of logical necessity.

II

At several places in his writings, notably in *Reconstruction in
Philosophy* and in *Logic: The Theory of Inquiry*, Dewey
seems to deny that the truths of formal logic and pure mathematics are *a priori*. We find Dewey saying in his *Reconstruction in Philosophy:* "Mathematics is often cited as an example
of purely normative thinking dependent upon *a priori* canons
and supra-empirical material. But it is hard to see how the
student who approaches the matter historically can avoid the
conclusion that the status of mathematics is as empirical as
that of metallurgy". And a little further on in this same book
Dewey says: "Logic is a matter of profound human impor-

tance precisely because it is empirically founded and experimentally applied".[4] Faced with these passages, one is led to say that Dewey does not believe that there are any *a priori* truths and therefore that he avoids both the problem of Kant and that of the logical positivists by denying one of their assumptions.

It might be said in reply that Dewey's use of the word "logic" is so different from that of Kant and the positivists that he would naturally, but irrelevantly, say that logic is *a posteriori*. For doesn't he hold that logic is a science insofar as "it gives an organized and tested descriptive account of the way in which thought actually goes on"?[5] And isn't this why Peirce said that Dewey regarded logic as the natural history of thought and not as a normative science?[6] The reply is certainly in order, but I do not think that it suffices to dismiss Dewey's views on logic as altogether irrelevant to the traditional controversy. For in that same passage in which he says that logic is a descriptive science, Dewey says that it is an art too. And when he calls it an art, he says he means that it "projects methods by which future thinking shall take advantage of the operations that lead to success and avoid those which result in failure".[7] And when he speaks of methods, he is thinking also of methods of inference which are formulated by the principles of formal logic. Therefore, he *does* join issue with Kant and the positivist, as is even more evident in his *Logic*. The fundamental theory of that book is that "all logical forms . . . arise within the operation of inquiry and are concerned with control of inquiry so that it may yield warranted assertions".[8] And when Dewey speaks of logical forms,

4. John Dewey, *Reconstruction in Philosophy* (New York, 1920), pp. 137–38; and Chapter II, *The Quest for Certainty* (New York, 1929).

5. *Ibid.*, p. 135.

6. *Collected Papers of Charles Sanders Peirce*, edited by Charles Hartshorne, Paul Weiss, and Arthur W. Burks (Cambridge, Mass., 1931–58), Volume VIII, Paragraph 190.

7. Dewey, *op. cit.*, p. 135.

8. John Dewey, *Logic: The Theory of Inquiry* (New York, 1938), pp. 3–4.

he says he is referring to principles like "if anything has a certain property, and whatever has this property has a certain other property, then the thing in question has this certain other property",[9] as well as to the traditional principles of identity, contradiction, and excluded middle.[10] He is not speaking solely of statements that might normally be assigned to the "natural history of thought".

Dewey speaks of such logical forms or principles as "conditions", "demands", "postulates", "requirements" of inquiry.[11] To engage in an inquiry, Dewey says, is "like entering into a contract. It commits the inquirer to observance of certain conditions".[12] Having agreed to engage in an inquiry, so to speak, you bind yourself, or promise, or agree to proceed in a way that observes a "rule" or "logical law" like "if anything has a certain property, and whatever has this property has a certain other property, then the thing in question has this certain other property". He says: "If you are going to inquire in a way which meets the requirements of inquiry, you must proceed in a way which observes this rule, just as when you make a business contract there are certain conditions to be fulfilled".[13] Such observance of logical rules is "at first implicit in the undertaking of inquiry. As they are formally acknowledged (formulated), they become logical forms of various degrees of generality".

This statement by Dewey may be used to bring out a number of important features of his view. First of all, and most important for the student of Dewey's theory of *a priori* knowledge, is the fact that postulated logical forms ("principles" or "rules", as Dewey calls them) may change in time. "Postulates alter as methods of inquiry are perfected; the logical forms that express modern scientific inquiry are in many

9. *Ibid.*, p. 17.
10. *Ibid.*, p. 11.
11. *Ibid.*, pp. 14–19.
12. *Ibid.*, p. 16.
13. *Ibid.*, p. 17.

respects quite unlike those that formulated the procedures of Greek science." [14] And here we seem to find a radical departure from a more traditional view of the truths of logic. The only sense in which they are necessary, for Dewey, is conditional: one must accept them at a given time if at that time our aim of successful inquiry requires us to accept them. Such principles are not imposed on inquiry from without, Dewey says over and over again; and therefore they are not "externally *a priori*", and they are not "*a priori* principles fixed antecedently to inquiry and conditioning it *ab extra*".[15] He says of a logical principle that "while it is derived from what is involved in inquiries that have been successful in the past, it imposes a condition to be satisfied in future inquiries, until the results of such inquiries show reason for modifying it".[16] This means that logical principles for Dewey are neither "arbitrary" nor "mere linguistic conventions". "They must be such as control the determination and arrangement of subject-matter with respect to achieving enduringly stable beliefs." [17]

It is just this instrumental feature of logical principles which leads Dewey to deny a sharp distinction between *a priori* principles of formal logic and *a posteriori* principles of natural science, and, in a sense, to deny the very existence of *a priori* knowledge. This is most explicit in his statement of a view which he says he derives from Peirce. (Whether Dewey is right in assigning this view to Peirce is of no interest to me at the moment.) Dewey speaks of "leading principles" as articulations of habits of inference which may be narrower or wider in scope. "Material" leading principles, which are relatively narrow, correspond to empirical generalizations, while those which formulate habits involved in *every* inference, in

14. John Dewey, *Logic: The Theory of Inquiry* (New York, 1938), p. 18.
15. *Ibid.*, p. 12.
16. *Ibid.*, p. 17.
17. *Ibid.*, p. 18.

spite of differences of subject-matter, are "formal". But it must be insisted that Dewey does not draw a distinction between these two kinds of leading principles on the ground that the formal principles are *a priori* while the material principles are *a posteriori*. Insofar as the two kinds of principles differ only in *width*, they differ, we may say, only in degree and not in kind. Basing himself on the model of a craftsman who "learns that if he operates in a certain *way* the result will take care of itself, certain materials being given", Dewey says that we discover that "if we draw our inferences in a certain way, we shall, other things being equal, get dependable conclusions".[18]

In this context Dewey does not formulate a radical distinction between an inference in accordance with a law of natural science and an inference in accordance with a law of logic. *Both* of them are governed or involve habits "that tend to yield conclusions that are stable and productive in further inquiries".[19] The fact that some leading principles are formal and others not, does not lead Dewey to say that the formal principles are justified independently of experience while non-formal principles depend on experience. In his view, I infer, a physical principle like conservation of energy is not justified in a way radically different from the way in which logical principles are justified.

> The position taken [he says] implies the ultimacy of inquiry in determination of the formal conditions of inquiry. Logic as inquiry into inquiry . . . does not depend upon anything extraneous to inquiry. The force of this proposition may perhaps be most readily understood by noting what it precludes. It precludes the determination and selection of logical first principles by an *a priori* intuitional act, even when the intuition in question is said to be that of *Intellectus Purus*. It precludes resting logic upon metaphysical and epistemological assumptions and presuppositions. The latter are to be determined, if at all, by means of what is disclosed as the outcome of in-

18. *Ibid.*, p. 12.
19. *Ibid.*, p. 13.

quiry; they are not to be shoved under inquiry as its "foundation." [20]

It is hard, therefore, to distinguish the justification of such principles from the justification of those which are, say, physical, for physical principles will also be determined "by means of what is disclosed as the outcome of inquiry". And so Dewey says:

> In the degree in which we understand what is done in inquiries that result in warranted assertions, we understand the operational conditions which have to be observed. . . . The conditions of the required operations (required in order that a certain kind of consequence may issue) *are as much matters of experience as are factual contents: which are themselves also discriminated in order to serve as conditions of a warranted outcome.* [My italics.] [21]

I conclude from passages like this in the *Logic* and from others in *Reconstruction in Philosophy* that Dewey, in some places at least, opposes a distinction according to which all truths of formal logic are *a priori* and all truths of natural science *a posteriori*, and, moreover, seems to deny the existence of *a priori* knowledge.

III

As I have already indicated, however, Dewey's reflections on the matter do not end here. Having led us to believe that he cannot draw a sharp epistemological line between logical and non-logical truths, he now proceeds to puzzle us by what he says about the distinction between "existential" and "ideational" propositions, as he calls them; and we become even more puzzled by his distinction between "generic" and "universal" propositions. For after implying that formal logic is

20. John Dewey, *Logic: The Theory of Inquiry* (New York, 1938), pp. 20–21.
21. *Ibid.*, p. 157.

just as empirical as physics is, Dewey now implies that the laws of physics are analytic *and* that they must be justified by experience. Let us examine the text in order to see how this comes about.

In his *Logic* Dewey makes a distinction between what he calls "existential" and "ideational" propositions which resembles that between synthetic and analytic statements. Thus Dewey says:

> Propositions . . . are of two main categories: (1) Existential, referring directly to actual conditions as determined by experimental observation, and (2) ideational or conceptual, consisting of interrelated meanings, which are non-existential in content in *direct* reference but which are applicable to existence through the operations they represent as possibilities.[22]

I realize, of course, that he follows this with a kind of pragmatic incantation, for he says that "in constituting respectively material and procedural means, the two types of propositions are conjugate, or functionally correspondent. They form the fundamental divisions of labor in inquiry".[23] But this is an experimentalist's blessing of a distinction which one does not expect to find Dewey making after he has criticized the "sharp division between knowledge of matters of fact and of relations between ideas". For all of Dewey's aversion to "shoving" abstract meanings under logical principles, he surreptitiously shoves them under his "ideational propositions", which might be called analytic by a positivist. And for all of his aversion, in the early pages of the *Logic*, to a sharp division between logical leading principles and material leading principles, does he not make this same sharp division when he formulates his distinction between implication and inference?

Were this the only *volte face* in the later pages of his *Logic*, one might say that Dewey is merely reverting to a position

22. *Ibid.*, pp. 283–84.
23. *Ibid.*, p. 284.

like that of Hume and the logical positivists. But once Dewey
begins to fall, there is no stopping him and before he is fin-
ished he is, I submit, a rationalist in the worst sense of that
word,[24] one who thinks that the laws of natural science are
established by examining the relations between concepts
alone. We may see why by asking what sorts of statements he
calls existential and ideational. Like so many of his predecessors (and successors) in the history of philosophy, Dewey is
struck by a distinction between two kinds of statements
which begin with the word "all". He speaks of "the ambiguity
of 'all' as sometimes having existential reference, in which
case it represents an inference having at best a high order of
probability, and sometimes having nonexistential reference,
when it stands for a necessary relation which follows, by definition, from analysis of a conception".[25]

In effect, he calls existential "all"-propositions "generic"
and ideational "all"-propositions "universal". Thus he says that
the statement "All men are mortal" may be construed as
meaning either "All men have died or will die"—in which case
it is, according to Dewey, a "spatio-temporal proposition"
and generic; or it may be construed as meaning "If anything
is human, *then* it is mortal", in which case it is *universal* and
states, says Dewey, "a necessary relation of abstract characters".[26] On the first interpretation, Dewey goes on to say, the
statement is inductive and matter-of-fact; on the second it is
valid, "if valid at all, by definition of a conception".[27] The pervasiveness of the error into which he has fallen becomes
clearer when we discover that he also construes contrary-to-
fact conditional statements of science as universal and hence
as valid "by definition". He says:

24. See Professor May Brodbeck's trenchant article, "The New Rationalism: Dewey's Theory of Induction", *The Journal of Philosophy*, Volume
XLVI (1949), pp. 780–91.
25. Dewey, *Logic*, p. 296.
26. *Ibid.*, p. 256.
27. *Ibid.*

In science, there are many propositions in which the clause
introduced by "if" is known to be contrary to conditions set
by existential circumstances; that is, to be such that they cannot be existentially satisfied, as "If a particle at rest is acted
upon by a single moving particle, then," etc. In such propositions, *if* and *when* designate a connection of conceptual sub-
ject-matters, not of existential or temporo-spatial subject-mat-
ters. If the word "conditions" is used, it now refers to a
logical relation, not to existential circumstances.[28]

Throughout the later chapters of the *Logic*, Dewey speaks of
the *necessity* of universal propositions as opposed to the con-
tingency of generic propositions, and of the analytic and definitional nature of the former. He also appears to hypostatize
meanings in spite of his protest against other philosophers
who do the same thing. Speaking of definitions, he says that
"in a definition a single symbol having a total meaning is resolved into an *interrelation* of meanings".[29] He adds that in
definition "conceptual meanings . . . are resolved into characters that are *necessarily* interrelated just because they are
an analysis of a single conception".[30] He also tells us that
mathematical statements are universal because they are abstract hypothetical propositions. And the grand climax of that
part of Dewey's *Logic* which flows from his contrast between
existential generic propositions and ideational universal ones
—a part which begins roughly around page 254 and continues remorselessly through about page 486—is the statement
on page 453 that all physical laws state a relation of characters, preferably in mathematical equations, and that "while
the latter have ultimate existential reference, through the
possible operations they direct, they are non-existential (and
hence non-temporal) in their content".

28. *Ibid.*, p. 255.
29. *Ibid.*, p. 343.
30. *Ibid.*

IV

How shall we sum up? I am inclined to say that Dewey's view of so-called *a priori* knowledge is inconsistent. The view set forth in *Reconstruction in Philosophy*, in *The Quest for Certainty*, and in about the first 150 pages of the *Logic*, is that there is no such thing as *a priori* knowledge. But if there isn't, then one might say that Dewey has dispensed with the need for a concept of analytic truth. Yet Dewey's distinction between generic and universal statements is not only founded on a distinction between analytic and synthetic statements, but it also leads Dewey to say, in effect, that there are analytic *a posteriori* statements. Therefore, he simultaneously disassociates himself from philosophers who have campaigned against positivistic complacency about the notion of analytic, and from those partisans of positivism who, while they are happy with analyticity, are horrified at the thought of an analytic *a posteriori* statement. Dewey seems to think that the laws of natural science are universal and therefore analytic and "definitory".[31]

The question naturally arises: How does Dewey get himself into his predicament? I can suggest one answer to this question without being sure of its diagnostic power. I believe that Dewey was unsuccessfully seeking a solution to the problem of lawlike statements, as it has been called more recently. This is suggested by the fact that his generic statement "All men have died or will die" differs from his universal "All men are mortal" in a way that is reminiscent of Goodman's distinction between a non-lawlike and a lawlike statement.[32] It is confirmed by the fact that Dewey proposes contrary-to-fact conditionals as examples of universal proposi-

---

31. See Ernest Nagel, *Sovereign Reason* (Glencoe, Ill., 1954), pp. 145–46, for a different interpretation of Dewey's views.

32. Nelson Goodman, *Fact, Fiction, and Forecast*, 2nd ed. (New York, 1965), Chapter I.

tions and that Goodman characterizes a lawlike statement as one that supports a contrary-to-fact conditional. Dewey was rightly aware of the fact that contrary-to-fact conditionals assert a *connection* between antecedent and consequent, in a sense a *necessary* connection. But, since he seems to have been tied in one part of his *Logic* to the positivistic view that all necessary connections are analytic and definitional, he could find no better way out than to call scientific laws definitional and analytic.

For all of these reasons I think that Dewey was a valiant figure in the struggle to solve the problem of necessity, but he was not the source of final truth. In one part of his thinking he was led to say that we cannot neatly characterize all of logic as *a priori* and all of natural science as *a posteriori*. But when he was trapped into saying that all of the laws of natural science are analytic, he revealed his confusion—so much confusion that it is hard to see how he could have consistently sustained his attack on social philosophies like that of Natural Law. Dewey, of course, was always suspicious of social doctrines dominated by what he calls "the conceptual approach". Even after his defense of the view that the laws of empirical science are necessary because analytic, he makes critical allusions in his *Logic* to those who defend the doctrine of Natural Law and the theory of intuitions of *a priori* necessary truths. He charges them with a failure to recognize what he calls "the three indispensable logical conditions of conceptual subject-matter in scientific method":

> (1) the status of theoretical conceptions as hypotheses which (2) have a directive function in control of observation and ultimate practical transformation of antecedent phenomena, and which (3) are tested and continually revised on the ground of the consequences they produce in existential application.[33]

But, one may finally ask, doesn't Dewey want to eat his cake and have it? He wants the hypotheses of social scientists (and

33. Dewey, *Logic*, p. 506.

moralists too) to be subject to alteration as circumstances and evidence changes, yet in his logical description of the aim of science he says that scientists seek analytic connections between abstract characters. How, in all consistency, can he say that *such* a connection will be falsified by appeal to experience? How can he consistently attack partisans of Natural Law like Aquinas? [34] One is bound to say that his doctrine of generic and universal propositions is not only untenable, but that it leaves him naked to his ideological enemies. No amount of pragmatic talk can undo his capitulation to rationalism in the later pages of his *Logic*. And while there are problems created by the more empiricistic doctrine set forth in *Reconstruction in Philosophy*, in *The Quest for Certainty*, and in the earlier parts of the *Logic*, I believe that these texts represent a healthier strain in Dewey's thinking on this subject.

34. See the Epilogue to the paperback edition of my *Social Thought in America* (Boston, 1957).

11. Value and Obligation in Dewey and Lewis [1]

The appearance of Professor C. I. Lewis' *Analysis of Knowledge and Valuation,* with its forthright defense of the thesis that all statements of value are empirical, presents an opportunity to examine the present state of pragmatic value theory and ethics. In particular it presents an opportunity to compare Lewis' views with those of Dewey on the relation between value and obligation. The third book of Lewis' *Analysis* presents a carefully worked out doctrine which closely resembles the one Dewey outlines in the tenth chapter of *The Quest for Certainty,* but these doctrines exhibit a great difference as well. The agreement and difference may be summarized by saying that whereas both Lewis and Dewey defend a view according to which value statements are empirical, Lewis, unlike Dewey, makes a distinction be-

1. Originally this essay appeared in *The Philosophical Review,* Volume LVIII (1949), pp. 321–29. A few pages of it were reprinted in my *Social Thought in America* (New York, Viking Press, 1949; paperback edition, Beacon Press, Boston, 1957). It was reprinted without changes or omissions in *Readings in Ethical Theory,* edited by Wilfrid Sellars and John Hospers (New York, Appleton-Century-Crofts, 1952). In the present version a few pages have been considerably revised in order to clarify the argument. The essay is reprinted here by permission.

tween value statements and ethical statements, according to
which the latter are not empirical. The purpose of this article
is to make some observations on this entire issue.

Dewey's central concern in this area is to distinguish between the *desirable* and the *desired* in a way that guarantees
a clear distinction between what he calls "de jure" statements
and what he calls "merely factual" statements; a *de jure* statement asserts the desirability of an object, whereas a merely
de facto statement asserts that it is desired. I do not think he
makes this distinction successfully, and I will try to show
why in the first part of this article.[2] Lewis, in spite of the similarity between his position and Dewey's, avoids what I think
is Dewey's error, but the manner in which he avoids it creates a problem for his theory of knowledge. In a postscript I
shall compare the difficulties facing Dewey's theory with
those which have been pointed out by almost all critics of
Mill's notorious analogy between the desirable and the visible.

Dewey is anxious to distinguish between the satisfying and
the satisfactory, the enjoyed and the enjoyable, the desired
and the desirable. Most of us would agree that the last of
these pairs of concepts illustrates an important difference—
indeed the most important difference in the theory of the
subject. Dewey objects to what he calls an "empirical theory
of values", according to which values are constituted by liking and enjoyment, so that "to be enjoyed and to be a value
are two names for one and the same fact". [3] But although he
denies this theory, he maintains that there is a connection between value and being desired, for he says: "I shall not object
to this empirical theory so far as it connects the theory of values with concrete experiences of desire and satisfaction. The
idea that there is such a connection is the only way known to

2. This problem has been discussed by C. L. Stevenson from another
point of view. See his *Ethics and Language* (New Haven, 1944), pp. 253–64.

3. John Dewey, *The Quest for Certainty* (New York, 1929), Chapter X.

me by which the pallid remoteness of the rationalistic theory, and the only too glaring presence of the institutional theory of transcendental values can be escaped". [4] Yet this is not the only condition he sets upon the solution of the problem. In connecting the desirable (value) with the desired, he must connect them in such a way as to show clearly that whereas the statement "*a* is desired now" is merely a statement of fact, the statement "*a* is desirable" is a factual statement which also has a "*de jure* quality". The problem, then, is to give an analysis of "*a* is desirable" when it is construed as meaning that *a* ought to be desired, which will render it an empirical statement, a statement which conveys empirical knowledge. What I will argue here is not that this is in general impossible, but rather that Dewey's particular method of solving the problem as set forth in the tenth chapter of *The Quest for Certainty* does not accomplish this difficult task.

The relationship between the desirable and the desired is not identified by Dewey in a way that makes me wholly confident of my interpretation of his view, but in many passages Dewey seems to suggest that this relationship resembles the connection between what Lewis calls "Value in Objects" and what he calls the immediate experience of satisfaction. "As a first approximation," Lewis says, "we might say that attributing value to an existent, *O*, means that under circumstances, *C*, *O* will, or would, lead to satisfaction in the experience of somebody, *S*." [5] Now it seems to me that there are many oc-

4. *Ibid.*, p. 258. It should be pointed out that my chief criticisms of Dewey are not affected by the conclusions of his controversy with P. B. Rice in *The Journal of Philosophy*, Volume XL (1943), for there Dewey reiterates his belief that there is a connection between value and satisfaction. What I am concerned with here is this *connection* rather than the nature of satisfaction. For this reason I do not consider Dewey's views on introspection and the subjective: they are not relevant in my opinion. If I were to enter this vexed problem, no doubt important differences would turn up between Dewey and Lewis, but no difference of that sort would interfere with their maintaining the agreement I discuss in the present article.

5. C. I. Lewis, *An Analysis of Knowledge and Valuation* (La Salle, Ill., 1946), p. 512.

casions on which Dewey speaks as though he holds this kind
of theory of objective value. For example, he says: "A *feeling*
of good or excellence is as far removed from goodness in fact
as a feeling that objects are intellectually thus and so is removed from their being actually so." [6] Many statements of
this kind lead me to believe that Dewey's view of the relation
between what is desirable and what is desired identifies it
with the relation which holds between the objective property
of being red and the appearance of red. It would seem that
according to Dewey we cannot infer validly that an object
has value simply on the basis of enjoying it casually, without
having instituted tests analogous to those which are instituted by the careful investigator of the objective color of
something. And it would appear that according to Dewey
only an object which satisfies us under conditions which are
analogous to the normal conditions involved in testing colors,
has value in his sense. Although there are other passages
which present difficulties for this interpretation, I believe
there is considerable evidence for holding that it does render
Dewey's meaning in some places. This interpretation has the
virtue of helping us understand a number of statements
which would otherwise be vague. We can understand more
easily now (or at least the writer can) what Dewey means
when he says that a judgment of value involves a prediction;
it also makes clear his analogy between statements of what is
immediately satisfying and statements which report what he
calls immediate "havings" in the perception of colors.

In addition, however, Dewey maintains that adjectives like
"desirable" and "admirable", appear in sentences which express what *should* be the case. He says: "A judgment about
what is *to be* desired and enjoyed is . . . a claim on future
action; it possesses *de jure* and not merely *de facto* quality. It
is a matter of frequent experience that likings and enjoy-
ments are of all kinds, and that many are such as reflective

6. Dewey, *op. cit.*, p. 265.

judgments condemn. By way of self-justification and 'rational-ization', an enjoyment creates a tendency to assert that the thing enjoyed is a value. This assertion of validity adds authority to the fact. It is a decision that the object has a right to exist and hence a claim upon action to further its existence". [7] Dewey thinks that statements of value are empirical statements to the effect that one *ought* to have certain attitudes, and for this reason he is more naturalistic in his view than Lewis. What I want to show, however, is that Dewey's ethical naturalism is subject to a serious difficulty. To this end I shall first formulate Dewey's view as clearly as I can.

First of all, Dewey distinguishes between a report of immediate sensation and a statement about an objective property of a thing. He seems to hold that if I look at an object a and say that a looks red to me now, my statement:

(1)   . a looks red to me now

is a report of a sensation, whereas if I say:

(2) a is (really) red,

I am not making a report about my immediate sensations. Dewey also seems to hold that statement (2) is equivalent to a statement that contains the expression "a looks red to y", for he seems to accept the statement:

(3)   "a is really red" is equivalent to "For every normal person y, if y looks at a under normal conditions, then a looks red to y".

Now, as I understand Dewey, these three statements have the following analogues:

(1') a is desired by me now

(2') a is desirable

7. *Ibid.*, p. 263.

(3′)   "*a* is desirable" is equivalent to "For every normal person *y*, if *y* looks at *a* under normal conditions, then *a* is desired by *y*".

However, if Dewey rests his case on (3′) he has not shown that (2′) has any more "*de jure*" quality than (2) has. Sentence (3′) tells us that "*a* is desirable" is equivalent to a general statement about what a normal person will desire under normal conditions; and sentence (3) tells us that "*a* is really red" is equivalent to a general statement about what a normal person will see under normal conditions. That is why we are led to wonder whether Dewey has, in accepting (3′), shown that "*a* is desirable" is a statement that "possesses *de jure* and not merely *de facto* quality". On his own showing, the statement "*a* is desirable" is no more *de jure* than "*a* is really red". For this reason one wonders whether the left-hand side of the equivalence (3′) shouldn't be "*a* is really desir*ed*" rather than "*a* is desir*able*".

Another way of making the same point is to say that if we accept (3′), then the left-hand side of the equivalence (3) should be "*a* ought to look red". But when we say that *a* looks red to a normal person who looks at it under normal conditions, do we mean that there is a *moral* obligation to see *a* as red? I do not think so. This statement expresses no moral claim and for that reason when we say that *a* is *desired* by any normal person who looks at it under normal conditions, we do not seem to be asserting a moral obligation.

I am not, I should add, concerned here with the general question whether "desirable", in the sense of "ought to be desired" or "worthy of being desired", can be analyzed so that statements like "*a* is desirable" are shown to convey empirical knowledge. I am merely interested in pointing out that the particular empirical or naturalistic interpretation which Dewey gives in the tenth chapter of *The Quest for Certainty* is defective in a subtle way. I am not concerned to criticize all of Dewey's writings on this theme, but I am not aware of any that supplements the view expressed in *The Quest for Certainty* in a way that obviates the difficulties in it. My chief criticism depends on the fact that the relation between "desirable" and "desired" is held by Dewey to be identical with that between "really red" and "appears red". But "*a* appears red" and "*a* is really red" do not differ in any way which would allow us to say that the first has a merely "*de facto*" quality, whereas the second has a "*de jure*" quality, to use Dewey's language. The fact that *a* is really red, to put it in another language, is no more *normative* than the fact that *a* appears red now. And since the fact that *a* is desirable (as Dewey construes it) is related to the fact that *a* is desired in precisely the way that the fact that *a* is really red is related to the fact that *a* appears red, it follows that "*a* is desirable" is no more normative than "*a* is desired". I conclude that Dewey has not succeeded in correctly analyzing "desirable" in the sense of "ought to be desired". I do not see how the statement "*a* is desired under normal conditions" can be viewed as synonymous with "*a* ought to be desired" without viewing "*a* appears red under normal conditions" as synonymous with "*a* ought to appear red", but I feel that this consequence is absurd, and hence fatal to Dewey's view.

Some philosophers who share my opinion on this might conclude that *any* so-called naturalistic definition of "ought to be desired" is refuted by an argument which is similar to the one I have offered above; but I am not convinced of this, and I want to repeat that my argument is directed solely against one naturalistic proposal. Some of the difficulties involved in a blanket rejection of the naturalistic program for analyzing "ought to be desired" appear in Lewis' work, I think, and so I turn now to his views on this question.

Lewis is convinced of the impossibility of a purely empirical analysis of the right and that which ought to be. So far as I can gather, he agrees with Dewey in construing objective value as a potentiality of objects whose realization takes place in immediate experience, in immediate satisfactions;

but he does not go on to construe having value so defined as identical with being desirable in any way that confers "*de jure*" status on judgments of value. Dewey does, and it is here that my difficulties with Dewey arise. Dewey is anxious to give an analysis of "desirable" in the "*de jure*" sense which will result in construing it as an empirical predicate. However, Lewis does not even attempt to do this because he holds that judgments of what ought to be, in particular judgments of what ought to be desired, are matters of ethics rather than of value. "The problem which delimits the field of ethics is not that of the empirically good or valuable but that of the right and morally imperative. To be sure, there is essential connection between rightness of action and goodness in that which this action is intended to effect. At least, it is with this general conception that rightness of action derives from value in the end, with which we should agree. But just at this point we should be careful that we do not illicitly connect the right and the good, before ever we have distinguished them." [8] Here we see plainly the gap between Lewis and Dewey, but it is here that new problems arise.

Lewis holds: "Valuation is always a matter of empirical knowledge. But what is right and just, can never be determined by empirical facts alone". [9] But if this is juxtaposed with Lewis' belief that there are only two kinds of knowledge —knowledge of empirical propositions and knowledge of analytic propositions—we find it difficult to see how he will classify ethical knowledge—knowledge of what is just, what is right, what ought to be. He has cut himself off from regarding ethical knowledge as empirical by definition of what is ethical. Can he regard all true ethical propositions as analytic? To be sure, Lewis regards *some* ethical statements as analytic, e.g., "No rule of action is right except one which is right in all instances, and therefore right for everyone". But it

8. Lewis, *op. cit.*, p. 552.
9. *Ibid.*, p. 554.

is not at all clear that he is willing to call *every* true proposition which involves the notion of *right* analytic, e.g., *it was not right of Brutus to stab Caesar*. In any case it does not follow from the fact that some principles of ethics are analytic that all ethical propositions are. *No rule of action may be right except one which is right in all instances* may be an analytic proposition for Lewis, but clearly the fact that it is analytic does not imply that the proposition, *Truth-telling is right*, is analytic. I point this out only because some readers of Lewis have concluded from the fact that he cites one ethical proposition as analytic that he holds that *all* true ethical propositions are analytic.

Yet if Lewis refuses to take this alternative (which does not seem defensible), what other alternatives are there for him? One is to surrender the view that all knowledge is exclusively and exhaustively divisible into the analytic and the empirical, but he seems to hold to this too confidently for us to expect that he will choose this course. Can he, then, face the conclusion that "knowledge" of ethical propositions is not knowledge at all? Several things he says suggest that he rejects this alternative. The problem is one that is immensely perplexing and is precisely the problem which leads Stevenson to *his* position.[10] We must observe, therefore, how Lewis' concluding remarks about the nonempirical character of ethical propositions (as distinct from value propositions) bring him closer to a position which he attacks in value theory. "The denial to value-apprehensions in general of the character of truth or falsity and of knowledge" is a denial which he describes as "one of the strangest aberrations ever to visit the mind of man".[11] But I should say that after showing successfully that value propositions *do* express empirical knowledge, he formulates a position in ethics which is closer in motivation to that

10. Stevenson, *op. cit.* I have in mind Stevenson's version of the emotive theory of ethical judgments.

11. Lewis, *op. cit.*, pp. 365–66.

of the "emotivists" than he thinks. For he has simply post-poned to ethics the problem that has troubled them in what he calls theory of value. In denying that ethical statements convey empirical knowledge, he joins with those who deny to apprehensions of what is right (as distinct from what has value) the character of empirical truth or falsity and of empirical knowledge. To be sure, he does not go on to treat judgments of right in the positive manner of the emotivists. But he does join with them in denying that ethical propositions are to be settled by appeal to factual considerations alone. However, I might remark here that it is not clear whether Lewis means to divorce ethical judgments from *all* appeal to fact or whether he means merely to say that in addition to factual considerations something else enters into a determination of what is right. Yet, if he holds the latter view, he must tell us what this something else is and how it enters.

The resulting situation in the ethics and value-theory of contemporary pragmatism may be summarized as follows. Dewey tries to translate statements of the form "*a* is desirable" into empirical statements. He does this by construing the property of being desirable as a disposition by analogy with objective characteristics like red as distinct from phenomenal appearances of red. This, I have argued, does not clarify or define "desirable" in the sense of "ought to be desired". Lewis regards "value" as an empirical predicate but avoids identifying what he and Dewey both call value (in objects) with what ought to be desired. Lewis holds that what ought to be desired is not a matter of value but of ethics, and for him ethics does not depend on empirical knowledge alone. But Lewis has also divided knowledge into the analytic and the empirical and has excluded anything like the synthetic *a priori*. How, then, will he classify and analyze propositions concerning what ought to be desired without making them all analytic and without appealing to something like the synthetic *a priori*? The disagreement between Dewey and Lewis on this question deserves notice as representing an important cleavage in American pragmatism, for Lewis has called himself a pragmatist on some occasions. Evidently pragmatism is united on the subject of value but not on obligation or justice. Dewey, in spite of a valiant attempt, has not given us a naturalistic account of obligation and Lewis forsakes the task as impossible. We may safely say, therefore, that contemporary pragmatism is still without a solution of the fundamental problem of ethics.[12]

Postscript on Dewey and Mill

In the original version of this article I made some remarks about the relationship between Dewey's views on the desirable and John Stuart Mill's views on this concept. In the present version I have withdrawn these remarks from their original position in the article because they interrupted the argument in a confusing way. However, because I think the remarks are still worth making, I present them here. I have, I think, presented them more clearly here than I did in the original version.

In a famous passage in his *Utilitarianism* Mill held that we can prove that a thing is desirable by showing that people desire it. He there leads us to suppose that he accepted the generalization:

(a)   Whatever people desire is desirable.

For how else could one justify the idea that one could *prove* a thing to be desirable simply on the basis of its being desired by people? Mill also said that one could prove that an object is visible by showing that people see it, and that the

---

12. I am indebted to Nelson Goodman for helping me clarify some of my ideas on the difference between "soluble" and "objectively red". Robert M. Browning's interesting article, "On Professor Lewis's Distinction between Ethics and Valuation", in *Ethics*, Volume LIX (1949), pp. 95–111, came to my attention after my article had been prepared for publication.

relationship between being desired and being desirable is analogous to that between being seen and being visible. Therefore Mill may be thought of as accepting the statement:

(b)   Whatever people see is visible.

One way of lodging a familiar complaint against Mill is to say that he overlooked an important difference between two kinds of adjectives ending in "ble": those that are dispositional terms like "visible" and those that are normative terms like "desirable." And it might be supposed that I lodged the same complaint against Dewey by protesting that he did not capture the normative element in the term "desirable" when he said in statement (3') above that "a is desirable" is equivalent to "For every normal person y, if y looks at a under normal conditions, then a is desired by y". For, someone might contend, asserting such an equivalence is tantamount to asserting that "desirable" is a dispositional term. Why? Because this equivalence is modeled on the equivalence asserted in (3) for "a is really red", an equivalence which shows that "really red" is a dispositional term. After all, when we say that a will look red if a normal person looks at it under normal conditions, we do assert that it has a certain disposition to appear in a certain manner under specified conditions.

Nevertheless, I want to say that the complaint I lodged against Dewey is *not* identical with that usually lodged against Mill. The point is that Dewey's analysis of "a is desirable" does *not* force him to say that whatever people desire is desirable, just as the analogous analysis of "really red" does not lead to the conclusion that *whatever* looks red to people is red. For a really to be red according to this analysis, the people to whom a looks red at a certain time must be people who are normal and who have looked at a under normal conditions. For a to be desirable, the people who desire a at a certain time must be people who are normal and who have looked at a under normal conditions. That is why we can't infer "*a* is really red" from "*a* looks red to me now", and can't infer "*a* is desirable" from "*a* is desired by me now".

However, the fact that Dewey may be said to have given a dispositional analysis of "desirable" which is not subject to the same strictures as those that are sometimes leveled against Mill shows that there are two uses of the expression "dispositional terms" which must be distinguished. In order to show this, I want first to contrast the terms "soluble" and "soluble in water". To say that *a* is soluble (period) is to say that *a* is capable of being dissolved. We mean merely that *a* will dissolve under *some* circumstances—and we do not say which. To say that *a* is soluble in water is to say that if *a* is put in water, it dissolves, and here we specify the condition that will result in *a*'s dissolution, namely, putting *a* in water. On the basis of this we can say that whereas we may not infer "*a* is soluble *in water*" from the statement that *a* dissolved at a certain time, we *are* inclined to infer "*a* is soluble (period)" from the statement that *a* dissolved at a certain time. If *a* dissolved yesterday, we suppose that there *were* circumstances which led it to dissolve and hence that it is soluble (period). But if we don't know that its having been in water led to its dissolution we may not conclude that it is soluble in water. Similarly, we may conclude that what people see is visible, but we may not conclude that because a man has seen an object it is visible at a distance of 3 miles. Being visible is like being soluble, but being visible at a distance of 3 miles is like being soluble in water.

It is now time to say that "really red" is a dispositional term like "soluble in water", and not like "soluble (period)". That is why we can't infer "*a* is really red" from "*a* looked red to me yesterday". Moreover, Dewey's assimilation of "desirable" to "really red" is what protects him from the complaints usually lodged against Mill. Dewey is not forced to say that whatever people desire is desirable. His troubles are of a different kind.

III. PHILOSOPHY AND CIVILIZATION

12. New Horizons in Philosophy [1]

The most arresting and most distinctive feature of philosophy in the English-speaking world today is concentration on linguistic and logical analysis. While dialectical materialism is the official philosophy of the Soviet bloc, and Western Europe continues to be strongly affected by existentialism, Britain and the United States are primarily the homes of what is called analytic or linguistic philosophy. Analytic philosophers are neither sponsored nor controlled by any government or political party, and they do not appeal to the Bohemian or the beatnik.[2] They invite both Marxist and existentialist scorn because they spurn the pretentiousness and murk of much traditional philosophy. For good reasons analytic philosophy has never become the favorite subject of the bistro or the *espresso* café, and it needs no proof of its seriousness. It re-

1. This essay was first printed in *The Saturday Evening Post*, 20 September 1960, p. 24 *et seq.*, © 1960 by The Curtis Publishing Company. It was reprinted in *Adventures of the Mind* (second series), edited by Richard Thruelsen and John Kobler (New York, Alfred A. Knopf, 1961), pp. 591–605; also in *Central States Speech Journal*, Volume XII (1961), pp. 188–96. It is reprinted here, with a few minor changes, by permission.
2. Had this essay been written later, I should have, of course, used the word "hippie" rather than "beatnik".

spects the values of the reasonable man rather than those of the irrational man, though it fully recognizes the existence of irrationality.

Analytic philosophy begins with an awareness of the fact that philosophy is not a rival of science and that it cannot provide us with another way of studying the world with which the scientist deals. When in the nineteenth century natural science grew so highly specialized, it became evident that nobody could encompass the whole of knowledge. And so the drift of philosophy was away from encyclopedism, away from thinking that the philosopher was a superscientist, a universal genius, a know-it-all.

Not only did it become evident that universal knowledge was humanly impossible, but it was seen how dubious it was to think that one could construct a system in which all our knowledge could be derived from a few philosophical principles, as the geometrical theorems of Euclid are deduced from his axioms. It was this mistake which resulted in the illusion that philosophers could dominate all knowledge through the command of a few pivotal truths. This may be called the metaphysical illusion, the product of a vast inflation of the powers and prospects of metaphysics, one of the oldest and most mysterious branches of philosophy.

According to tradition, metaphysics is the most fundamental of all disciplines. The first part of the word "metaphysics" is derived from the Greek *meta*, meaning "after", so that the subject was conceived as that which went beyond the problems of physics. Physicists, some metaphysicians said, deal with material things, biologists with living things, mathematicians with numbers, points, and lines. But the metaphysician cuts a much wider swath; indeed he takes the whole cloth as his province, for he studies being *as such*. Not any particular being or limited class of beings, but just plain being, since the traditional metaphysician is the spectator of all time and eternity.

It took philosophers a long time to realize that the number

of interesting things that one can say about all things in one fell swoop is very limited. When you lump together such different items as kings, cabbages, bits of sealing wax, numbers, thoughts, and electrons in order to say what they all have in common, you are likely to discover that what they have in common is the fact that they exist. You say very little through the effort to become supremely general.

Having reached this conclusion about the most central of philosophical disciplines, some philosophers asked themselves just what was left for them to do. If all of existence could be parceled out to different scientists who worked so effectively by specializing, and if the philosopher was unable to supply any significant first principles which could neatly order the tangled forest of modern science and information, what was the philosopher's function in the intellectual world? Once philosophy was everything. Now it threatened to become nothing.

Fortunately the story of philosophy did not end here. There were some who did not desert the battered, beleaguered ship. They knew that there were nonmetaphysical questions of large import which had always been asked by philosophers and which had to be asked more relentlessly than ever in an age of scientific specialization. One of these questions—short, but powerful—was "What do you mean?" The patron saint of philosophy, Socrates, had spent most of his time asking it, often to the discomfort of those with whom he conversed in Plato's *Dialogues* and to the immense delight of centuries of readers who watched Socrates puncture humbug and ironically examine ideas which could not stand the test of honest logical criticism. The question "What do you mean?" could be directed even at scientists. It was the tiny candle which had flickered since antiquity, which had never gone out even in philosophy's darkest days. It was used to light a philosophical bonfire by a generation of thinkers at the turn of the century—Ernst Mach, the Austrian philosopher-physicist who influenced Einstein; Bertrand Russell and

G. E. Moore in England; Charles Peirce and William James in the United States. They sparked the various new explosive movements of the twentieth century—pragmatism in the United States, logical positivism in Austria, and Cambridge analysis, so called in honor of the English university where it first flourished.

No matter how far scientific specialization went, it left the possibility of asking Socrates' question. In fact, the more the scientists specialized, the more their preoccupation with description, experiment, observation, and prediction robbed them of the time and energy needed for the clarification of their fundamental concepts. Physicists before Einstein had failed to be sufficiently clear about the notions of space and time, and biologists were not always prepared to give comprehensible answers to the question "What is life?". Even mathematicians were foggy about the idea of number and had fallen into serious paradoxes. Here, then, was an opportunity for philosophers to cooperate with scientists in an effort to elucidate the basic concepts of special sciences, instead of pretending that the philosopher possessed a mysterious key to all scientific doors. The revival of the Socratic question "What do you mean?" as applied to the words of the scientist, thus preserved for the philosopher a central, if not regal, position. He was no longer a surveyor of everything, but rather a careful student of language who at this stage of the analytic movement tended to concentrate on the terms of natural science and mathematics. The most brilliant monument to this pre-World War I era in philosophy was the three-volumed *Principia Mathematica* of Russell and Whitehead.

After the First World War the harvest of this intellectual activity was reaped by younger philosophers who described themselves as logical positivists. Philosophy, they said in going beyond Russell and Whitehead, was nothing but the philosophy of science. And philosophy of science, as someone put it, was philosophy enough. A story was told of a philosopher of the old school who came into the office of his department during the '30's and overheard two of his younger colleagues arguing about the meaning of a physical theory. The disputants grew more and more intense, and just after one shouted, "What do you mean by saying that space is curved?", the other yelled, "What do you mean by saying it's not?" The first, not to be outdone, then produced that classic in philosophical oneupmanship: "What do *you* mean by 'mean'?". At this point the old professor could not contain himself and spoke up for his own generation as he interrupted the conversation to say, "Good morning, gentlemen. If that means anything to you".

The professor's greeting pointed a moral. It revealed a grave limitation in the conception of meaning itself. For the logical positivist a meaningful utterance was simply one that could be verified or falsified. And verifiability and falsifiability, it was said, were limited to scientific statements. Small wonder that a greeting like "Good morning" was said to be meaningless. But much more than "Good morning" was at stake. For by these same narrow standards, poetry and ethics, in addition to metaphysics, were all nonsense.

At this point in its history, analytic philosophy was at its furthest from the humanistic tradition. The verifiability theory of meaning was to the positivist in the 1930's what the guillotine was to the French Revolution, and like the guillotine it destroyed indiscriminately. It was one thing to attack metaphysics, another to say that every poetic or moral utterance was meaningless. And it did not help to add that moral and poetic language had what was called "emotive meaning", or the capacity to stimulate emotions. That was often a polite way of sweeping much of human language under the rug, to put it where the positivist could conveniently avoid it, indeed walk all over it while he puzzled about the meaning of "space", "time", and "number".

It soon became evident that the question "What do you mean?" had been conceived too narrowly. It tended to direct the philosopher's attention only to language in which knowledge was communicated. Under Plato's influence, philosophers had identified the meaning of a term with an abstract concept, thinking of the word on the page as expressing a cloudy entity in Plato's realm of ideas. And therefore they tended to think that only declarative sentences, such as "Socrates is a man", had meaning as they conceived it. On this theory the command "Socrates, come here!" was strictly nonsensical. And so was the exclamation "Great Socrates!" because obviously it was hard to suppose that there was some weird resident of Plato's realm called "Great Socrateshood" which could serve as the meaning of the exclamation.

Partly because of these consequences and other more technical difficulties, and partly because of the intellectual mood created by the aftermath of the war, the influence of logical positivism waned perceptibly in the '40's. Unfortunately, however, the phrase "logical positivist" continued as an epithet which was wrongly applied to anyone with the faintest interest in the philosophy of language. For that reason an entirely different attitude in analytic philosophy has been hidden from public view. It is dominated by the idea that the philosopher should ask of utterances and writings not what their Platonic meaning is, but rather what their *use* is. This attitude is usually identified with the late Ludwig Wittgenstein, who was the leading philosophical figure at Cambridge University after the days of Russell and Moore, and who influences contemporary philosophy mainly through his posthumously published writings and through his loyal disciples.

As is so often the case in the history of ideas, a simple suggestion, undoubtedly present in the minds of many others who had failed to stress it sufficiently or to carry it out as brilliantly as Wittgenstein did, caught on among a great number of English and American philosophers after the Second World War. I am not a follower of Wittgenstein, and I regard a good deal of what he has said as dubious; but in the history of recent philosophy he is a liberating force. Once he said plainly and insistently that the main subject matter of the philosopher was the behavior of human beings trying to communicate with one another, a whole new world seemed to open up to the analytic philosopher, the many-sided world of language in all of its employments. Not just the language of scientific assertion and proof, for man does not communicate by assertion and proof alone. He greets, exclaims, exhorts, commands, judges, describes, promises, and does many other things with words. And all of these linguistic activities have now become fair game for the philosopher who has abandoned the Platonic version of the question "What do you mean?".

What should the analytic philosopher do, now that he has been shown these new horizons, now that he has been freed from the restrictive idea that he is merely a logician of natural science? In the remainder of this essay I should like to formulate and illustrate my own answer to this vital question.

Philosophers have an unprecedented opportunity to clarify the language which men use in the writing of history, in morality, law, religion, politics, and education, to take the most challenging examples. And so I might label my viewpoint "institutionalism" in order to suggest that one of the primary tasks of philosophy is to analyze, compare, and contrast language as it is used for purposes of communication within these different institutions. While communicating in these situations, men use language in a variety of intertwined ways which express their beliefs, hopes, their needs, and their values; and one job of the philosopher is to draw an intellectual map, to provide a coherent picture of the interconnections between these different modes of speech, feeling, and thought.

Language is a cultural instrument, and it must be seen in its cultural setting. Those who fail to view it in this way and who instead regard it as a collection of dead sentences fall into two related errors. One may be called formalism and the other essentialism. Formalism is the tendency to view language as if it were an inscription on a scroll or a monument rather than as the living, complex, subtle tool that it is. Essentialism is the idea that the philosopher can look at these dead words and, without attention to their use, summarize the essence of complex forms of communication. Philosophers given to such oversimplification have said that religion is merely a belief in God. Law has been defined as the command of the sovereign. History has been glibly summarized as the effort to report what actually happened in the past. Questions in each of these areas have been separated sharply from questions of morality. The icy hand of overabstraction guides the writing of those philosophers who think that merely by examining the *forms* of words, they can characterize the essence of religion, history, or law. Their most common assumption is that by looking at any kind of language one can *always* single out those statements in it which are factual, objective, and descriptive, and separate them sharply from statements of value. And this assumption, I think, is a mistake, notably when it is applied uniformly to the writings of historians and the language of lawyers. It is often the result of a failure to study the actual processes of law and historical writing, a failure which is encouraged by the formalism and essentialism of which I have spoken.

Of course, I do not wish to deny that *sometimes* we can make a distinction between statements of fact and evaluations in a given context. For example, two men can agree that someone has told a lie and yet judge his lying differently. In such cases our conclusion about the lying may be reported in a conjunction of a factual statement and a moral statement, "Jones lied, and it was wrong of him to do so". Here another person is logically free to agree with the first or factual part of the conjunctive statement, while he denies the second if his moral viewpoint is different from ours. But a careful study of communication, especially in history and law, brings to light a kind of blended or hybrid language which defies any effort to decompose it into factual and moral parts that may be accepted or rejected independently. There are, I believe, uses of language which are simultaneously descriptive and evaluative, and which cannot be broken down into the assertion of a factual statement and an evaluative statement which may be judged separately. The person who speaks or writes in this way is doing two inseparable things at once, stating a matter of fact and evaluating, and therefore his audience must take or leave his speech as a whole. To acknowledge this possibility is to abandon certain conventional modes of classifying language which have dominated the history of philosophy.

My contention is that this hybrid kind of language is most commonly found in an institutional setting. It is too large, sprawling, and complex for textbooks of logic, for they are too often dominated by a passion for neatness and an interest in classifying isolated statements. Therefore, in order to illustrate and clarify what I have in mind, I shall turn to a basic problem in the philosophy of history and another in the philosophy of law. History is an institution insofar as no civilized society can live without some image of its past. And no one can deny the pervasiveness of legal institutions.

One of the historian's concerns is to report particular facts, and another is to present a connected picture of the past. The first expresses itself in simple declarative statements, such as "Caesar crossed the Rubicon", and the second in lengthy sequential narratives about the life of some person or the development of a society or a nation. And narrative is not usually studied by formal logicians. It is one thing to report the simple fact that Caesar crossed the Rubicon, but it is another to present Caesar's biography or the history of Rome. By holding fast to this distinction between statement and narration, one can see a profoundly important distinction between two ways in which value judgments operate in history. When the historian is assessing the evidence for individual statements of fact, his value judgments—whether on political or religious matters—are properly distinguished from his factual conclusions. But when he is forming his narrative, the historian is often unable to separate these two parts of his thinking. To show this let us consider some illustrations that are closer to home than Julius Caesar.

If we say that George Washington crossed the Delaware we make a statement which is as "objective" as most statements made in history books. It is accepted or rejected on grounds that are not likely to include the values of the historian who makes the statement. The situation changes dramatically, however, when we are asked to choose between two general narrative histories of the United States. Here we are not faced with a short descriptive question about one man's actions at a certain time. And here our values do play a part in determining which of two general histories we should write or prefer. Take, for example, the difference between general histories of the United States which take the Federalist point of view and those which are Jeffersonian in their slant.

Professor Samuel Eliot Morison points out that sixty years ago it was difficult to find a general history of the United States that did not, as he puts it, "present the Federalist-Whig-Republican point of view, or express a very dim view of all Democratic leaders except Grover Cleveland". But by the middle of this century the fashion had changed, and it was then equally difficult to find a good general history of the country "that did not follow the Jefferson-Jackson-Franklin D. Roosevelt line". Morison says that he was converted to the latter as a young man when he discovered in his first researches on New England Federalism that "the 'wise and good and rich' whom Fisher Ames thought should rule the nation were stupid, narrow-minded and local in their outlook". But isn't it clear that Morison's conclusion presupposed values which some other historian might not share? And is it not clear, therefore, that the historian who tells a story following a "line" is engaged in an undecomposable blend of description and evaluation?

Something similar is true of the history of philosophy. The historian of philosophy does not expound the views of all human beings who have philosophized. Consciously or unconsciously he adopts standards of philosophical excellence by which he judges who is to be admitted into his history. Doctrinal agreement with the historian is not the standard, but his history incorporates a judgment of importance and interest which rests on values that another historian of philosophy might easily reject. Any Catholic reader of histories of philosophy which skip lightly over the medieval period will understand what I mean.

When a historian believes that a certain political tradition is superior to another, he tends to see the history of the country as a development of that tradition. And when we see that history in terms of another tradition, we are no more in a position to say he speaks falsely than we would be if he and we were to see certain trick figures in psychology books differently. The reader may have seen the illustration that can at one moment be seen as a rabbit's head and at another as a duck's.

Well, the historian who tells the story of the United States in Jeffersonian terms because he admires that tradition is a little like the man who always sees the duck-rabbit as a duck because he likes ducks more than rabbits. And we who evaluate his history are likely to praise it in the degree to which he sees the past as we see it in the light of our values. I think that opposing narrative historians sometimes confront each other as rabbit-loving rabbit seers confront duck-loving duck seers.

Some historians are loath to admit this because they view the problem absolutistically. They think of the general historian of the United States as confronted with an "actuality" whose main line is either Federalist or Jeffersonian and not both. They tend to assimilate the logic of narrative history to the logic of historical statement, and to hold that the general historian of the United States who is preparing to write his book is faced with just as objective an "either-or" as the historian who is trying to decide whether Caesar crossed the Rubicon. They argue that the Jeffersonian line or the Federalist line is *the* line which the main stream of American life has followed, and they refuse to allow that anything as ambiguous as the duck-rabbit turns up in their subject. But can they define the notion of a main stream in a completely objective manner? Can it be explained so as to make it possible for historians to converge on it in anything like the way in which scientific students of rivers locate *their* main streams? I doubt that it can, even though I am willing to grant that no one has said the last or even the next-to-last philosophical word on this subject. Until those words are spoken, historians should admit that one man's duck might be another's rabbit.

The historian must grant that in some parts of his work he engages in a blend of fact finding and evaluation, and that when he pretends in such cases to be recording merely what happened, he is not being accurate about the nature of his enterprise. Moreover, it is impossible to see what could be meant by saying that we can treat the narrative as a conjunction of factual statements and value judgments so that the reader can distinguish them and test them independently. It makes no sense to ask us to remove the Jeffersonian slant from a Jeffersonian history in order to see whether the remainder is factually true. And this is because the value orientation does not figure detachably in the narrative as it figures in the conjunction "Jones lied, and it was wrong of him to do so". The value orientation pervades or colors the narrative and he who would call the narrative a good one must be sympathetic to this coloring and orientation. He must therefore judge the history as a whole, simultaneously guided by the evidence and his values.

Historical narrative is not the only mode of discourse in which the language of value and the language of fact are not related conjunctively. The law presents us with a similar kind of complexity. Take the case of a statute forbidding the entry of a vehicle into a public park. One might be tempted to say that whether anything is a vehicle is a question of fact, settled by purely empirical means and having nothing to do with the values of those who are trying to find out whether it is a vehicle. One dictionary at hand says, "VEHICLE: That in or on which a person or thing is or may be carried". But suppose that the statute had been enacted before the existence of roller skates. And suppose that a case were to come up in which it was necessary to decide whether a pair of roller skates was a vehicle. Surely the judge might hesitate before saying with a straight face that because a pair of roller skates is something "on which a person or thing is or may be carried" it should be excluded from a park by the statute.

When the judge reaches one of these puzzling examples, he might be moved to ask two questions. He might ask what the enactors of the statute would have said if roller skates had existed when they enacted the statute. This is a straightforward factual question of a kind that can rarely be answered with confidence. But even if it could be, its answer would not be decisive in all cases like this. The judge might more sensibly ask what social good or evil would be brought about by regarding a pair of roller skates as a vehicle and hence keeping it out of a public park. And this is a straightforward value question, the answer to which can play a vital part in the judge's effort to answer the question, "Are roller skates vehicles?". It shows that in the process of answering what is on the linguistic surface a question of fact, the judge can advert to his own values, to his own ideas of what is good for the community.

What shall we call this hyphenated process of looking-at-the-roller-skates-and-deciding-whether-it-is-good-to-call-them-vehicles? We may not have a simple name for it, but it is surely a mode of linguistic activity. It is not logically analyzable into two activities which may be judged independently, like walking and talking. It is not analogous to the combination of separable processes that lead us to the conjunctive conclusion, "Jones lied, and it was wrong of him to do so". If the judge in the roller-skate case were asked what he was doing, he might fairly reply, "Trying to decide whether roller skates are vehicles". And if asked to introspect further and to break down the activity into two separate processes, one of which was merely looking and another merely evaluating, he might be unable to do so.

What general significance should be attached to the existence of these hybrid processes in historical and legal thinking? First of all they show that when we turn to language in a complex cultural setting—the telling of stories and the settling of legal disputes are basic to most civilizations—we find uses of language that cannot be adequately understood if we remain prisoners of an exclusive and exhaustive dichotomy of language into the factual and the evaluative. Some linguistic activities are in a sense both. Reflecting on such modes of thinking and language makes the philosopher aware of a certain narrowness in the traditional philosophical classification of language. The case of the narrative shows that there are modes of discourse which go beyond the simple, isolated statements treated by logicians who work with science and mathematics as their models. The philosopher of language who looks at law and history discovers modes of speech which require new philosophical categories.

This is not all. The philosopher who moves in this direction comes to see that the philosophy of language is not a dreary grammatical exercise. For once he begins to think about modes of discourse in a cultural setting, he will come to see that there are many others which transcend the word and the statement. The religious believer finds it impossible to characterize his religion merely by reference to a few propositions that he accepts. For religion is an organic unity of theological belief, moral attitude, emotional reaction to liturgy, view of human nature, and much more. Those who accept the same religion agree on many issues of value and fact which cannot always be separated.

The philosopher who tries to understand the use of religious language will meet in even more complicated form the sort of thing encountered in our discussion of history and law. He will find himself more and more concerned with the description and the evaluation of blends of thinking, feeling, and doing. In short, with ways of life. And by dealing with ways of life he will come closer to the concerns of the ordinary man. The philosopher who begins by recognizing that a narrative is more than a mere conjunction of factual and evaluative statements, or who sees that some linguistic activities of lawyers fall under hybrid categories not usually acknowledged by philosophers, will soon see a whole new world of language opening up before his eyes. Philosophy of science is not philosophy enough. The philosopher must broaden his vision to civilization itself.

Such a philosophical student of human institutions need not be a mere reporter of linguistic behavior. He can also stimulate new ways of thinking and speaking. But the philosophic institutionalist should emulate the good and effective legislator who studies the customs of his land before he draws up new statutes. If the philosopher conceives of his function in this broad and generous way, he will help restore philosophy to its deserved central place in the intellectual world. Not through empty speculation about "being as such", but through a deeper understanding of man gained from a study of his ways of communicating with his fellow men.

13. *Darwin, Marx, and Materialism* [1]

Professor Jacques Barzun's purpose in *Darwin, Marx, Wagner: Critique of a Heritage* is to give "a critical account of mechanistic materialism in science, art, and social science" from the days of its great apostles down to ours. The dust jacket informs us in a more striking way of Mr. Barzun's comprehensive review of the three great *isms* that "threaten the individual and his solution to the problems of life". That the promises of the jacket are not simply the over-enthusiastic outbursts of the publisher becomes very clear as the author fights the reader's way through Darwin, Marx, and Wagner. All of them, he claims, separated man and his soul, all of them believed that "things were the only reality—indestructible matter in motion", and all of them helped people think that "feeling, beauty, and moral values were . . . illusions for which the world of fact gave no warrant". This is the thesis of the book, but it is far from the only kind of utterance that appears in it. Presumably in support of this thesis,

1. This first appeared as a review of Jacques Barzun's *Darwin, Marx, Wagner: Critique of a Heritage* (Boston, Little, Brown and Company, 1941) in *Partisan Review*, Volume VIII (1941), pp. 431–35, copyright 1941 by Morton White. It is reprinted with a few changes.

Mr. Barzun brings out material of all varieties: biographical data, facts concerning the readers of the terrible trio, pronunciamentos in biology, references to the development of economic theory, detailed esthetic analyses, materials from the history of music, opinions on the method of science, its significance for our lives, values, problems, etc., etc. Reviewing the book becomes quite difficult under these circumstances. For this reason I shall treat some of the many, far-flung statements separately.

The Metaphysics

Nothing is more shocking than Mr. Barzun's utter lack of conscience about using the phrase "mechanical materialism" precisely. We learn that a mechanical materialist is someone who separates man and his soul, someone who thinks that nothing exists but concrete material objects, someone who doesn't think that beauty, feelings, and moral values exist, someone who thinks that the world is cold and that man's will is powerless. If one tries to get further than this, one is at a loss, except, perhaps, for learning that a mechanical materialist is someone who *reduces* all observable phenomena to matter. That a writer working with criteria as vague as these could ever be in a position to declare anyone a mechanical materialist is incredible. And yet Mr. Barzun damns three tremendous figures, using his unclear definition and depending, not on detailed textual evidence, but on impressions of how cold and alien the world felt after putting down a book or leaving an opera by one of them.

Where the criteria used are a little less lyrical, Mr. Barzun's statements cease to be unclear and become obviously false. For instance, where do Darwin and Marx (I don't know about Wagner) deny the *existence* of beauty, feelings, and moral values? And consider that supposedly accurate phrase "reduction to matter". What Mr. Barzun means by it is hardly fathomable in these pages. But perhaps we take him too literally; perhaps he does not mean that Darwin, Marx, and Wagner *say* explicitly what he attributes to them, but that they seem to imply it or suggest it in some way. His interpretation of Wagner's leitmotif is typical of this kind of analysis. The leitmotif represents, and when an artist, especially a composer, uses representative devices, he is concerned with the *materials* represented. Therefore we have evidence of Wagner's *materialism*. Because Darwin thought that random variations appear and that useful ones are preserved and inherited, and because he thought that human beings were subject to this process of natural selection, he was, in Mr. Barzun's eyes, a mechanical materialist. And because Marx believed that there were uniformities in history, and that there were limitations upon the action of single individuals, he too was a mechanical materialist. Leaving aside the analysis of Wagner's leitmotif, one can only come to the conclusion that to seek regularities in human behavior, in short, to use scientific method, is to be a mechanical materialist. Apparently Mr. Barzun finds it impossible to believe both that there are biological and social laws and that man's will is not powerless. That Darwin believed men consciously sought goals is indicated by the fact that the whole theory of natural selection is modeled after the *willed* activity of breeding. And that Marx thought men were not powerless is indicated by the fact that he held out the possibility of barbarism if they did not use their power to produce a better world.

The Science

All of the metaphysical accusations go hand in hand with elaborate references to the special fields of Darwin, Marx, and Wagner. De Vries, Bateson, and Mendel are trotted out as having produced the refutations of Darwin. Jevons, Cournot, Walras, and Menger are spoken of with great intimacy as the destroyers of Marx. The collapse of mechanism in physics is described with equal authority and even mathematical logic is tortured into the service of some of the more grandiose claims.

By far the most forceful "scientific" statements occur in connection with Mr. Barzun's innuendoes about the present state of evolutionary biology. Now it is a commonplace that Darwin asserted many false propositions and that he was ignorant of certain important facts concerning heritable variations. It is also well known that Bateson and De Vries performed a very valuable function in criticizing Darwin. But the impression given by Mr. Barzun is that these men and Mendel had unearthed material which completely demolished the theory of natural selection. Yet an examination of the work of competent contemporary biologists leads to no such rash conclusions. Patient study of the whole subject of heritable variations has led the best workers in the field to hold that the so-called *mutations* perform the function originally assigned by Darwin to his variations. Given these random mutations, the Darwinian process may begin to operate. Rather than examine the evidence presented by contemporary biologists, Mr. Barzun is content to rest upon the work of Bateson alone, impervious to the whole literature which has grown up as a result of discussion of his work. Mr. Barzun refers to a book by one, I think, contemporary biologist, who points out that the causes of mutations are not known. But it is interesting that Mr. Barzun neglects to say that work is being carried out in an attempt to solve just this problem —for instance the work of H. J. Muller upon the connection between X-rays and the mutation process. The only inference that can be drawn is that Mr. Barzun has been blinded by his dislike for Darwin into an unscientific neglect of evidence, which, no matter how much one is opposed to "scientism", is a serious omission, particularly when one is discussing a scientific question.

The failure to consider scientific questions in a scientific way is repeated by Mr. Barzun in his metaphysical, methodological, and ethical discussions of subjects which come

under the heading of economics. The most flagrant examples
occur in the discussion of Marx on value. Consider the following statement: "Marx's notion of value is thus at bottom
identical with the Matter of the physicist—an absolute, homo-
geneous, measurable abstraction, which is imagined as lying
beneath the surface qualities of things".[2] Now surely this is a
totally irrelevant comment. What does the word "absolute"
denote? Why the reference to Matter altogether? Apart from
all questions of the truth of the theory of value, is there anything *logically* incorrect in saying that two commodities
which exchange for each other have the same exchange-
value? Why isn't it possible to define a function, *equality of
exchange-value*, in this way? And what is methodologically
unsound about trying to show that the exchange-value of
commodities will be equal if the amount of socially necessary
labor-time put into them is also equal? The only relevant
objection to this would be that it is false, and no amount of
methodological nonsense can serve as a substitute for patient
empirical analysis if one wishes to prove that it is false. Mr
Barzun's objection is completely irrelevant.

The same type of comment on value appears when he summarizes the difference between the classical and marginal
utility theories of value. He says: "The classical and Marxian
views were that value arose from labor embodied in things.
The new view asserted that value arose from human awareness of comparative usefulness in a world where goods are
scarce. Value was a psychological as well as an objective
fact".[3] It is hard to gather anything from Mr. Barzun's book
which will clarify this last statement. And when we read a little further on that "the significance of utility, banished by
Marx in favor of labor, was . . . reaffirmed" by the marginalists, and also that these marginalists showed that "things have

2. *Darwin, Marx, and Wagner*, p. 150.
3. *Ibid.*, pp. 218–19.

value because we want them",[4] we are completely at a loss.
For now it appears as though Marx and Ricardo had never
distinguished between use-value and exchange-value, and
that it took the marginalists to confirm Hamlet's statement
that "there is nothing either good or bad, but thinking makes
it so".

The Moral

The growth of marginal utility economics, Mr. Barzun tells
us in hushed tones, was a sign that "mind was creeping back
into the world of things". Expelled by Darwin and Marx, the
mechanists, it began its stealthy return trip in the latter part
of the nineteenth century, and arrived safely home by the
time Mr. Barzun's last chapter appeared. For there *mind* is
enthroned, and given its proper due. And what support it is
supposed to find in contemporary science! Quantum theory,
relativity theory, Jamesian psychology, and psychoanalysis,
all of them are simply so much confirmation for Mr. Barzun's
philosophical contentions. Here is one of them: "Events are
. . . the result of our wishes and our notions, our wills and
our brains, acting in conflict or co-operation with the physical world".[5] Here is another: "The law of contradiction on
which Hegel based his logic dogs our mental steps so long as
we confuse the conceptual with the actual, and it is only recently that a logic of relations has sought to replace a logic of
identities in an effort to make reason less unreasonable".[6] It
would be dignifying these last statements to call them false,
for to be false statements must at least be meaningful. To
present them as the assured results of twentieth-century science is to add insult to injury.

4. *Ibid.*, p. 221.
5. *Ibid.*, p. 9.
6. *Ibid.*, p. 391.

The History

The history of ideas is an important, fascinating, and far-reaching subject. Workers in it must be capable of understanding ideas in many fields and also able to correlate them with various cultural, non-intellectual phenomena. It is with this in mind, I suppose, that Mr. Barzun spends so much time on the personalities of Darwin, Marx, and Wagner, and their disciples. If Mr. Barzun were interested only in recording facts about these men, this might be understandable. But since the essay is critical, and tries to cast doubt upon the truth or beauty of what they created, it becomes important to ask whether the slander is at all relevant. What significance, even if they were true, would the attacks on the personalities of Darwin, Marx, and Wagner have? It is one thing to be told that Darwin was not a thinker,[7] that Marx was prurient, and that Wagner was an ingrate, but given the information one pauses between deprecatory remarks to ask what connection they have with the major point of the book. And one asks this question under the guiding influence of the author. For nothing, he keeps insisting, is so terrible as the genetic fallacy.

There is one other theme that deserves examination. It involves the reverse of the genetic fallacy, perhaps best called "the fallacy of consequences". Pragmatists and instrumentalists have succeeded in convincing many people that theories are to be tested by observing their consequences. Unfortunately, many of the converts understand by "consequences" the reactions of the people who read the book in which the theory is presented. This fallacy is not the fallacy of origins, but is equally vicious. The formula is simple. Prove a man has been read and quoted favorably by a fascist, and he becomes a fascist. Prove that someone who read Darwin urged the destruction of all social reforms, and refute the theory of natu-

7. *Darwin, Marx, and Wagner*, p. 92.

ral selection. The tendency appears throughout Mr. Barzun's book, and is one of the many things in it which are irrelevant to its thesis.

The Book

The book is not very good. Perhaps Mr. Barzun puts his own finger on the reason when, in explanation of the alleged failure of Darwin, Marx, and Wagner, he says: "The explanation is that none of our three men was content to stay within his specialty. Darwin made sallies into psychology and social science; Marx was a philosopher, historian, sociologist, and would-be scientist in economics; Wagner was an artist-philosopher who took the Cosmos for his province".[8] But consider Mr. Barzun, who makes more than sallies into philosophy, history, economics, sociology, and art.

8. *Ibid.*, p. 10.

14. Social Darwinism and Dewey's Pragmatism [1]

One of the most illuminating accomplishments of Richard Hofstadter's extremely informative book, *Social Darwinism in American Thought, 1860–1915,* is to show convincingly that not all Americans who admired evolutionary thought derived from it the laissez-faire conclusions of the influential sociologist William Graham Sumner. For example, Lester Ward was a sociological "meliorist" who encouraged active intervention in the social process; and Ward was not alone. Between the Civil War and the First World War, many American thinkers dissented from the social doctrines of Sumner and Herbert Spencer, for example, Henry George, Edward Bellamy, preachers of the social gospel, Herbert Croly, and John Dewey; and some of the most interesting parts of Hofstadter's book are devoted to those who believed that mutual aid and social solidarity, rather than rugged individualism, are natural outgrowths of evolutionary development. However, in spite of Hofstadter's skill in depicting the nature and background

1. This essay originated as a review of Richard Hofstadter's *Social Darwinism in American Thought, 1860–1915* (Philadelphia, University of Pennsylvania Press, 1944) in the *Journal of the History of Ideas,* Volume VI (January 1945), pp. 119–22. It is reprinted here, in considerably revised form, by permission.

of this anti-Spencerian, anti-Sumnerian variety of evolutionism, his treatment of John Dewey's relationship to
evolutionary thought is in certain respects misleading. Therefore, because Dewey's variety of pragmatism was probably
more distinguished and more lasting in its influence than any
of the other American movements affected by evolutionary
doctrine, I wish to say something about his pragmatism
which is intended to clarify its historical background. In particular, I want to argue (1) that we should not underestimate
the extent to which Dewey's early philosophical idealism encouraged his political activism nor exaggerate the role that
Darwinism played in making him an activist and (2) that we
should not be misled into supposing that because Dewey's activism led him to reject Spencer's notion that human beings
cannot or should not intervene in the social process, Dewey
was forced to abandon scientific determinism.

In connection with my first point, I am inclined to disagree
with Hofstadter's view that Dewey's activism emerged as a
critique of Hegelianism. According to Hofstadter, Hegelianism, as it was usually interpreted in America, was politically
conservative; and Dewey, Hofstadter correctly maintains,
was originally a Hegelian. In this way, however, Hofstadter
may give the erroneous impression that Dewey began as a
Hegelian conservative and turned away from conservatism
only when he became a pragmatist who "preached the effectiveness of intelligence as an instrument in modifying the
world".[2] Furthermore, when Hofstadter says that Dewey's
skepticism about laissez-faire doctrine was a "natural consequence of his experimentalism",[3] and that the "spectator
theory of knowledge" which Dewey attacked so vehemently
in his pragmatic phase was "pre-Darwinian",[4] Hofstadter may
lead the reader to think that it was contact with Darwin's

2. Hofstadter, *op. cit.*, pp. 114–15.
3. *Ibid.*, p. 117.
4. *Ibid.*, p. 115.

thought that led to Dewey's activism, and even that his early idealism was an obstacle to his arriving at this position.

The historical facts as I see them are somewhat different. I should emphasize that in his idealist days Dewey was not politically conservative and that he did not have to wait for the influence of Darwin to make him an activist in his theory of knowledge [5] or his politics. It is true that he was, from his early days, critical of Spencer, but the criticism he then leveled against him was idealist in character. Dewey was in those days heavily influenced by T. H. Green, the Oxford idealist who so vigorously opposed laissez-faire individualism; and Dewey's teacher, G. S. Morris, was an anti-Spencerian idealist who insisted on the active nature of the mind in a way that prefigured Dewey's own attack on the "spectator theory of knowledge".[6] Therefore Dewey was disposed to criticize passivity in politics and in the theory of knowledge well before he came to admire the ideas of Darwin and William James. This is evident in Dewey's early anti-Spencerian article, "Ethics and Physical Science",[7] and in his idealist crit-

5. See my *Origin of Dewey's Instrumentalism* (New York, 1943), *passim*.

6. See the last chapters of George S. Morris, *British Thought and Thinkers* (Chicago, 1880). Morris' Hegelianism should not be identified with that of W. T. Harris. Hofstadter relies on Merle Curti's *Social Ideas of American Educators* (1935) for his statement that American Hegelianism was socially conservative. But this is based on Curti's chapter on Harris, in which he speaks of Hegelianism "committing" Harris to a *laissez-faire* attitude (p. 343). Yet Curti, in his chapter on Dewey, remarks that Dewey, "unlike Harris, . . . had come under the influence of the more socially liberal English neo-Hegelians" (p. 503). Morris wrote very little on practical politics, but in at least one place he "heartily" recommended the volume *Essays in Philosophical Criticism*, edited by A. Seth and R. B. Haldane (1883), and referred especially to an essay by Henry Jones, "The Social Organism". The volume was dedicated to Green, and Jones' essay was, among other things, a criticism of Spencer. Dewey has recently spoken of the volume's influence on his own work. For Morris' remark, see his essay "The Philosophy of State and of History", *Methods of Teaching History*, edited by G. S. Hall (second edition, Boston, 1902).

7. *Andover Review*, Volume VII (1887), pp. 573–91.

icism of Maine's *Popular Government*, "The Ethics of Democracy".[8] In the latter Dewey speaks of the need for an "industrial democracy", "a democracy of wealth" in which "all
industrial relations are to be regarded as subordinate to
human relations, to the law of personality". A similar view
emerges in a letter to William James in which Dewey describes what he regarded as the "practical bearing of idealism".[9] In short, Dewey originally opposed Spencerian laissez-faire doctrine from an idealist point of view which did
not encourage passivity; his epistemological and political activism antedated his Darwinism and his pragmatism; and
therefore we should not exaggerate the Darwinian or the
pragmatic ancestry of his activism. True, he later fortified his
activism by appeals to Darwin, but neither Darwin nor James
introduced him to the views and attitudes summed up by the
use of that word.

I turn now to Dewey's views on determinism in order to
emphasize—in contrast to what I think is Hofstadter's view—
that we should not link Dewey's opposition to laissez-faire
with a supposed opposition on his part to determinism. Focusing on Dewey's criticism of Spencer and on Dewey's belief
that men can change the world in which they live, Hofstadter is inclined to see Dewey as an anti-determinist because
Spencer is a determinist. Hofstadter often uses the expressions "passive determinism" and "fatalism" to describe Spencer's thought. And because he disagrees with Spencer's belief
that there are social laws which make it impossible to meddle
with the "natural" historical process, Hofstadter seems to associate political passivity with a belief in the deterministic
doctrine that there are laws of social behavior. It is in this
vein that he says: "Spencerianism had been the philosophy of

8. University of Michigan Philosophical Papers, Second Series, No. 1 (Ann
Arbor, 1888).
9. Ralph Barton Perry, *The Thought and Character of William James*
(Boston, 1935), Volume II, pp. 518–19.

inevitability; pragmatism became the philosophy of possibility".[10] But this epigram is misleading because it creates the impression that since Dewey disagreed with Spencer's idea that we cannot or should not interfere in the social process, Dewey denied that we can establish true generalizations about social behavior. One might conclude from Hofstadter's remark about pragmatism being the philosophy of possibility that Dewey held that *anything* is possible in human affairs, and therefore that we can never arrive at so-called laws of social behavior. But I do not find this in Dewey's thought during the period that Hofstadter examines.[11] Leaving aside Dewey's not altogether clear remarks about Heisenberg's principle of indeterminacy in *The Quest for Certainty* (1929), I think it may be said that the pragmatic Dewey encouraged the search for social regularities; and if one believes that there are social regularities, then one is committed to the belief that certain social phenomena are *im*possible. Furthermore, the search for regularities in social behavior need not lay a foundation for political acquiescence or passivity. On the contrary, in certain social situations the very opposite is true. Political passivity frequently arises from skepticism about our capacity to establish any general truths about society, and hence about our capacity to predict the outcome of our efforts to change it.

Having offered these criticisms of Hofstadter's treatment of Dewey's pragmatic activism, I want to make clear that I nevertheless believe that his book is an excellent study of Social Darwinism. I would add that it is a refreshing antidote to books which attempt to show Darwin as an apostle of brutality and a destroyer of morality. Moreover, Hofstadter does

10. Hofstadter, *op. cit.*, p. 103.

11. At one point Hofstadter says parenthetically that "Dewey has shied clear of James's assertion of freedom of the will" (*op. cit.*, p. 116), but does not seem to realize that this requires considerable qualification of his own statement that "Spencerianism had been the philosophy of inevitability; pragmatism became the philosophy of possibility".

not venture any pretentious declarations on the present status of Darwin's theory; he wisely leaves biology to the biologists. But he does make his main point brilliantly: that there were as many American followers of Darwin who were mild, reasonable advocates of fraternity and social welfare as there were strenuous-lifers and ruthless imperialists. For this relief we owe Hofstadter much thanks even though we may find it necessary to diverge at points from his view of the historical background of Dewey's pragmatism.

15. E. H. Carr on the Nature of History[1]

E. H. Carr is an unusual historian if only because he feels a need to examine the foundations of his discipline and does not avoid philosophical reflection as if it were a debilitating disease that might permanently impair his capacity to write history. In his book *What Is History?*, Carr insists that the historian should know what he is doing, and is old-fashioned enough to think that if a historian says something causes something else, he ought to have some glimmering of what causation is. Moreover, Carr rightly thinks that historians should be prepared to talk coherently about the grounds on which they select some facts for inclusion in their narratives and exclude others.

For venturing into the turbulent waters of philosophy, Carr deserves the highest praise. His distrust of obscurantism is also refreshing, and his optimism bracing. Yet, while one can applaud Carr for striking blows against philistinism and irrationalism, and for being courageous and thoughtful

1. This first appeared as a review of E. H. Carr's *What Is History?* (New York, Alfred A. Knopf, 1962) in *The New Leader*, Volume XLV (1962), pp. 27–28, copyright © 1962 by The American Labor Conference on International Affairs, Inc. The essay is reprinted here by permission.

enough to ask philosophically interesting questions about historical knowledge, one cannot applaud all of his answers.

There are, broadly speaking, two kinds of questions that Carr takes up. Some are very general and are discussed without special attention to the language and thought of the historian; for example, the topic of free will vs. determinism. But Carr's views on such matters are far less stimulating than those he advances on a second class of problems that are of particular interest to the historian, problems such as those having to do with objectivity and selection. Here the terrain is much more familiar to Carr and so he is able to move about on it in a livelier and more graceful manner—despite the fact that he comes to extremely dubious conclusions.

In discussing historical objectivity, Carr begins with the familiar observation that every historian must decide what facts to incorporate into his narrative. And in making causal statements he must select from among the many factors that play a part in the production of historical events. Upon what rational basis does he do so? Apparently Carr is in search of a standard which will allow the historian to justify his selection of certain facts and causes as "real", and this search he virtually identifies with the effort to answer the question, "What Is History?". Carr seems to think of the discipline of history as having an essence that may be discerned by locating an objective basis for the historian's selections. He who finds this Archimedean point and mounts his lever on it will lift out of the ocean of past facts all those that are really and truly historical. He shall be called a real historian, while those who fail to discover this point are doomed to wallow in relativism, subjectivism, and cynicism.

Carr's search for one stable standard of selection finally leads him to the view that the real historical facts and causes must somehow be linked with the future of society. A historian in search of an objective standpoint must first discern the road of progress and then paint his picture of the past accordingly. When he knows how things will progress, he can say what was significant in what went before. Although Carr sometimes writes as though we can never know what specific form progress will take because we are locked in our own culture and imprisoned by our parochial values, at other times he suggests that if we wish to know what the progressive aspects of the future will be, we must ask ourselves who will have power then, for power is objectively measurable. In these more concrete, more lucid, but more Hegelian moments, Carr regards the historian as *obliged*, on pain of forfeiting his claim to objectivity, to depict the past in conformity with a prediction about who the successful will be.

It is certainly idle to argue in a purely logical way with a historian who is so impressed by success that he wishes to make it the hero of his history. One may persuade him to enlarge his vision, but one ought not try to prove theorems to him. On the other hand, one may easily argue with—and refute—Carr if he claims to have a foolproof argument demonstrating that historical objectivity consists simply in telling the story of the past with an eye on the successes of the future. It is absurd to hold that only such future-directed and power-dominated history is "history properly so-called". History is a vast and varied discipline, and surely historians do not forfeit their titles or abandon their offices when they concentrate on the politically and economically powerless or on the defeated. Nor do they become idle cynics when they write the history of thought rather than the story of how force triumphed.

Carr correctly points out that historical selection is always dictated by a value judgment made by the historian. But Carr's own focusing on future power is also dictated by a value judgment. His mistake—a classic one in the history of philosophy—is to suppose that his own judgment can be shown to be *the* objective one and all others shown subjective by appealing to the essence of history, properly so-called. Carr's conception of history is surely not borne out by an examination of what all historians do, nor by a study of the use of the word "history". And if he is merely recommending that history turn itself into the discipline he describes, there is no objective reason in his pages, or out of them, for supposing that the only facts worth recording are those that presage the powers that be or will be. I therefore cannot share Carr's view that the historian should attend to the career of the victorious in order to escape cynicism. On the contrary, it seems to me that only by eschewing Carr's view can the historian escape cynicism, *properly so-called.*

16. *Richard Hofstadter on the Progressive Historians* [1]

The editors of the *American Historical Review* will forgive me, I hope, if I depart momentarily from the austere standards formulated in their "Suggestions for Reviewers", by saying that when they asked me to write a notice of Richard Hofstadter's admirable book on Beard, Turner, and Parrington I felt at first like a Ph.D. who hears the words, "Is there a doctor in the house?". I am not a member of the historians' guild and do not have one of their licenses to prescribe or heal; but since I have studied certain aspects of the Progressive period, I finally decided to accept the invitation to treat, as it were, this long-expected book. I say "long-expected" not because I had known that Hofstadter was writing it, but because I had long surmised that so distinguished a historian would sooner or later be led to study the aspect of the Progressive era he deals with in this work. I remembered how self-denying he was, for example, in his *Age of Reform*, where he insisted that he was not concerned with what he called the high culture of the period, not concerned with its

1. This was first printed as a review of Richard Hofstadter's book of the same title in *The American Historical Review*, Volume 75, (December 1969), pp. 601–3. It is reprinted with few changes.

best but with its most characteristic thinking, and not concerned with its intellectuals but rather with those he called
"middle brow writers". Now, in a burst of well-earned self-in-
dulgence, Hofstadter has lifted his eyes from the muckrakers
toward three of the more high-browed intellectuals of the
Progressive period; and, having looked that far up, he has
even been led to discourse philosophically on the nature of
historical writing.

Hofstadter's four main concerns are: to place Turner,
Beard, Parrington in the history of American thought; to give
us some insight into their lives and personalities; to evaluate
their more specific historical views in the light of more recent
research (and in Parrington's case more recent literary criticism); and, finally, to assess in a more general way their emphasis upon the role of conflict in American history as epito-
mized in Turner's famous statement that "we may trace the
contest between the capitalist and the democratic pioneer
from the earliest colonial days".

In carrying out the second and third of his concerns, Hofstadter makes his greatest contribution. He has a dazzling
command of the enormous literature stimulated by Turner's
treatment of the frontier, by Beard's work on the economic
interpretation of the Constitution and of Jeffersonian democracy, and by Parrington's almost obsessive preoccupation
with whether American writers were or were not in touch
with reality. By forcefully exercising this command, Hofstadter exposes his subjects' errors of fact, the defects of some of
their explanations, and the inadequacy of some of their value
judgments, all without denying that they called attention to
something that cannot be omitted from American history. On
the other hand, Hofstadter seems to me less successful in locating his three men in the history of thought, and in his
more general reflections on the role of factors like the frontier, economics, and conflict in American history.

In trying to place Turner, Beard, and Parrington in the history of American thought, I think that Hofstadter underesti-

mates an important element of continuity between them and their predecessors, namely, an antipathy to the large American city. Hofstadter rightly says that the Progressive historians "took the writing of American history out of the hands of the Brahmins and the satisfied classes", but perhaps the brevity of his forty-page sketch of pre-Turnerian historiography prevents him from making clear that the middle western Populistic, antiurban agrarianism of the Progressive historians perpetuated, in a certain respect, an attitude toward the large American city that had been typical of the eastern Brahmin historians. Prescott, in his correspondence, called New York the "Yankee Babylon" and once vowed that he would never stay there for more than three days. Russel Nye's biography of Bancroft (1944) makes clear Bancroft's feeling that farmers are the true material for a republic and that city merchants are parasites on them. In 1878 Parkman wrote an article on "The Failure of Universal Suffrage",[2] maintaining that in American cities the diseases of the body politic were gathered to a head, that in them "the dangerous classes" were most numerous and strong, that in them "the barbarism that we have armed and organized stands ready to overwhelm us", and that these "cities have become a prey". And then there are Henry Adams' waspish views, explained in the fifth chapter of *The Intellectual Versus The City*, by Lucia White and me, on what Adams regarded as plutocratic and Jewish American cities. In short, the Brahmins fired at the growing American city from a Boston that was fading out, whereas Turner, Beard, and Parrington fired at it from a Populist Middle West that wanted in.

Therefore—and this will lead me to my comments on Hofstadter's fourth concern—the Progressive historians were distinguished from their American predecessors less by their antiurban values than by their notion, sufficiently emphasized by Hofstadter, that the frontier or the economic factor played

2. *North American Review*, Volume CXXVII (1878), pp. 1–20.

a central or decisive role in American history. Not *the only* role, they granted, just as a man who says that the dryness of the powder was the decisive factor in bringing about an explosion will grant that the spark was also a factor. The question that any student of Beard and Turner must face is that of analyzing what they meant, or could have meant, by saying that economics or the frontier was central or decisive. On this question Hofstadter is not very helpful. He says, for example, "a very large part of what historians differ about boils down to questions of emphasis, to arguments about how much stress we want to put on this factor rather than that, when we all admit that both were at work. And I see no way of arriving at a final consensus on questions of this kind. I take comfort in a remark Carl Becker once made in objecting to the very idea of a definitive history: 'Who cares to open a book that is without defect or amiable weakness?' ".[3] With all due respect to our author and Becker, I must say that it is silly to take this kind of comfort. It is also surprising that poor Turner and Beard should be so forcefully criticized by one who believes what Hofstadter says in the above passage, or by one who, like Hofstadter, asks but cannot answer the question: "By what calibrations do we measure and compare the weight of such grand imponderables as the frontier, as against the nonfeudal inheritance of America, or its Protestant background, or its ethnic mixture?".[4] If Hofstadter cannot weigh the importance of one contributing factor as against another, on what ground can he say that the Turner factor or the Beard factor is *not* central or, for that matter, that anything is not central? That historians should not be able to arrive at a "final consensus" on which factor is central is not surprising, but that they should not have any clear conception of centrality seems to me depressing so long as they keep making assertions about what is or is not central.

3. Hofstadter, *op. cit.*, pp. xv–xvi.
4. *Ibid.*, p. 122.

I do not think that this problem can be solved merely by calling attention to "the rediscovery of complexity in American history" and the "new awareness of the multiplicity of forces" that developed in the 1950s; nor do I think that Hofstadter can avoid the responsibility of analyzing what is meant by saying that economic interests are not central by declaring that "the old Progressive antinomy between ideas and interests, between appearances and reality has been dissolved"—whatever that means. Neither is the problem solved by saying that recent historians like Bernard Bailyn have shown that ideas and attitudes "must be taken into consideration" if we are to understand the background and the effects of the American Revolution.[5] In his brilliant study, *The Ideological Origins of the American Revolution,* Bailyn is not merely concerned to *take into consideration* the ideological, political, and constitutional aspects of the Revolution, nor content merely to put economics on a par with ideology and politics as elements in a complex set of forces. He pointedly says that "the American Revolution was above all else an ideological, constitutional, political struggle and not primarily a controversy between social groups undertaken to force changes in the organization of the society or the economy".[6] But what does "above all else" mean and what does "primarily" mean? These questions must be answered by those who agree with the Progressive historians as well as by their critics; and, until they are, I do not see how we can make very confident assertions about who is right in the controversy. And when Hofstadter tries to resolve such controversies by saying that they all boil down to questions of emphasis, I am reminded of a story.

A rabbi in a small Russian village was conducting a judicial hearing, and his wife was sitting on the bench with

5. Hofstadter, *op. cit.*, p. 443.

6. Bernard Bailyn, *The Ideological Origins of the American Revolution* (Cambridge, Mass., 1967), p. vi.

him. The first disputant came and told his story; the rabbi stroked his beard and told him, "You are right!". The first disputant left and was followed by the second, who told a contrary story. The rabbi stroked his beard and said to him, "You are right!". After the second disputant left, the rabbi's wife turned to the rabbi and asked, "Rabbi, they told opposite stories. How could you tell each of them that he was right?". The rabbi stroked his beard and said to her, "You are right!".

17. Edgar Z. Friedenberg's Philosophy of Education[1]

Who would have thought thirty years ago, when I took a deadly course in what was called education, that in the year 1965 America would produce a specialist in that subject who could refer knowingly to Gide's *actes gratuits* and to *Der Rosenkavalier*, quote Ortega y Gasset favorably, write stunningly about the feelings of high school students, and defend the life of the gentleman? One might just as well have predicted that America would, in the words of the late J. L. Austin, produce a goldfinch that quoted Virginia Woolf. And yet Professor Edgar Z. Friedenberg is just such a rarity. While crying out against the leveling tendencies of the American high school and of American society, he uses all the statistical means and modes at his disposal, and discourses learnedly about autonomy and empiricism; yet during the whole procedure his prose sparkles and his heart aches for the neglected humanist in the eleventh grade. He believes that in our mass society too many high school students have been turned into

---

1. This essay first appeared as a review of Edgar Z. Friedenberg's *Coming of Age in America* (New York, 1965), in *The New York Review of Books*, Volume IV (17 June 1965), pp. 9–11, and is copyright © 1965 by Morton White. It is reprinted with minor changes.

opportunists and that the sensitive adolescent intellectual has as good a chance of coming through the American high school happily as an honest man in a Madison Avenue public relations firm.

Although I disagree with a great many things in Frieden-berg's *Coming of Age in America,* I want to say at once that it is extremely well written, that it is provocative, and that it ought to be read by anyone interested in the education of ad-olescents. No reader with a shred of feeling can help being touched by Friedenberg's concern for children who don't fit into the mold created by their dreary peers, petty principals, and petty bourgeois teachers. And who can bring himself to deny that our high schools should encourage more respect for privacy, for inwardness, and for all of the other things that Friendenberg summarizes by his use of the modish word "subjectivity"? But it is one thing to speak out movingly for all of these things, and another to write a philosophically co-gent and sociologically penetrating study of the vast subject covered by this book. When Friedenberg is not accurately and delicately recording how his subjects, as he calls them, feel, but lecturing us, for example, on the nature of mass so-ciety and the evils of empiricism, he is much less winning, much less persuasive, and—greatest failing of all for one of his philosophical persuasion—much less authentic.

I have written some friendly and some fighting words. Let me try to justify them. First I turn to the best part of the book. Armed with statistics, with style, and with a nice sup-ply of irony in his soul, Friedenberg makes a striking assault on "The Structure of Student Values". That chapter takes up more than a third of the book. In preparation for it he spent a full year testing and interviewing twenty-five students in each of nine high schools, and he tried very hard to pick his subjects in a random manner. His procedure was in essence the following. He invented an imaginary high school called "LeMoyen", as well as a set of six connected narrative epi-sodes about it. Associated with each of these episodes was a

series of nine cards, each of which bore a comment on the episode. The student was asked to evaluate these nine card-
comments. One of Friedenberg's most instructive episodes
was called "The King's Visit", in which the students were told
that the king of a country not unlike Denmark was to visit
their high school, a king interested in meeting "spirited
young people". They were also told that "such young people
as were to be chosen should be persons to whom the school
could point with pride as expressing what was finest and best
about their school". Then the students were given cards
which carried little descriptions of fictitious candidates, and
their task was to rank them for the honor (or job) of meeting
the king. Their top choice 69 per cent of the time was either
one of two rather dull characters. The first was a well-
groomed, polite valedictorian called Karen Clarke, who was
"completely in command of herself in any situation" and "the
perfect model of what a high school student ought to be".
Next came Elfrieda Eubanks, who "is so sweet that you
couldn't help liking her, and everybody at LeMoyen does.
She's president of the Girls' Athletic Association and a sure
thing for the Chamber of Commerce's Best All-Around Girl
Award this spring".

Since Friedenberg interviewed the students, he was able to
talk to them about their reasons for their choices. On the
basis of his privileged access to their narrow minds, he tells
us that the reason why 69 per cent of them made Karen or
Elfrieda their first choice is that nearly all of them thought
they were being faced with a problem in the establishment of
good public relations. Although they were to pick the "finest
and best" of their school, and had a wide-open field in
construing those words, they insisted on interpreting the
"finest and best" student as the one who would make a good
impression, and thought that to make a good impression one
would have to "know how to talk to the king", to be "well-
rounded", and to be a "good mixer". One certainly could not
be sloppy, like Scotty Cowen, the school genius, mathemati-

cian, chess player, and literary editor. The students also shied away from an unkempt orator and basketball player called Johnny Adams, because, like Scotty Cowen, he does only what he *feels* like doing. In general, to use Friedenberg's own words, his subjects' responses to "The King's Visit" showed their dependence on external judgment as more important than self-approval and internal coherence, their suspicion of specialized personal competence unless directed and controlled by the school or the group for social purposes, and their skepticism that the king's visit could have any other purpose than good public relations.

We need not go into more detail about Friedenberg's methods nor about the sort of conclusion that he draws on what might be called the first (and best) level of his analysis. He has great gifts in reporting how children feel about well-rounded people, mixers, sloppy people, and unshaven basketball players; and his observations are brilliantly formulated and cogently defended. But it is important to point out that Friedenberg does not limit himself to such homey observations about his subjects. Like so many behavioral scientists who study values, he tries to rise to a higher level on which he begins to use the terminology of philosophy, and here is where the reader begins to have a certain amount of difficulty in understanding or believing what he has to say. Here we are not completely at Friedenberg's mercy, for he is making inferences from premises and by steps that are before our eyes. The students didn't *tell* him that they didn't like Scotty Cowen because they didn't value autonomy: Friedenberg inferred that they didn't from statements which they made and which he reports to us.

I do not object in principle to such inferences, but I don't understand what Friedenberg means by the word "autonomy". Does he think that an autonomous person does what he feels like doing *without any* attention to the interests or wishes of others in his group, and that autonomy in this sense is an absolute value that his subjects are wrong not to share?

Surely Friedenberg believes that sometimes when we do what we feel like doing, without attention to the interests of others, we act wrongly, and therefore that autonomy as such is *not* an unqualified good. Under what conditions, then, is it a good? Friedenberg doesn't say. I hope the reader will excuse me if I sound excessively Socratic, but I know no other way of calling attention to Friedenberg's lack of philosophical acuity.

Let me give a more crucial example of the same defect. Friedenberg criticizes his young subjects (and our society) for being addicted to empiricism, but what is empiricism as Friedenberg understands it? He thinks the students exhibited it in their reaction to "The King's Visit" because they chose as their representative someone who would make a favorable impression. They confined themselves to asserting what Kant calls an imperative of skill. If you want the king to be impressed, they seemed to say, send him Karen and Elfrieda; but don't ask us whether he *should* be impressed by drags like them. To be an empiricist in this sense, then, is to avoid ethical assessment and, more particularly, to choose a nonethical rather than an ethical interpretation of words like "finest" and "best" when presented with a situation in which one might interpret the words in either way.

So far, Friedenberg's analysis is very illuminating; and it is greatly to his credit that he reveals this unfortunate tendency by a masterly use of well-designed statistical techniques. But he is not content with calling the students empiricists in his first sense. This is evident in what he says about them when they are faced with the episode called "The LeMoyen Basketball Team". Here the cards are stacked so that they *must* make a moral judgment: they can't do otherwise if they are to answer the question. So Friedenberg cannot accuse them of empiricism as previously defined, and therefore he accuses them of being empiricists in another sense. What is that? When they appeal to the idea of equality of opportunity and insist that Kevin McGuire should not be kept off the team because of his race or religion, Friedenberg still condemns them because, although they appeal to a moral principle, "they don't really care whether their idea of how a democratic society works makes sense, because to them understanding something means knowing how to handle it; it does not mean being able to relate it to a larger, metaphysical whole". Now Friedenberg has his poor subjects coming and going. To avoid his disapproval, they must not only construe all value questions as moral questions when they have the choice but also be able to relate their conclusions to "a larger metaphysical whole" when they answer moral questions. Does Friedenberg tell us what he means by this dark saying? Not at all, and so by the time we and Friedenberg leave LeMoyen's corridors together we begin to worry about his power to guide us through the clouds of sociology and philosophy that loom ahead.

Indeed, we begin to suspect that Friedenberg may not know what he is talking about in the higher realms, and such suspicions are more than confirmed by later chapters in which he begins to talk about the highest aims of education. Earlier, when he is being so lofty about the empiricism of the students and deplores their failure to establish contact with larger metaphysical wholes, the reader may think that Friedenberg is some kind of rationalist who wants children to be taught how to forge a logical link between their moral judgments and ontological structures, as the saying goes. But when we come to the last chapter we find this kind of scholastic logic-chopping is as far from Friedenberg's mind as it could possibly be. From this point of view, the trouble with the argumentative boy is that he is not a gentleman; and what Friedenberg wants to cultivate is inwardness and subjectivity. Hence his sociological hauteur about I.Q. tests, which, he says, reward a cognitive style that is especially bourgeois. While they demand a verbal facility and a familiarity with abstract symbolism and with the goods, services, and proper social attitudes of the middle class that make it

very difficult for lower-status children to give the right answer, they also penalize any youngster who approaches the
test with the stance of an amateur, however gifted. Now it
may be that "lower status" children are penalized by I.Q.
tests, but I cannot agree that amateur juvenile seers are dis-
advantaged by having to understand "abstract symbolism".

As the clouds lift a bit we can see the lack of originality in
Friedenberg's theorizing. Building on a well-worn tradition
in nineteenth-century thought, he thinks that our mass society has encouraged the empiricism of bureaucrats and the
"abstract symbolism" of shopkeepers in the name of equal opportunity. And so, in conformity with an anti-intellectualist,
romantic stereotype that I find indefensible, he sees middle-
class boys calculating, experimenting, climbing, never evaluating, avoiding metaphysics, and paying no attention to their
inner lives. Therefore, in another familiar move, Friedenberg decides that we must play both ends against this middle
class. We must revive the amateur, the gentleman, with his
humanity and trustworthiness, his sense of style and personal
integrity, his taste for intimacy, and his contempt for calculation. But where, in this society, shall we find him? Mainly in
the slums, says Friedenberg in a burst of inverted snobbery
that allows him to eat and have his cake of custom. Friedenberg will beat Madison Avenue, as a knowing New Yorker
might say, by joining Madison Street. But as one who knows
a good deal about Madison Street, I can testify that while humanity, integrity, and trustworthiness certainly flourish there,
they do so in about the same degree as they do on most other
residential streets of the world. And even with due attention
to what he says about Dr. King and Medgar Evers, I cannot
take seriously Friedenberg's statement that "one hardly ever
encounters examples of aristocratic bearing among any . . .
contemporary Americans" besides Negroes. Nor can I take
seriously his proposal that we set up federally supported
boarding schools for "culturally deprived" children who show
signs of becoming gentlemen in his sense while other more
conventional adolescents continue in public and private

schools. I see no objection to giving special encouragement to the distinguished of all kinds, whether they be sensitive, bright, or both; but it seems grotesque to form a special institution for those who seek primarily to "understand the meaning of their lives and become more sensitive to the meaning of other people's lives" while their contemporaries are segregated in other schools, presumably doing geometry, physics, and social studies as they learn about space, time, and mass society.

What is to be said in a more general way about all of this? For one thing, that Friedenberg's own intellectual limitations and his prejudices in favor of *Gemeinschaft* are mirrored in his educational ideals. What he can't do, namely, reason analytically, he demotes; and what he can do, namely, respond sympathetically, he promotes. But just as inwardness is not enough when one wants to be a philosopher of education, so the cultivation of inwardness is not the only or the highest aim in educating the young. I am sure that we have sinned in our failure to develop a respect for intimacy in our children, but I am also sure that we have sinned in our failure to develop their power to think. I am not talking about power in physics and mathematics. I mean the ability to reason clearly and consecutively about matters of the greatest human importance. I deny therefore that what we need today is only or mainly to resist the depredations on inwardness conceived as narrowly as Friedenberg conceives it, for modern society has victimized the mind in a more thorough way. It has discouraged not only those (in and out of high school) who want to understand "the meaning of their lives and become more sensitive to the meaning of other people's lives and relate to them more fully" but also those who want to think coherently and honestly about politics, literature, religion, history, science, law, and, of course, education. Therefore, if we want to battle effectively against the encroachments of mass society we must try to protect not only the poet against the philistines, but also, to put it simply, the philosopher in us all.

Friedenberg may speak with authority about his subjects

while they are in high school, but others of us know what
they are like after they escape; and we don't think that their
only or chief failing is their lack of taste for intimacy, inwardness, and integrity. Besides, I don't quite see how the young
people at Berkeley and Selma—some of whom Friedenberg
may have been studying at LeMoyen—could have risen up in
their wrath if Friedenberg were altogether right about their
personalities or about the deadening effect of mass society on
their emotions.[2] My plea, therefore, is for something broader,
deeper, and more radical in the reconstruction of our educational aims. We must do everything possible to encourage the
union of analytic power, culture, and feeling in our students.
I would remind Friedenberg that the great critics of industrial society have not labored to show simply that our culture has neglected the claims of sensibility, but rather to
show that it has severed or alienated sensibility from intellect
and experience. Their educational message, then, is not that
we should weep only for the eleventh-grade poet who is no
good at math, or simply to realize that there is such a thing
as the "high creative" as well as the "high I.Q." student. We
must teach our young people to cease being well-rounded
squares, LeMoyen style; but we must also educate them to be
whole men—to use a phrase that has unfortunately been cor-
rupted by others besides Barry Goldwater. For the whole
man, unlike the beatnik and the gentleman "C", is capable of
thought *and* feeling, of analysis *and* empathy, of learning *and*
loving, all of which we and our society desperately need. And
if only Professor Friedenberg could have brought himself to
see this he might have produced a much better book than the
interesting and challenging book he has written.

2. I remind the reader that these lines were first published in 1965—before
the disturbances at Columbia and Harvard, where some LeMoyen alumni
may have been doing graduate work.

18. *The University in Transition*[1]

Arthur Schlesinger reports in *A Thousand Days* that John F. Kennedy exclaimed soon after his election, "How am I going to fill these 1,200 jobs? . . . All I hear is the name Jim Perkins. Who in hell is Perkins?". At the time vice-president of the Carnegie Corporation and later president of Cornell, James Perkins, it seems, was recommended for virtually every post Kennedy had to fill; and Perkins' excellent book, *The University in Transition*, goes a long way toward explaining why. Its publication also makes it possible for everyone to discover that James Perkins is a distinguished administrator who has challenging ideas on a topic of vital concern today— the American university.

The basic premise of Mr. Perkins' argument is that the university is primarily concerned with knowledge, a truth so

1. This first appeared as a review of James A. Perkins' *The University in Transition* (Princeton, 1966) in *The New York Herald Tribune Book Week* (6 March 1966), p. 1 *et seq.*, and is reprinted here by permission. It has not been changed even though the university has changed. I should have written a somewhat different review after witnessing the events at Harvard in the spring of 1969, but nothing that happened there has caused me to alter the general opinions I advanced in my review. Indeed, I am more convinced than ever that they are true.

often neglected or so foolishly contested that he deserves
great credit for calling it to our attention once again. We
must also thank him for giving us none of the usual double-
talk about the nature of knowledge. According to Perkins, it
is won by rational inquiry; and he spares us the customary
nonsense about how painters have knowledge in their fingers
and how dancers have it in their toes, and how the heart has
reasons that reason never knows.

In its concern with knowledge, according to Perkins, the
American university differs from similar institutions of the
past and present because it accepts all three of the following
jobs: acquiring new knowledge through research, transmit-
ting it directly to the young, and making it available to society in the spirit of public service. The great German universities of the nineteenth century concentrated on research,
while traditional Oxford and Cambridge were most occupied
with undergraduate instruction, but none of them, says Perkins, supplied information or advice to those faced by practical problems, at least not on the scale we know today in
America. Today, when knowledge itself, the student popula-
tion, and society's demand for professional assistance are in-
creasing at an astonishing rate, the American university is in
a state of crisis unprecedented in the history of the academic
world. Having agreed to run a three-ring circus, it is now
watching the rings expand to the point where the tent is not
big enough to hold them, where the clowns, the lion-keepers,
and the animals dash about madly in all directions, and
where the whole show often spills riotously into the streets.
Mr. Perkins describes the crisis in more sedate prose. He says
that the American university may lose its internal cohesion
and therefore its capacity to run its own affairs. He also says
that it may lose what everyone is afraid of losing these days
—its identity.

First let us consider what Perkins proposes to do about the
problem of internal cohesion. Essentially, he tries to cheer us
up by telling us that bigness as such is not a curse, provided

that the three main parts of the American university develop in proportion to each other. If, as it were, the torso should get bigger, he would make sure that the brain and the limbs become better able to direct and carry it. Therefore he rightly insists that the university should not accept outside contracts unless they result in the improvement of research and teaching. How this advance on three fronts can be accomplished he does not say in great detail, but leaving aside some reservations about his plan that I shall express later, I think it is sensible and that it may provide some much-needed guidance for those who must lead the advance.

What about the university's identity-crisis? What should its distinctive role be in a world that is full of other knowledge-able institutions—foundations, institutes, research centers, and independent undergraduate colleges? Because the university is the only one of these organizations that discovers, teaches, and applies knowledge, Perkins rightly regards it as a unique and pivotal institution which stands halfway up the academic scale of being. Poised as it is, however, between the philanthropoids on Madison Avenue and the little angels in General Education, the university must, like man himself, be more than versatile if it is to survive and prosper. It must unite with other universities to form what Perkins calls "systems" which do more than cooperatively build and operate laboratories and synchrotrons. The moral is that if universities don't hang together in this world of mounting costs and large-scale planning they will hang separately. If they fail to unite, they will not be able to resist the inroads of unwarranted political authority, which is always ready, as the saying goes, to rush into a vacuum.

Having indicated how much I admire the outline of Mr. Perkins' argument, I must now add a few reservations about it. I am not sure whether they involve me in flat disagreement with him or whether our differences are simply those of emphasis, but I think they should be aired in either case. First of all, it seems to me that Mr. Perkins' organic metaphor of the harmoniously functioning three-part university often leads him to suggest that the three parts are of equal importance, and this I cannot admit. He sometimes writes as though the American university should assign equal weight to research, instruction, and public service; but I would dispute this. I don't think that our universities have come to this point and I don't think they ever should. I sympathize with students who come to the swinging doors of government offices asking, "Is my teacher in there?". Having a drink at those heady springs is one thing, but staying out all night is another. Maintaining the harmony of the parts is fine but harmony does not imply equality, and I would have been happier if Perkins had said in a loud and clear voice that the two principal functions of the university are teaching and research, with public service a distinct third.

I would have been happier, too, if Perkins had said that in rendering public service the American university should not be too monotonous in its choice of customers. It should not work only or preponderantly for the military even if it should be the case—and I do not think that it is—that such circumscribed labor would best maintain its internal harmony or augment its power. Moreover, I think it should devote itself more than it now does to noble tasks like improving primary and secondary education, whose aims are, after all, more closely related to the university's than those of any other institution in society.

Finally, I come to a point which demands the greatest emphasis of all. Now that the American university is so active in supplying knowledge to other parts of our society, it has an inescapable responsibility to evaluate the ends for which that knowledge is to be used. Not only must it ask whether accepting certain contracts will redound to the benefit of the university, but it must ask whether it will redound to the benefit of mankind. Some may say that this moral concern will require the university to abandon its primary concern with knowledge, but I disagree. I think that there is such a thing as knowledge of good, bad, right, and wrong, and that the university is as good a place in which to learn it and teach it as any in our society. Whatever one may think of some of the student demonstrations and teach-ins, many of them reveal a heartening concern with the moral problems created by an increasingly heartless world. More than ever, therefore, it is the responsibility of the university to help students transform their more admirable feelings into defensible beliefs and actions, for by doing so it may keep both students and professors from becoming mere technicians in the service of goals they never examine. The truth about prime numbers, electrons, DNA, the Civil War, and mass society is not enough for today's American university. It also needs the truth about what individuals and governments should and should not do with the knowledge that universities make available to them.

In one of the places where Mr. Perkins addresses himself to such questions, he says that "the university's function is to serve the private processes of faculty and students, on the one hand, and the large public interests of society on the other". But clearly the university that is to serve *large* public interests must try to determine what those interests are and what they are not. Engaging in moral analysis and criticism, therefore, is the logical consequence of that fateful step which the American university took when it moved beyond the limited roles of nineteenth-century German universities and traditional Oxbridge. If it critically examines the ends it is asked to serve and serves only those that pass muster, it will go a long way toward convincing the American student that his teachers are still dedicated to liberal education, the civilized life, and the free society he is required to read about as a freshman but often advised to forget about when he becomes a graduate student seeking research grants. It will also keep faith with what Mr. Perkins rightly calls its ancient and noble ancestry, and in particular with a man called Socrates.

19. *Reinhold Niebuhr on the Irony of American History*[1]

Reinhold Niebuhr is an eloquent preacher and a shrewd political analyst; and while his book *The Irony of American History* shows many of his virtues it is mainly the work of a theologian defending religious views about the nature of man and history. These views have been praised by many agnostic liberals who do not accept Niebuhr's version of Christianity but I do not see how they can praise them without falling into inconsistency. Of course, they may consistently admire many of Niebuhr's practical judgments on specific political issues and they may even find some of his more general psychological observations appealing. But Niebuhr's claim to fame as a *thinker* is based on the theology which he advances in such books as *The Nature and Destiny of Man,* and any one who cannot subscribe to that theology is logically bound to reject Niebuhr's fundamental views on the irony of American history.

Niebuhr adopts a Christian point of view which he con-

1. This first appeared as a review of Reinhold Niebuhr's *The Irony of American History* (New York, 1952) in *New Republic,* Volume 126 (1952), pp. 18–19, copyright 1952 by Harrison-Blaine of New Jersey, Inc. The essay is reprinted here by permission.

trasts with Marxism and with liberalism. Christianity, he says, is inclined to an ironic view of history. "Irony," as some dictionaries define it, is a word used to describe a "state of affairs or events which is the reverse of what was, or was to be expected; a result opposite to and as if in mockery of the promised or appropriate result". This definition doesn't require our expectations to be *self*-defeating since it allows them to be defeated by events external to themselves; expectations don't necessarily lead to their own ironic defeat in the manner of Hegelian theses giving rise to their antitheses. But according to Niebuhr's definition we have an ironic situation only when virtue becomes vice *through* some hidden defect in the virtue; when strength becomes weakness *because* of the vanity to which strength may prompt the mighty man or nation; when security is transformed into insecurity *because* too much reliance is placed on it. In this way, according to Niebuhr, Jeffersonian ideals have led to their own opposite in domestic affairs, and in foreign affairs an originally "innocent" nation now finds itself the custodian of the atomic bomb; in this way the "perennial moral predicaments of human history have caught up with a culture which knew nothing of sin or guilt".

We need not list the other ironies which Niebuhr discusses. What interests us is Niebuhr's message for those who are concerned with the future of mankind. In what way is the recognition of these ironies instructive and helpful? How can we overcome them? Niebuhr answers: by recognizing the fragmentary character of human wisdom; by recognizing that man is a creature as well as a creator of the historical process; by accepting the mystery and complexity of things; by realizing that "man cannot rise to a simple triumph over historical fate".

By contrast how do empirically minded men react when they see their hopes and ideals "cruelly refuted" by history? Usually by trying to find out what their mistakes were, by asking what they might have done to have avoided the ironic outcome, by using the method of trial and error. Having adopted a policy which has failed, we try another in the hope of improvement. We suppose that we can alter our actions and expectations in order to diminish the probability of a second defeat. We do not suppose that we can devise schemes which will be perfect but neither do we imagine ourselves sinners in the hands of an anonymous force which always determines that our hopes will be denied, that our plans will be destroyed, and that our predictions will be falsified by a Cartesian demon. We do not think of ourselves as actors in a drama of human history "under the scrutiny of a divine judge who laughs at human aspirations". We recognize limits to what we can do at any given moment but nevertheless assume that some ironies can be avoided in the future; as empiricists we are humble because we accept the possibility that some of our predictions will be falsified. All of this is in keeping with the pragmatism Niebuhr respects in common men and practical politicians but when philosophers and social scientists work in this spirit it is labeled "nineteenth-century rationalism", "Enlightenment optimism", and "pretentious social science"—the three bugbears of Niebuhrians.

When Niebuhr attacks doctrinaires who believe with "fanatic certainty" in the theory of inevitable progress we can agree with him, as would every sensible liberal thinker of the twentieth century. However, the refutation of this theory is based on the study of history, the results of psychology, and the observation of the social behavior of human beings. Yet none of these considerations make it reasonable to suppose that we can't improve our situation by progressively diminishing certain political, economic, physical, and psychological obstacles. To suppose that we can improve our situation and avoid the repetition of irony is not to suppose that we can reach a perfect state, nor is it to suppose that we can become identical with what Niebuhr has called "the whole"— whatever that means. If all that Niebuhr did was to oppose simple-minded optimism or the view that men are gods, we should embrace him as a sane partisan of the empiricism and pragmatism he assigns to wise American politicians. But surely Niebuhr wants us to learn more than that from him, since that is much too naturalistic and modest. Niebuhr believes in the doctrine of Original Sin, according to which man is necessarily evil. Yet this doctrine is just as indefensible as the theory of inevitable progress and, ironically enough, it rests on faith—a faith which has engendered even more "fanatic certainty" than that which theorists of inevitable progress assign to *their* view. The truly emancipated mind must reject both of these dogmas.

Niebuhr is thought by many to be the philosophical Atlas of liberal politics who supports liberalism with a tough, realistic faith in man's sinfulness whereas others have offered nothing but "pretentious social science", the "shallow optimism of the enlightenment" and "nineteenth-century rationalism". I dissent heartily. Liberalism needs no support from "ultra-rational presuppositions"; it need accept no obscure dogmas about "historical fate"; it cannot accept such monstrous falsehoods as "Nothing that is worth doing can be achieved in our lifetime" (p. 63). Everyone is entitled to come to a mature recognition of man's finitude in his own way, but I do not believe that our great need is a sense of awe, a sense of contrition, and a sense of gratitude for the divine mercies which are promised to those who humble themselves.

20. *Advocacy and Objectivity in Religious Education*[1]

I am very grateful to the editors of the *Union Seminary Quarterly Review* for kindly inviting me, at Professor John A. Hutchison's generous suggestion, to reply to his discussion of my collection of essays, *Religion, Politics, and the Higher Learning*, especially as Professor Hutchison seems so anxious to understand me, to help me dispel my "prejudice", and to inform me "in all good will" who my friends are. No author can fail to be moved by such solicitude on the part of a reviewer. Unfortunately, however, Hutchison's exposition of my point of view is not distinguished by any great effort to avoid the danger which is present in all polemically oriented exposition. Perhaps he would remind me here of his view that there is always a tension between the attitude of attachment and the attitude of detachment required by critical reason. In which case I must say that I am sorry that he could not have made a more strenuous effort to overcome that tension, a

---

1. This is a reply to Professor John A. Hutchison's review of my *Religion, Politics, and the Higher Learning* (Cambridge, Mass., Harvard University Press, 1959). His review and my reply both appeared in the *Union Seminary Quarterly Review*, Volume XVI (May 1961)—the review on pp. 397–402; the reply on pp. 403–7. I reprint my reply without any changes.

more strenuous effort to understand and to report my beliefs as presented in my book.

Under the circumstances I must try myself to communicate to readers of the *Review* the gist of what I was trying to say. In doing so I am reminded of the pianist who had just played a sonata, who was asked by an unsympathetic member of his audience just what the sonata meant, and who in reply sat down and played the sonata all over again. I suspect that my re-rendition may be of more use to those who have not read my book than it will be to Professor Hutchison; but I hope that even he will be in a better position to evaluate my views after he has listened to a new performance of one of the movements, as it were, a performance that I shall speed up at places and pedal differently in order to emphasize tones that seem to have escaped his attention.

The basic question to which I addressed myself in the title essay of my book was: "Should secular undergraduate colleges give instruction in religion?". And by instruction *in*— the preposition is very important—religion I meant instruction in a spirit of advocacy. My answer to the question was "no" for a variety of reasons, some of them having to do with the nature of religion and some of them having to do with the fact that I was considering the needs of a secular undergraduate college. Religion, I said, is more than a cognitive affair. It is more than a matter of believing truths of the kind that the teacher of mathematics or physics or logic can usually explain and defend. Acceptance of a religion, I said, usually involves the adoption of certain moral, social, political, and esthetic attitudes, an attachment to a certain liturgy, for example. It also leads the believer to have certain kinds of feelings peculiarly associated with the religion he believes in. To be religious, therefore, is to adopt a certain total way of life. Beginning with this as a premise, I argued that instruction *in* religion is bound to be specific, bound to articulate and defend one religious way of life. Instructors in religion in the sense specified would not teach their students to be religious in general; they would teach them to be Jews, Catholics, Protestants, or Mohammedans, for example. This being so, I concluded that such instruction should not be offered by college faculties which could not conscientiously choose one religion as *the* best religion or *the* true religion. Moreover, it seemed to me that the effort to give instruction in a small number of favored religions would pose the same difficult question of the worth or superiority of one family of religions. In addition, I think it would be unwise to offer competing courses in which different religions are taught in a spirit of advocacy precisely because of the total character of religious devotion to which I have alluded. The emotional fervor with which some people accept their religion, and the political implications of some religions would, where serious instruction *in* religion were given, contribute to an atmosphere in which the central aim of such an undergraduate college as I had in mind, the pursuit and communication of knowledge, would be seriously obstructed.

Even if the reader of Mr. Hutchison's review were to gather from it that I believe what I have just set forth, he might not realize that I make no objection whatever to what I call instruction *about* religion. I fully agree that such an effort at objective instruction ought to be made. I suggest that it ought to be made in departments like anthropology, literature, history, psychology, and sociology; but I do not wish to deny that under certain circumstances the subject might better be taught by members of a separate department of religion. The question whether the history of religion, for example, should be taught in a department of history or in a separate department of religion cannot be answered in an *a priori* way.

Moreover, the issue is not one that merely concerns the title or the guild of the teacher. It concerns the spirit of his teaching. I never argued that a professor of religion as such is bound to engage in special pleading. And I am happy to hear that Professor Hutchison is inclined to wager that there has been no more special pleading in his classrooms than in mine. (I might say, however, that as he has very little reliable knowledge of what goes on in my classrooms, his asseveration would have been more appropriate if he had limited himself to what goes on in his own classroom.) I also want to inform him that he is quite wrong when he says that the position I advocate "if carried out consistently, would exclude all religious adherents from the academic community or at least from any study in which religion might be involved". I made no such assertion, of course, and I do not see how he could have derived this conclusion as an implication of any assertion that I did make. I suspect that he does so only because he adds one of his own premises to my argument, namely, that no religious adherent can teach *about* religion in an objective manner. I agree that it might be difficult, but I pointed out in my book that many great teachers of religion have tried successfully to do just that: for example, the late George Foote Moore and more recently Professor Harry A. Wolfson, the former a Protestant who taught the world and his pupils so much about Judaism, and the latter a Jew who has taught with such great distinction about Christianity. I repeat that Professor Hutchison manages to attribute views to me that I do not hold, in part because he disregards my distinction between advocacy and objectivity in religious education, and in part because he implicitly attributes to me his own views on the limits of objectivity. And, as I have already suggested, his failure to interpret me accurately may well be an ironic example of his own pessimistic views about a scholar's capacity to be disinterested.

A related pessimism about my candor leads him to overdo his reading between my lines when he implies that I was making an invidious comparison between the faculty of the Harvard Divinity School and the Harvard Department of Philosophy. I said nothing in my book about the faculty of the Harvard Divinity School save to call attention to the distinction of two of its great members, Moore and Wolfson. For this reason it is exceedingly unfortunate that Professor Hutchison should have marred his review by suggesting that I assert that Harvard theologians "are engaging in religious propaganda", and by saying that I "seem consistently to assume that Harvard Divinity School maintains a credal or confessional requirement for its faculty". I asserted nothing of the kind; I assumed nothing of the kind. There are so many genuine philosophical issues between us that Mr. Hutchison might have taken more trouble to deal with what I said explicitly and less in speculating about my views on matters I did not treat.

I should like to conclude with a remark on Mr. Hutchison's statement that "A final chapter brackets Reinhold Niebuhr with Walter Lippmann and attacks both as enemies of the kind of liberalism which the author professes". Readers of the *Review* are entitled to know that in my essay "Original Sin, Natural Law, and Politics" I say that Dr. Niebuhr is shrewd, courageous, and right-minded on many political questions but that I cannot accept his, or Mr. Lippmann's, philosophical views on the foundations of politics. I call attention to this because it might not be evident to readers of Mr. Hutchison's review. My "prejudice", as Mr. Hutchison calls my opposition to some of his own views or those of his friends, is not as pervasive as Mr. Hutchison would have the reader think. I am very sorry that he could not have exerted his good will toward me in a more Kantian spirit. Kant, it will be recalled, said that exhibiting good will involves summoning all the means in one's power to achieve something. I doubt that Professor Hutchison has done this in his effort to understand and report my views.

21. Jacques Maritain: Philosopher in the Service of His Church[1]

No one who reflects on the life and work of Jacques Maritain can fail to observe the contrast between his influence and that of most philosophers of the twentieth century. Maritain is known throughout the world and regarded by countless laymen as a source of insight and wisdom, though one can easily name several twentieth-century Americans and Englishmen of far greater intellectual power and philosophical originality who are virtually unknown to the general public and who have almost no impact on it.

One of the most obvious reasons for this difference is Maritain's laudable interest in matters of general concern, his preoccupation with questions that stir the minds of ordinary men and intellectuals who are not technically trained in philosophy. He is widely read in history, literature, and political theory; he is a facile writer and a friend of writers; he is a

1. This essay is the result of joining together parts of two reviews of books by Maritain: one a review of his *Man and the State* (Chicago, 1951) in *The New Republic,* Volume 124 (9 April 1951), pp. 18–19, copyright 1951 by Harrison-Blaine of New Jersey, Inc.; the other a review of his *Moral Philosophy: An Historical and Critical Survey of The Great Systems* (New York, 1964) in *The New York Herald Tribune Book Week,* 19 July 1964, p. 3.

philosopher of religion and a commentator on manners and morals.

In trying to explain Maritain's greater influence one might go further and say that French philosophers, by contrast to their Anglo-American colleagues, are notoriously cosmopolitan; as Plato might have said, they stay close to the cave. They are habitués of salons and cafés, and not commuters from split-level houses to hair-splitting seminars. All Parisian professors know that man cannot live on epistemology alone, and Maritain is a Parisian professor. But before one can even apply the rules of the syllogism to that pair of premises, one's mind runs to another city that is of even greater significance in understanding the impact of Maritain—the city of Rome.

Maritain has been one of the chief philosophical spokesmen of the Roman Catholic Church in our century, and the Church has need of technically trained advocates who can move with ease from religion to art, to politics, to history, to literature. On all of these subjects it has positions that must be defended; for all of these subjects it claims to provide a synoptic world-view by means of which it extends its influences from the city of Rome to the world. The impact of Maritain is therefore in great measure the impact of Catholic thought on our times. It is obvious that Maritain's defense of the Catholic faith has contributed greatly to making him the force that he is. What Maritain has done to earn the respect and support of his Church is especially well illustrated in two of his books, *Moral Philosophy* and *Man and the State*.

Moral Philosophy is called a historical and critical survey of the great systems of moral philosophy, but almost 350 of its 468 pages are devoted to an attack on Hegelianism, Marxism, Comte's positivism, the existentialism of Kierkegaard and Sartre, Dewey's pragmatism, and the philosophy of Bergson. After a brief survey of the moral philosophies of the Greeks, of the impact of Christianity, and of Kantian ethics, Maritain turns to his main concern, which is to defend a Catholic moral philosophy against its chief intellectual opponents in the nineteenth and twentieth centuries. His book is therefore not a history of moral philosophy so much as an apologetically motivated polemic that is conducted at times with great ingenuity, and at times with an emphasis that reflects his idiosyncratic approach to the whole subject.

The last feature is strikingly illustrated in the excessively long treatment of Comte. I should not have thought that Comte's version of positivistic ethics was worth ninety pages —one-fifth of the book—when there is virtually nothing on the ethical theory of logical positivism. I should not have thought that the ethical views of Marxism deserved fifty pages when neither Hume, nor Bentham, nor John Stuart Mill, nor G. E. Moore are treated at all. Even Kierkegaard, Sartre, and Bergson are granted less space than Comte, who never completed a treatise on ethics and whose ideas on the subject Maritain is forced to reconstruct from a posthumously published sketch and from whatever he can glean from Comte's other writings.

All of these defects, however, are minor by comparison to the defects of the ethical views that Maritain himself defends —the doctrine of Natural Law as he conceives it. It is the instrument with which Maritain tries to "unmask" the errors of all those he belabors. For Maritain, as for most moral philosophers, the main task is to discover or provide a rationale for our moral judgments. What, he asks, do these judgments mean, and on what grounds do we make them? According to Maritain, the answers to these questions cannot be found in what he calls the science of phenomena. Phenomena are the objects of sensory experience, the objects of empirical science, and therefore one cannot base one's moral judgments on a study of them. According to Maritain, moral philosophy must have its own objects, which must be investigated by methods that transcend those of physics, chemistry, biology, history, sociology, economics, and psychology. And most non-Catholic moral philosophies fail, he says, because they locate the ground of our moral judgments in something factual and phenomenal.

Hegel and Marx, he argues, identified right action with the furtherance of the aims of an actual historical institution like the state or the working class; Comte worshipped humanity itself; and Dewey did not go beyond the natural desires and goals of men when he analyzed ethical concepts. In opposition to all of them Maritain holds that moral judgments of right and wrong are ultimately based on principles that must be established not by examining the observable behavior of individual men but rather by penetrating man's essence or nature, which is a super-sensible entity. We must peer into this and when we discover what it is to *be* a man, we shall supposedly be able to develop a foundation for the moral principles in the Decalogue by using the techniques of metaphysics.

In *Man and the State*—a series of lectures commissioned by the Walgreen Foundation in an effort to provide democracy with more than a pragmatic defense—Maritain shows that the doctrine of Natural Law is more than the scholastic philosopher's stone—it is his rock; it supposedly underlies all our political rights. A piano, Maritain tells us with Aristotelian simplicity, has as its end the production of sounds and if it doesn't produce them it must be judged worthless. A good piano is one that plays; it successfully attains its end, and if it doesn't, not only is it not a good piano, it is not a piano at all. We may say, therefore, that a piano is by definition a keyboard instrument that emits musical tones when its keys are struck, and use the definition as a standard for good pianos. This much we can take, but surely not the supposed analogy with man which is then drawn for the purpose of explaining Natural Law. Pianos are artificial, but men are not; and only by assuming a theological dogma can we say that men, like pianos, are constructed for certain purposes. Men may *seek* ends, but that is another matter. We may formulate a standard for good pianos by reminding ourselves of the purposive definition of a piano, but we cannot speak of "the ends of men" and "the ends of pianos" without exploiting ambiguity or dogma. Men *seek* ever so many things that Maritain would call evil, so that he can hardly discover a series of moral laws merely by observing what goals men *do* seek. What Maritain wants is a series of moral laws describing how men *ought* to behave, and these he cannot get merely by distilling the essence of man.

Aristotle hoped to define man's highest good by emphasizing his difference from all other animals—his rationality. But if all men are rational, how absurd it is to set up rationality as a goal to be sought! It is sometimes replied that the Aristotelian definition of man requires only a minimum of rationality, and then it is urged that what man *ought* to do is to improve on his distinguishing feature. But man may also be defined as the only animal that lies and yet this would hardly imply that he should devote himself to a life of prevarication. At this point, Maritain might appeal to a distinction between the *essence* of being a rational animal and the *accident* of being a liar, but this appeal is based on a logical doctrine, which is intimately connected with the dubious distinction between analytic and synthetic statements. Therefore Maritain cannot effectively defend the doctrine of Natural Law by such a move—or so it seems to me.

In my opinion the kernel of truth in the doctrine of Natural Law is conveyed in the idea that we may always make moral appeal beyond the decisions of any state or group of people. But this truth is obscured by the effort to rest Natural Law on the notion of essence, and misused by those who hold that the Church is the best interpreter of Natural Law in specific moral cases. If the Church is the best interpreter of Natural Law, why shouldn't the Church have the secular power it had in medieval times? This is an embarrassing question for neo-scholastics, and it should be said on Maritain's behalf that he really opposes the view that the Church can ask kings to expel heretics, or use "the rights of the spiritual sword to seize upon temporal affairs for the sake of some spiritual necessity". But it is important to remember that this handsome disavowal of medievalism does not itself derive from Natural Law but rather from a recognition of practical necessity. "The Church," according to Maritain, "does not lose any of the essential rights she has claimed or exercised in the past"; she merely renounces the exercise of them now in the interest of the good both of the Church and society. In short, the trouble with theocracy is that now it won't work. In criticizing some of his over-eager co-religionists Maritain reminds those who would "require that the State make all non-Christians and non-Orthodox second-rate citizens" of "the consequences that such a claim would entail, not only for themselves but for the very work of the Church in the world". In short, Maritain advises the holder of the spiritual sword to keep it in its sheath, but Maritain does not rest his advice on moral scruples that flow from Natural Law. He rests it on pragmatic considerations, on cold considerations of political necessity. Not a very Walgreenian doctrine.

Liberals will duly note Maritain's assurances, born of a speculative philosophy of history, that the time will never come again when the civil power will be the secular arm of the Church; but they must remember that the *right* to return to a "sacral regime", according to Maritain, is zealously guarded by the Church and is restricted only by its *own* conception of its *own* good and that of society. They will appreciate Maritain's declaration that men mutually opposed in their philosophies may come to a merely practical agreement about a list of human rights, and they may even quote his observation that it is too much for the state "to judge whether a work of art is possessed by an intrinsic quality of immorality" when they attack the suppression of "sacrilegious" movies. But they ought to remain unmoved by the philosophy which animates this book, for it is contrary to reason and experience.

No doubt this consideration will not faze a devout believer like Maritain, for whom mystery is not an obstacle. But I must say that Maritain's doctrine of Natural Law rests on an incomprehensible ontology that cannot provide a rational man with a basis for his moral convictions. This is not to assert that there are no universally accepted moral principles— there may well be. Nor is it to assert that we have no bedrock moral principles for which we might be willing to die. On the contrary, by not trying to support our fundamental principles with an ontology, we show that they *are* bedrock, that *we* take responsibility for living in accordance with them, and that *we* are prepared to die in defense of them.

I cannot see what is gained by resting our moral principles on metaphysical entities when those entities are more obscure, and their existence more dubious, than the principles we rest on them. Moreover, when we recall that Aquinas believed that a principle which was not self-evident to an ordinary man might be self-evident "to the wise", we become aware not only of the anti-democratic potential of the doctrine of Natural Law but also of the ease with which it can lead to a moral philosophy which justifies the actual state of things. One can see how it might be used by a man or an institution—a dictator, a state, or a religion—in order to present a "rational" apology for its repressive actions, and according to the doctrine of Natural Law as understood by Maritain such power is certainly vested in anyone who has the power to say what the essence of man really is.

Once the philosopher comes to the conclusion that he can penetrate the essence of man and in this way find out what the really true moral principles are, he obviously can play a grander role than that played by his more modest colleagues. He does not limit himself to the technicalities of epistemology; he provides a ground for rules by which he thinks all men ought to live. But the philosopher who expands his idea of what his job is in this way, while he remains within the confines of certain institutionalized religions, moves from the level of mere technique to the level of dogma, and not to the heights of free and unobstructed vision. His job is cut out for him in advance by others and his views are more predictable than those of his less influential colleagues. His influence is won at a price that some philosophers are not willing to pay.

22. The Open Mind of
Robert Oppenheimer [1]

A reader like the present one, who believes that the Oppenheimer case produced one of the great injustices of our time,
might be tempted to seize his book, *The Open Mind*, as an
occasion for defending him once again, for pointing out the
large number of instances in which Oppenheimer vigorously
attacked the policy of the Soviet Union, and for emphasizing
the extent to which his career as a scientific statesman
brought him into direct conflict with the Russians on the international politics of the bomb. Yet it is well to resist this
temptation here, not only because of the absurdity of trying
to reargue the case in a few paragraphs after so many thousand pages have been devoted to it, but also because yielding
to the temptation would be extremely unfair to the author of
a book that deserves serious consideration in its own right.

In this book Dr. Oppenheimer has brought together eight
essays, four of which state his views on the tortured problem

1. This first appeared as a review of Robert Oppenheimer's book of essays
The Open Mind (New York, 1955), in *The New Leader*, Volume XXXIX (30
January 1956), pp. 25–26, copyright © The American Labor Conference on
International Affairs, Inc. It is reprinted, with a few minor changes, by per-
mission.

of controlling atomic weapons, and four of which reveal him as a deep, sensitive, acute commentator on the relation between science and the culture of our time. He presents these essays without any advocating preface, without any reference to his ordeal, without apology. We are therefore reminded of the dignified way in which he replied to reporters after the AEC's decision was rendered: by referring them to the simple, terse statement of the physicist Smyth's dissent from the majority verdict. We are also reminded, more obliquely, of a premonitory story which Oppenheimer told in another connection in 1947:

"One day in a clearing in the forest, Confucius came upon a woman in deep mourning, wracked by sorrow. He learned that her son had just been eaten by a tiger; and he attempted to console her, to make clear how unavailing tears would be, to restore her composure. He left, but had barely reentered the forest when the renewed sounds of weeping recalled him. 'That is not all,' the woman said. 'You see, my husband was eaten here a year ago by this same tiger.' Again Confucius attempted to console her and again he left only to hear renewed weeping. 'Is that not all?' 'Oh, no,' she said. 'The year before that my father too was eaten by a tiger.' Confucius thought for a moment, and then said: 'This would not seem to be a very salutary neighborhood. Why don't you leave it?'. The woman wrung her hands. 'I know,' she said, 'I know; but, you see, the government is so excellent.'"

It is encouraging to know that Robert Oppenheimer did not leave the neighborhood after being subjected to his infamous ordeal. In this volume, he addresses his profound and moving voice to one of the perplexing philosophical problems of our time: the relation between science and society. What he says is in refreshing, challenging contrast to much of the cant we hear today about the defects of rationality as a way of dealing with our moral, social, and political problems. Oppenheimer's view is made more poignant and more commanding by the fact that he admits that "In some sort of crude sense which no vulgarity, no humor, no overstatement can quite extinguish, the physicists have known sin; and this is a knowledge which they cannot lose". Those who have seen Hiroshima even recently will know what he means. But the sin Oppenheimer speaks of is not Original Sin, nor does he think that Hiroshima forces us to abandon the categories of rationality in making our moral decisions. In spite of Oppenheimer's personal suffering and his guilt about his association with the most devastating death-dealer of all time, Oppenheimer does not contritely abandon the tradition of the Enlightenment. On the contrary, Jefferson is the thinker whom he quotes with most sympathy on the relation between science and politics. He praises Jefferson for being confident that an increased understanding of the world will lead to progress, for being convinced that barbarism cannot stand up against inquiry and enlightenment, for believing that as men know more they will act more wisely and live better, for realizing that science, in the long run, cannot flourish in an undemocratic society.

"What are the lessons that the spirit of science teaches us for our practical affairs?" Oppenheimer asks. And he answers: that we must reject authoritarianism and dogmatism, and keep our minds open to all the evidence bearing on the problems that concern us. This is the message of a brilliant, cultivated man who symbolizes in a complex way the triumph and the travails of natural science in the twentieth century.

23. John Dewey: A Great Philosopher of Education[1]

When I first picked up John Dewey's *Lectures in the Philosophy of Education: 1899*, its title brought chilling thoughts of the darkest and loneliest parts of university libraries, those sad stacks devoted to what used to be called pedagogics. And as I had spent part of my youth studying the background of Dewey's thought, I knew that a good deal of late nineteenth-century philosophy could be dull beyond belief. From the pages of the editor's accurate introduction, old forbidding terms and figures leaped forward—Froebelianism, Pestalozzianism, Herbartianism, William Torrey Harris, George Sylvester Morris—and my heart sank even deeper. Yet I pressed on in disregard of every counsel of prudence, and I am very glad that I did. When I began reading Dewey's text, I was lifted high above its intellectual milieu and I marveled once again at a great thinker's ability to speak across time to readers of another age. I was amazed by the contemporary relevance of

1. This was first printed as a review of Dewey's *Lectures in the Philosophy of Education: 1899*, edited by Reginald D. Archambault (New York, Random House, 1966), in *The New York Times Book Review*, 24 July 1966, p. 10 *et seq.*, and is copyright © 1966 by The New York Times Company. It is reprinted, with one minor change, by permission.

244

a course of lectures that began just after the Spanish-American War.

They were delivered by Dewey at the University of Chicago in the winter term of 1898–99, and were taken down verbatim by a student who hectographed them and sold them to other students eager to understand the master's words by all means at their disposal. The published version, edited by Mr. Archambault, clearly demonstrates to those who need such demonstration that Dewey was one of the most profound of all educational theorists. No really significant general principle that is accepted today escaped him, and it is obvious that he approached his task with more wisdom, learning, analytical power, and concern for the child than anyone has been able to marshal since his death.

I can testify to Dewey's insight on the basis of some experience with a recent effort to revitalize the high-school curriculum in social studies. He knew that total coverage in history is an absurd goal and that much can be gained by the use of what he called "representative topics", which bring structural unity to facts by using them as illustrations of concepts and generalizations in social and natural science. He also knew that by studying technology in its historical setting, the student can come to understand something about the interplay between scientific advance and social demands, and about the integrity of culture.

In confirmation of Dewey's views I have seen with my own eyes how a tenth-grade class studying the Industrial Revolution can be captivated and really learn a great deal while it examines the development of the steam engine from a technological, economic, and social point of view. Instead of being made to memorize the familiar dreary and mindless list of inventors' names, they can be given an exciting and instructive exercise which leads them to see why the engine developed from the versions of Newcomen and Savery to that of Watt as a result of technical ingenuity and economic need.

I know of the students' ability to reinvent the steam engine after receiving some preliminary information about some of the devices and scientific knowledge that preceded it. I know how delighted they are to see that their history course deals with something they have also encountered in their science course, and how Dewey would have nodded with knowing approval at hearing about this. I am also convinced, on the basis of another part of the program I am working on, that we shall be able to "bring to consciousness the method of science", to use Dewey's phrase, in a unit on Charles Darwin— which examines his theory of natural selection, its logic, and its revolutionary impact on the world.

All of this and more Dewey anticipated in 1899. To his eternal credit, however, he was more than a pedagogical technician, since he saw the school in larger terms, as a force that would break down barriers of class, color, and nation. He also knew before C. P. Snow that the humanities and the sciences are not two cultures, and a half-century before Wittgenstein he said that "a use of language that did not tell somebody else something would not be a language at all". He saw that the child's interest had to be captured before any education could begin, but he clearly distinguished between interesting a child and humoring him. Dewey argued that the child's active nature cried out for sympathetic guidance instead of merely mechanical drill, but he knew the difference between action and aimless activity.

Dewey realized that the growth of urban industry and science were two of the most important facts of modern society and that its highest political ideal was democracy, but he knew how abrasive and divisive the modern city can be and that genuine democracy cannot flourish there in the absence of fraternal feeling. And, though he believed that the school, by cultivating local loyalties and neighborly feeling, might help re-create the sense of community that had prevailed in rural America, we can be sure that if he were alive today he would have condemned the kind of neighborhood parochialism that merely masks prejudice and perpetuates segregation in the schools.

When one sees how much energy Dewey devoted to the education of the young and their teachers, one is reminded that he was a professor who tried all his life to combine research, teaching, and social service at their highest levels. He wrote technical philosophical books and articles, he prepared assiduously for his classes (as these lectures show so well), he encouraged his students sympathetically, and he tried harder than any other American academic of his generation to leave society better than he found it. His service to society, however, was as liberal in spirit as his teaching and his research—for it was dominated by a desire to keep children, their parents, and even philosophers from leading stunted lives.

And so, although I disagree with many of Dewey's philosophical views, I admire him without reservation for the remarkable range of his intellectual interests and his unceasing efforts to apply the tools of philosophy to the problems of men. These lectures reveal a figure who towered over the age of McKinley and the educational thinkers of the gray nineties, for by 1899—the year, incidentally, in which Dewey published his "School and Society"—he had already demonstrated that he was one of the greatest of all philosophers of education.

24. A Tribute to
Harry Austryn Wolfson[1]

In 1935 Harry Austryn Wolfson delivered a lecture at the College of the City of New York when I was an undergraduate there. I do not remember what he lectured on—probably on his favorite, Spinoza—but I do remember the spell he cast upon me. He simply overwhelmed me. I had already been taught to admire great scholarship in the history of philosophy but had never before been exposed to the real thing: a dazzling display of Latin, Greek, Hebrew, and Arabic, an impeccable command of the text on which he discoursed, and a prodigious knowledge of its background and its impact on the philosophical tradition. To me Wolfson became a symbol of awesome scholarship, philological accomplishment, and devotion to learning. I saw him as a scholar's god, to be admired by mortal philosophers and historians, but never to be approached.

Fifteen years passed and I had the good fortune to become Wolfson's colleague on the Harvard faculty. He was, in his majesty, taking time off from studies in Jewish and Mohammedan thought to lecture to students in my department on

1. This first appeared in *Mosaic: A Jewish Student Journal*, Volume IV (1963), pp. 34–35. It is reprinted, without change, by permission.

248

ancient, medieval, and modern philosophy; but I was still too overcome by my boyhood vision of his magnitude to try to get to know him. Moreover, Emerson Hall was not his permanent habitat: he merely visited it on periodic excursions from his real home, Widener Library. It was only when I had the further good fortune to have my study translated to that Cambridge version of Solomon's House in Bacon's *New Atlantis* that I really came to know Wolfson. Not only did I enter the house, but at last I also got to know Solomon himself. Soon I enjoyed the pleasures of a daily walk with him from Widener to what is rightly called Wolfson's Table at the Faculty Club, of summer foraging with him at the Wursthaus and the Waldorf Cafeteria when the Faculty Club shut its doors, and of talking with him about the condition of man, to say nothing of women and children. At last I had the opportunity to see that my boyhood hero was not only immensely learned but also truly gentle, charming, and warmhearted. I saw that he combined the way of science with the way of wisdom in the tradition of those philosophers he admired most. And then the fun began, as he reminisced about Europe, the Lower East Side, and Scranton, Pennsylvania; offered bits of shrewd advice that so many of us treasure; reflected on Harvard in the good old days and Harvard in the bad old days; and gave other touching signs of his humanity.

In this year of celebration (1963) others will speak more fully and more authoritatively of Harry Wolfson and his work, for I am a mere neophyte in the cult. As a comparative newcomer to his world, it is hard for me to believe that he— the first to enter the library and the last to leave it, the first to get a point and the last to forget it—is seventy-five. I wish him new joys as he begins the next quarter of a century, chasing down ever more references in the stacks, deepening our knowledge of the history of philosophical thought, and brightening the lives of his friends.

25. The Later Years of
George Santayana[1]

I have always thought that Bertrand Russell was right in not taking George Santayana seriously as an analyst of knowledge, of truth, and of essence—Santayana's favorite concept;[2] and I have thought for a long time that William James and John Dewey were justifiably irritated by his snobbishness, coldness, and reactionary sentiment. As a metaphysician and epistemologist Santayana lacked great depth and logical power, and for one who set himself up as a moralist he seemed to me strangely lacking in sympathy for human beings. Because Daniel Cory, who has edited the volume of letters, *Santayana: The Later Years*, has done little to expound or defend Santayana's philosophy, he has not forced me to change my view of Santayana's position in the history of metaphysics and epistemology; but he has certainly led me to see more warmth, wisdom, and generosity than I had ever

1. This is a slightly revised version of a review of *Santayana: The Later Years: A Portrait With Letters*, edited by Daniel Cory (New York, 1963), in *The New York Herald Tribune Book Week*, 20 October 1963, p. 6. The essay is reprinted here by permission.

2. See Bertrand Russell, *Portraits from Memory and Other Essays* (New York, 1956), pp. 94–95. However, Russell does acknowledge certain philosophical debts to Santayana in ethics, *op. cit.*, p. 96.

seen in Santayana before. In the letters that Cory prints and in his description of his relationship with Santayana from the philosopher's sixty-third year in 1927 to his death in 1952, Santayana does not appear as the representative of "moribund Latinity" that James knew, nor as the patent-leather stylist that Russell found so boring to read. We no longer find him generalizing waspishly on the subjects of Judaism, Positivism, Liberalism, Pragmatism, and all of the other failings that he identified with the City of New York—whose philosophers, with great forbearance, have been the first to praise him and the last to be offended by the rudeness of some of his published statements about their thoughts and attitudes.

In these letters another Santayana emerges in a story whose plot is relatively simple. A world-famous philosopher is living in Italy, having gone to Europe after abandoning his Harvard professorship fifteen years earlier. He receives an essay on his philosophy from the twenty-two-year-old Cory and replies by saying that it is the best interpretation of his thought he has ever read. The young and impecunious admirer expresses a desire to meet his hero, the hero offers to defray his travel expenses from England to Italy, and the admirer accepts. The "young Barbarian", as Santayana praisingly calls him, plays pool (and later golf), and is much concerned about the standing of the New York Giants, but after six weeks Santayana asks him to become his secretary and to help him with the preparation of "The Realm of Matter". Astonished, but thrilled and honored, Cory accepts.

Before long another philosophical expatriate enters the story—Charles Augustus Strong, whose deceased wife was the daughter of John D. Rockefeller and who therefore lives comfortably. Strong also hires Cory as secretary and companion, and by that time two old lonely men have brightened up their lives and lightened the financial burdens of a loyal, jolly friend who, among his other duties, criticizes their manuscripts, converses and corresponds with them, and brings them gossip of the outside world. For this Cory earns himself

a lifetime fellowship set up in Strong's will and a secure repu-
tation as Santayana's Eckermann. He also becomes the source
for two stories that will never cease to interest Santayana's
future biographers.

According to Cory, Santayana once said to him that he,
Santayana, "must have been" a homosexual in his Harvard
days, though "unconscious of it at the time". Upon this Cory
comments: "If he was a man with the feelings of a woman, he
was not aware (until well into middle life) what this might indicate to a Freudian expert", and then adds in a protective
spirit: "When he did finally suspect something 'unconventional' in his psyche, I am certain it only hardened a predilection to renounce the world as much as was compatible with
living a rational life devoted to his labors".

Santayana's renunciation of the world, as Cory makes clear
in his second big story, meant no renunciation of Santayana's
naturalism. Just before his death Santayana told Cory that if
he should die while Cory was away, Cory was not to be misled by any reports about his last hours. He was, he pointed
out, living in a Catholic nursing home, where it was expected
that a man should die like a Christian, but Cory was warned
that if he ever heard reports that Santayana had *requested*
extreme unction he was not to believe them. Santayana
added that it might be difficult to avoid receiving it—
especially if he were in a semi-unconscious state, and "that he
might even go so far as to nod his head in approval, if he felt
that by so doing he could avoid all 'fuss and bother.'"

These stories are more touching than any I have ever
heard about Santayana, and there are many others in the
book that are equally so. They show, for example, that Santayana could be fatherly to Cory, sweetly understanding of
poor old Strong, appreciative of the young Robert Lowell's
genius, and shrewdly objective about his own limitations and
those of some of his admirers. He was, therefore, a better and
wiser man than at least one of his readers had taken him to
be. Just as Eckermann announced, "This is *my* Goethe", so

Cory might well say, "This is *my* Santayana", but Cory's Santayana is so much more winning than the one that many of us have been carrying around in our heads that we owe Cory a great debt of gratitude.

26. Memories of G. E. Moore[1]

G. E. Moore was at once the most distinguished and the most admirable philosopher I have ever known personally, and I am sure that my feelings are shared by many philosophers all over the world. I also feel sure that he would have wished me to confine myself to analyzing or criticizing his philosophical views on this occasion, but I am moved to talk also—even primarily—about Moore as a teacher, about Moore as a guide and inspiration to young philosophers, and about Moore as a man. I should like, in some of my remarks, to make those of you who knew him feel his presence once again and to give others some impression of his character and of his impact on several generations of philosophers in England and America. And I hope I can do this without indulging in the kind of sentimentality which he avoided so successfully all of his life

1. This was delivered as a talk on the Third Programme of the British Broadcasting Corporation; it was also delivered at Columbia University on 15 January 1959 during a meeting in memory of Moore. It was printed in *The Listener*, Volume LXI (30 April 1959), pp. 757–58; also, in a slightly longer version, in *The Journal of Philosophy*, Volume LXII (1960), pp. 805–10. The latter version was reprinted in *Studies in the Philosophy of G. E. Moore*, edited by E. D. Klemke (Chicago, 1969), pp. 291–97. It has been allowed to stand with few changes.

even though he was a man of deep and delicate feeling, as anyone could tell by listening to him sing Brahms and Schubert *lieder*.

While he was lecturing at Columbia in the early forties he and Mrs. Moore lived in a tiny flat off Amsterdam Avenue, and some of you will remember how, at a certain point in the evening, if you coaxed him just a little bit, he would go into his bedroom, where the piano was because the livingroom was so small, and play and sing while you listened in the livingroom. And in 1945, when he was seventy-two, he wrote me from Cambridge: "Now that our youngest son is living with us, I have the pleasure of constantly playing duets with him. I think you get to know music better if you play it yourself, however inadequately, than if you merely hear it".

Moore would have said the same thing about philosophy, I am sure. You get to know *it* better if you play it yourself, than if you spend your life merely listening to others, recording them, and playing them back to yourself and your students. It was this passion for doing philosophy independently that made Moore such an exciting and encouraging teacher.

Young philosophers at Columbia were not altogether unprepared for Moore when he visited there in 1942. Some of our teachers had made us aware of the value of clarity in philosophy, but the accepted view was that philosophy required great learning in the sciences and history, or technical expertise in logic, or a professional fondness for wisdom. And Moore was deficient in all of these respects. We had been taught that the theory of perception was a waste of time, that anti-naturalism in ethics was a dreadful heresy, and that Cartesian dualism was even worse. But Moore believed in them all. We had also been assured by political experts in the thirties that the situation in philosophy had become even more poverty-stricken than it was when Marx had described it so scathingly—that bourgeois philosophers were now not only not changing the world, they were not even interpreting it; instead they confined themselves to interpreting *words*, under the counter-revolutionary influence of Moore and his allies.

You can imagine, therefore, how militant young New York philosophers, raised on the teachings of Morris Cohen, Carnap, Dewey, or Marx, might have been struck by a fresh dose of Moore. He deviated from almost every New York doctrine —pragmatic, positivistic, or naturalistic. He spent one term trying to analyze the concept of *seeing* and introduced us to the despised sense-datum. He spent another worrying about the *ordinary* use of the words "if-then", after the logicians had assured us that nothing but the "horse-shoe" was worth talking about. He repeated (though with diminished confidence) his published statement that goodness was a non-natural quality. He insisted that he was quite distinct from his body, and one day said that his hand was closer to him than his foot was. He showed no inclination whatever toward encyclopedism. He announced to scandalized empiricists that he believed in the synthetic *a priori*. He seemed utterly unconcerned with changing the ways in which we speak about the world, to say nothing of the world itself.

In short, Moore challenged most of our philosophical beliefs, attitudes, and prejudices. And yet knowing him and talking with him when he was about seventy and when I had just received my Ph.D. provided one of the most refreshing episodes in my philosophical education. Why? He did not persuade me, I am bound to say, of the validity of a single one of his main philosophical doctrines. But he was living proof of the importance of honesty, clarity, integrity, and careful thinking in philosophy. Moore never asserted anything that he did not believe was true; he never said that a statement followed from another unless he was absolutely convinced that it did; he never said that he understood when he didn't. And how many philosophers are there of whom one can say this? These qualities of Moore meant more to me when I began to stand on my own philosophical legs than all of the machinery of *Principia Mathematica*, than all of the learning of the learned, than all of the wisdom of the ancients. When later I read John Maynard Keynes' reminiscences of Moore as he was at the turn of the century, I could see how deeply ingrained Moore's qualities were. I could also see why they had been so affecting in Cambridge, England, for I felt the same excitement and intellectual pleasure in Moore's presence when he was seventy as Keynes and his friends had felt when he was thirty. The same purity, the same incredible simplicity, the same lack of bluff—they were all still there at the end of his life as they had been at the beginning.

"Do your philosophy for yourself", I have suggested, was one of Moore's great messages to the young. And he helped you do it yourself. He gave you the feeling that there was something like a method in philosophy. And this made you feel the comparative unimportance of arriving at the same doctrines as he did. I believe that Moore, more than any of his distinguished contemporaries, communicated to his students the feeling that they should share his method even when they did not accept his philosophical beliefs. Characteristically, however, Moore shied away from talking of his method, as the following excerpt from a letter shows. It was written by William Frankena after a conversation with Moore in 1949: "One bit of conversation was about Keynes' *Two Memoirs*. I asked Moore if he knew at the time that he was having such an influence on Keynes, etc. He said, approximately, 'No, I didn't. I used to hear them speak of "The Method" sometimes, and understood that it was regarded as mine, but I never did know what it was' ".

Moore may never have known what the method of his philosophy was, but Moore was unusually agnostic on such matters. It fitted in with his dislike of philosophical pomposity. A student of his, however, could not fail to observe a few characteristic gestures and grimaces. You watched him begin by disentangling the different senses of the expression in which he was interested, and then, after he specified the sense with

which he was concerned, he would consider the various pro-
posals for analyzing it. Almost all of them, it seems in retro-
spect, he found defective. "*Surely,* the word so-and-so doesn't
ordinarily mean that," he said, as he wrinkled his nose. Or
then there was that characteristic conversation-stopper as he
wagged his head violently: "I shouldn't have thought anyone
could possibly say that *that*'s what we ordinarily mean by
that expression!" Because he was so cautious about saying
that one expression meant the same as another, Moore
seemed to be left with a set of *un*analyzable concepts in one
hand, and in the other a set of concepts about whose analysis
he was never certain. The result was that one of the greatest
philosophical analysts of our age found it hard to point, in all
honesty, to a single successful analysis of an important philosophical idea.

Part of the reason for Moore's failure as a constructive analyst is to be located in the difficulty surrounding the notions
of *meaning, synonymy,* and *analytic* which are so central to
Moore's conception of analysis. He may have been shy about
characterizing his method, but in *The Philosophy of G. E.
Moore* he was prompted to say something revealing about
the nature of analysis as he conceived it—among other things,
that you must be sure, before you can say that you have
given an analysis of a concept, that the expression which expresses the *analysandum* must be *synonymous* with any expression which expresses the *analysans.* Moreover, Moore
says in the same place that a fuller discussion of the topic of
analysis would require a discussion of the distinction between
an analytic necessary connection and a synthetic necessary
connection, because, he says, the necessary connection between the *analysandum* "*x* is a brother" and the *analysans* "*x*
is a male sibling" is analytic, while other necessary connections are synthetic. At this point he says: "It seems to me . . .
that the line between 'analytic' and 'synthetic' might be
drawn in many different ways. *As it is, I do not think that the*

two terms have any clear meaning". [2] I venture to call this support from Sir Hubert to those who have been campaigning against complacency about the idea of analyticity. But one is tempted to add that if the word "analytic" doesn't have any clear meaning, then Moore's phrase "giving an analysis" doesn't either. And this is one reason why Moore had justifiable doubts about so many of the "analyses" he considered.

Now I wish to insist that in spite of such fundamental difficulties in Moore's method Moore was a pedagogical genius, because he allowed you to see that even if his own conception of analysis was too stringent or too obscure for effective use, something like analysis was of fundamental importance in philosophy. For then you might weaken the requirements for a successful analysis, as Russell and his followers do when they ask for no more than extensional identity between *analysandum* and *analysans*. Or you might say with Wittgenstein that the meaning of the term under consideration is its use; or that philosophers should look for its use rather than its meaning. But in either case you would be building on Moore's conviction that clarification is a central task of philosophy.

So pertinacious and candid was Moore in his search for clarity that he had to admit, as we have seen, that the notion of analysis which was so central in his thinking was itself unclear. It was this same candor and this same pertinacity which made him so admirable. A few typical stories may show why. In telling them I feel fortified by Moore's own statement that "stories, whether purporting to be true or avowedly mere fiction, [had] a tremendous fascination for [him]". The stories that follow purport to be true and *are* true, approximately.

At Columbia in the early forties Moore held an informal

---

2. *The Philosophy of G. E. Moore*, edited by P. A. Schilpp (Evanston, Ill., 1942), p. 667. The italics are mine.

seminar to which students and members of the faculty came. One day, after Moore had made a particularly slashing attack on some doctrine in epistemology, a graduate student asked: "But, Professor Moore, why do you spend so much time refuting *that* doctrine; *surely* [this emphatic use of "surely" he had learned from Moore] no one holds it". To which Moore replied, in a rising crescendo of rhetorical questions: "*No* one holds it? *No one* holds it? *No one holds it?* But Montague holds it—don't you, Montague?" Professor Montague rolled his eyes and nodded his head affirmatively.

There was never a consideration, you see, which was to get in the way of *finding* the truth, never any sense that a distinguished colleague's pain should get in the way of *saying* what was true. And this was of immense educational value. For Moore was not nasty in these belligerent moods. He was not sarcastic. He was a simple, direct Englishman who did not speak or write with his eye on the gallery. He made the young feel that by using their wits they might say things of value in philosophy.

One day a Columbia colleague of Moore's was looking for a book by Whewell—the famous Dr. Whewell who played such a great part in the history of Moore's own college, Trinity. He met Moore as he was looking for the book in the offices of *The Journal of Philosophy*. As his colleague took the book down from the shelf he showed it to Moore, thinking that Moore would certainly know it, and asked him what he thought of Whewell. To which Moore replied without the slightest sign of embarrassment and even with a sly twinkle: "You know, I've *never* read Whewell. Should I?." I don't remember what the colleague said in reply.

Just two more typical stories. When I was staying with the Moores in Cambridge, England, in the spring of 1951, Mrs. Moore came into the room after dinner to announce that Bertrand Russell was about to speak on the B.B.C. Long silence. "Moore," she asked (she called him "Moore" when she didn't call him "Bill"), "Moore, don't you think we ought to listen to

Russell? I feel an obligation to listen to him. Don't you?" And then there was another awfully long pause as Moore puffed on his pipe. One felt that Moore was tuning in on him*self*, to see whether *he* felt that obligation. After the pause he reported with utter seriousness: "Dear, *I* don't feel any obligation to listen to Russell tonight".

Lest this give a misleading impression of Moore's attitude toward Russell—as expressed in my presence, at any rate—I should supplement it with a story which reverses the picture somewhat. One night in New York Mrs. Moore was commenting on Russell's lawsuit against Albert Barnes to recover his salary after their dramatic falling out in the forties at the Barnes Institute. Mrs. Moore said that while Russell was probably right, he shouldn't have stooped to the point of suing Barnes. "Moore wouldn't have done that. Would you have, Bill?" Once again there was the long puff on the pipe, but this time Moore said, "Oh yes I should have, dear".

You will now see why I say that I have never known a philosopher with more integrity. Some in this audience may not agree with my high estimate of Moore as a philosopher. But I hope that no one—either in this room or out of it—will deny that he possessed in the highest degree those moral and intellectual qualities that every great philosopher should have. Once I heard a man say after a sharp exchange with Moore: "I hate Moore's mind". I can only say that I had many a tough bout with Moore that I lost, but I never came out of one with any doubts about how I felt about Moore *or* his mind. I loved them both.

Index

Adams, Henry, 206
Addams, Jane, 20, 25, 26, 27
Allen, Gay Wilson, 34-40
Ames, Fisher, 180
Aquinas, St. Thomas, 154, 239
Archambault, Reginald D., 244n, 245
Aristotle, 14, 40, 47, 136, 237
Ashley, William James, 59
Austin, J. L., 210
Austin, John, 45-46, 47n, 48n, 56, 58, 62, 64
Ayer, A. J., 112-17, 120

Bailyn, Bernard, 208
Bain, Alexander, 38
Bancroft, George, 206
Barnes, Albert, 261
Barzun, Jacques, 186-93
Bateson, William, 188, 189
Beard, Charles A., 41, 42, 43, 45, 51, 63-67, 204-7
Becker, Carl, 207
Bellamy, Edward, 194
Benda, Julien, 33
Bentham, Jeremy, 45-46, 47n, 56, 58, 62, 64, 235
Bentley, A. F., 66

Bergson, Henri, 38, 234, 235
Berkeley, George, 111

Caird, Edward, 44
Carlyle, Thomas, 17
Carnap, Rudolf, 256
Carnegie, Andrew, 8
Carr, E. H., 200-203
Cleveland, Grover, 180
Cliffe Leslie, T. E., 59
Clifford, W. K., 89, 99-100
Cohen, Morris R., 49n, 69-70, 256
Coleridge, Samuel Taylor, 13, 16, 87, 88, 90, 111, 116
Comte, Auguste, 74, 234, 235, 236
Condorcet, Antoine-Nicolas de, 70-71
Cory, Daniel, 250-53
Cournot, A. A., 188
Crèvecoeur, J. Hector St. John, 89
Croly, Herbert, 194

Darwin, Charles, 36-37, 38, 43, 44, 99, 111, 186-93, 195-99, 246
De Vries, Hugo, 188, 189
Dewey, John, 9, 10, 12, 13, 14, 21, 24-29, 31, 40-46, 49n, 51-55, 57, 58, 59n, 62, 63n, 65, 67, 74-75, 96, 97, 102, 103, 107-09,